D0949742

NATIONAL UNIVERSITY
LIBRARY   SAN DIEGO

The
RABBI
and the
HIT MAN

ALSO BY ARTHUR J. MAGIDA

How to Be a Perfect Stranger

Prophet of Rage: A Life of Louis Farrakhan and His Nation

The Environment Committees

The
RABBI
and the
HIT MAN

A True Tale of Murder, Passion, and the
Shattered Faith of a Congregation

Arthur J. Magida

HarperCollins*Publishers*

THE RABBI AND THE HIT MAN. Copyright © 2003 by Arthur J. Magida. All rights reserved. Printed in the United States of America. No part of this book may be used or reproduced in any manner whatsoever without written permission except in the case of brief quotations embodied in critical articles and reviews. For information, address HarperCollins Publishers Inc., 10 East 53rd Street, New York, NY 10022.

HarperCollins books may be purchased for educational, business, or sales promotional use. For information, please write: Special Markets Department, HarperCollins Publishers Inc., 10 East 53rd Street, New York, NY 10022.

FIRST EDITION

Printed on acid-free paper
Library of Congress Cataloging-in-Publication Data is available upon request.

ISBN 0-06-621067-4

03 04 05 06 07 ❖/RRD 10 9 8 7 6 5 4 3 2 1

The heart is deceitful above all things.
Who can understand it?

—JEREMIAH 17:9

Where there is truth, justice shall surely follow
and then will come peace.

—PIRKE AVOT

CONTENTS

PART ONE

THE MURDER

The night that Rabbi Fred Neulander came home and found his wife's dead body poking out from underneath the brown coffee table in the living room was when it all began: his infamy, his indignity, his public shame, and his private fear. Carol lay facedown on the floor. Her head was angled to the right; the back of her skull was bashed in. Blood and brains were everywhere, splattered on the walls and furniture, soaking into her blue pants and vest, her gray long-sleeved blouse, her white bra, even into her gray socks. More blood had collected underneath her, drenching the white carpet. One of her fingers was almost severed. Both of her hands were bruised, though her attacker had not taken any of the jewelry she wore: two gold bracelets, two gold rings, and a Seiko watch with a black band. One leg of the coffee table was stained with her blood. On the surface of the table, a silver tea set still sat, undisturbed.

Twenty years before, Neulander had founded a temple in southern New Jersey. Thanks to his powerful sermons and even more powerful personality, M'kor Shalom had grown into the largest Reform congregation in that part of the state. A religious leader of his experience and dynamism was expected to know the answers to everything, or at least to know where to get them. There was nothing in the Torah or the Talmud that could make sense of the horror Neulander came home to that night. Yet his calm demeanor over the days that followed was impressive. Barely a month later, he would write in his temple's newsletter that only "through a spiritual strength that comes from outside me can I be free from the captivity of rage and bewilderment." That, of course, was Neulander the rabbi. Neulander the man—and the widower—kept his thoughts to himself.

1

"There's Blood over Everything"

The sixteen-mile drive from M'kor Shalom to Crescent Burial Park normally took twenty minutes, but so many people joined the funeral procession for Carol Neulander that nearly an hour was required. Police and state troopers were stationed at major intersections to hold back other motorists so that the caravan could wend its doleful way across the landscape. All along the route, commercial enterprises that typified the best—and worst—of the Garden State were copiously in evidence. A BMW dealer whose "Ltd." after its name connoted a certain British classiness (even though BMWs are as Teutonic as any car can get); a splattering of capacious diners, appropriate symbols of an area totally lacking a culinary identity; a small, beige cottage whose neon sign advertised PSYCHIC/TAROT CARD READINGS; and an unending series of motels, sometimes up to eight in a row, featuring "free Continental breakfast"—watered-down orange juice, instant coffee, doughnuts plucked from cardboard boxes.

The procession inched north on Route 73 for a few miles, then turned south on Route 130 until arriving at Crescent Burial Park. This was the largest Jewish cemetery in South Jersey, yet there wasn't enough room for the multitude of cars. Some people parked on the long, narrow road that stretched the entire length of the cemetery; others hunted for space on neighboring side streets. The hearse and the family's limousines went straight to the far end of the cemetary. Pallbearers carried the plain pine coffin to the burial plot thirty feet away, followed by Carol's children, her siblings, and, of course, her husband. A rabbi who had been friends with Fred and Carol recited verses from Psalms that didn't quite provide the intended comfort:

> For He will give His angels charge over thee,
> To keep thee in all thy ways . . .
> Because he has loved Me, therefore I will deliver him;
> I will see him securely on high, because he has known My
>   name . . .
> With a long life, I will satisfy him,
> And let him behold My salvation.

The freshly dug ground of Grave D in Plot 910 of Section F was just behind the tall green fence that separated Crescent Burial Park from the modest homes bordering on it. Not the best place to raise kids, but an inexpensive one. Carol Neulander would be laid to rest next to her in-laws, Sally and Ernest Neulander. Their tombstones lay to the right of Grave D. Off to the left were smaller markers for five children unrelated to the Neulanders. They had died in infancy, some on the very day of their birth: Ellen Shaya. Joshua Adam Brodsky. Eli James Lewis. Baby Carson. Baby Dana Emdur. Carol Neulander had never known them, but she might have been pleased to spend eternity with them. After all, she had been a kind and devoted mother of three, and her interest in children had led her to major in child and adolescent psychology in college.

After more prayers were said, the casket was lowered into the ground and the mourners took turns shoveling dirt on it, according to Jewish custom. The thud of earth on the casket's hard surface was intended to remind people of the absolute finality of death. At last, it was time for the ritual recitation of the *kaddish,* the prayer that asks for peace for the deceased:

> *"Yisgadal v'yiskadash sh'mai raba, b'olmo deev'ro chir'usai v'yamlich malchusai b'chayeichon uv'yomeichon v'chayai d'chol bit yisroel, ba'agala u'viz'man kariv v'imru: Amen.*

("May your Great Name be magnified and hallowed in the world according to Your will and may Your reign be quickly established, in our own lives and our own day, and in the life of all of Israel, and let us say: Amen.)

> *"Y'hei shmei raba m'vorach l'alam ul'almenu almaya. Yitborach v'yishtabach v'yitpa'ra v'yitromam v'yitnasei, v'yit'hadar, v'yi'ale v'vit'halal sh'mei d'kud'sha b'rich hu, l'ile min-kol-brichata v'shirata, tush b'chata v'nechemata, da'amiran b'alma, v'imru: Amen.*

("May your great name be blessed for ever and ever! All praise and glory, splendor, exaltation and honor, radiance and veneration and worship to the Holy One of Blessing, even beyond any earthly prayer or song, any adoration or tribute we can offer, and let us say: Amen.)

> *"Y'hei sh'lama raba min-sh'maya, v'chayim aleinu v'al-kol-yisroel, v'imru: Amen.*

("May there be great peace from the heavens, and life for us and for all of Israel, as we say: Amen.)

> *"Oseh shalom bimromav, hu ya-aseh shalom aleinu v'al kol yisra'el, v'imru: Amen."*

("May the one who makes peace in the high heavens send peace for us and for all of Israel, as we say: Amen.")

Then, the family turned to pass through two parallel lines of relatives and friends uttering a prayer of consolation: *"Ha'makom yenachem et'chem b'toch she'ar avelei tziyon vi'Yerushalayim."* ["May the Lord comfort you among the other mourners of Zion and Jerusalem."] Finally, Fred Neulander and his children—Matthew, Benjamin, and Rebecca, all young adults—left the cold November winds for the comfort of the limousine and the somber journey back to the house where Fred had found Carol's lifeless body. She had still been wearing the gold necklace with six small diamonds that Fred had given her a few years earlier on their wedding anniversary. In eight weeks, they would have celebrated their twenty-ninth anniversary.

On the Tuesday night of Carol's murder, Fred had stayed at the synagogue later than usual. M'kor Shalom was always busy on Tuesdays, with choir practice in the evening and lots of meetings for adults while their kids attended religious classes. Fred Neulander wasn't teaching that fall, but as M'kor Shalom's senior rabbi it was his prerogative, if not his duty, to monitor the religious education programs. It was odd, though, that he chose to do so on that particular night. Aside from a brief visit the previous Tuesday, he hadn't stopped in on any of the classes for almost a year. One reason he'd avoided choir rehearsal was because its director—the temple's cantor—had told him she didn't like his behavior. He'd wave to her from the back of the room or walk up to her and whisper, commenting on her teaching or telling her about an upcoming meeting, sometimes even sharing gossip. These appearances disrupted rehearsals and caused the cantor and choir to lose their focus.

On the night of the murder, Neulander sat in on a confirmation class taught by Gary Mazo, his assistant rabbi, from about seven-thirty to almost eight o'clock. Then he headed to choir practice, where he did exactly what the cantor had asked him not to do. He walked down the middle of the aisle and stood smack in the center of the room. He couldn't have been any more noticeable.

"How ya doing, Rabbi?" called out a choir member.

"Great," he answered, swinging his arms. After a few moments, he left. Next he showed up at another class Mazo was teaching that night—a class on Jewish responsibility—and stayed for about twenty minutes. In the temple's vestibule, Neulander met a local schoolteacher and her husband, a retired FBI agent, who had just attended an Alcoholics Anonymous meeting at the temple. The three of them spent nearly half an hour discussing Judaism. Finally, around eight-fifty, Neulander went to his office to pick up his coat and headed home for the second time that day. He'd stopped home around six o'clock, spending an hour or so over dinner with his son Matthew, who'd temporarily moved back in with his parents after a few semesters at Tufts. Carol was expected home around eight, later than usual, because of an after-hours business meeting.

The drive from M'kor Shalom to the Neulanders' residence at 204 Highgate Lane was a quick eight minutes: three left turns, then a right. Like most of the houses on the block, theirs was a comfortable two-story, middle-class residence with four bedrooms, an attached two-car garage, a dining room, and a large remodeled kitchen. The family room, equipped with fireplace, track lighting, a piano, and lots of books, led through sliding doors to the backyard. People on Highgate had steadily updated these houses over the years, although nothing about the architecture or the nature of the improvements was unconventional or especially elaborate. The Neulanders' home was no fancier than that of any of their neighbors. Among Fred and Carol's friends were lawyers and doctors of considerable means; some had second homes on the Jersey shore or on Nantucket, others indulged in lengthy European or Caribbean vacations. The Neulanders had no such room for extravagance in their budget.

When their kids were around, Fred and Carol spent much of their time hanging out in the family room, which had been built for just that: being together, whether relaxing, reading, watching TV, kidding around, or having a heart-to-heart talk. But it was rare these days to find all the Neulanders home at the same time. Rebecca, twenty-four, was a graduate student at Temple University in Philadelphia. Nineteen-year-old Ben was in his second year at the University of Michigan in Ann Arbor. The only child living at home, twenty-one-year-old Matthew, had a full schedule. He was a premed student at Rutgers during the day and an emergency medical technician at night.

When the rabbi parked his black Acura in the driveway, Carol's car was already there. Entering the house, he spotted two drops of blood on the hardwood floor in the hallway, then saw Carol's body on the floor of the living room. "It was so repulsive and frightening and horrible," he later said. "I just couldn't stay in the room." He fled to the kitchen, picked up a cordless phone and banged out the numbers 9-1-1. When an operator answered, he stuttered into the mouthpiece, "I, I, ah, just came home and my wife is on the floor and there's blood all over. I . . . I . . . I . . . don't know what to do . . . There's blood all over . . ."

"Does she appear to be breathing?"

"I . . . I . . . can't tell. I don't think so."

"You can't tell?"

"I can't tell. Do I touch her or should I do anything? . . . I don't think so. Oh, my God."

"No, no. Just calm down. I want you to calm down. That's what I want you to do . . . just leave everything the way it is, sir. And stay on the phone with me until the police officers get there . . ."

"Ah . . . ah . . . She's not moving. She's not breathing . . . ah, ah . . . *Jesus.*"

"Do you see any weapons around her, sir?"

"No, I don't see anything. I don't see a thing . . ."

"Just leave everything the way it is, sir, and stay on the phone with me until the first police officers get there."

"Ah, ah . . ."

"Do you need an ambulance? Are you all right?"

"Oh, sh . . . I don't know what all right is . . . There's blood over everything."

"Don't touch her . . ."

"Oh, my God! Oh, my God! Oh!"

"We're sending somebody down."

"No, wait a minute. I've got another problem. My son is an EMT . . . He's gonna hear this call. Ah, ah . . . Oh, God! Did you hear? Do you understand what I'm saying?"

"I understand exactly, sir. But we have nothing to do with the EMTs . . ."

"Oh, my God! Oh, my God!"

Matthew Neulander, who had just taken a patient to a local hospital, was listening to the radio in his ambulance when he overheard the 911 dispatcher send an ambulance to 204 Highgate—to *his* address. Next, the radio blared that the home owner had found his wife lying in a pool of blood. Matthew grabbed his car phone and dialed Mike Tasch, his best friend on the EMT team. "Get the fuck over to my house," he screamed when Mike picked up. "Get the fuck over to my house. It's my mom. It's my mom."

It took Tasch a few moments to identify Matthew's voice. But once he separated the voice from the fear, he jumped into his gray 1990 Nissan pickup and drove, he said, "like a madman, which is what you do when you get a call like that from a friend."

Tasch used every inch of his oversized tires to race over to Matthew's house—running through traffic lights and stop signs, flashing his headlights to warn other drivers to let him pass, ignoring one woman who was yelling that he was "driving like an idiot," and slamming the brakes so forcefully in front of the Neulanders' house that he skidded on the wet autumn leaves covering the ground. He narrowly missed colliding with the front end of ambulance 1397, which was pulling in just as he was.

Steve McCann, the driver of 1397, was halfway to the Neulanders' house, responding to the 911 call, when he heard on his radio that Matthew was on his way. He rang up Matthew on the two-way radio to tell him not to bother. The job was covered. Matthew screamed that it was *his* house and he was going anyway.

McCann grabbed oxygen and some first aid supplies from the back of his ambulance and sprinted toward the front door. He was joined by Tasch. Both men noticed the rabbi standing in the driveway. The cordless phone from the kitchen was still in his hands. Tasch was disturbed by how "calm and relaxed" the rabbi appeared to be. "It was unreal," Tasch later recalled. "I couldn't believe this man had just found his wife murdered."

In the three years Tasch had been on the ambulance squad, he'd seen "lots of people who'd discovered bodies—bodies of people they loved. Most wanted to know how they could help. Or they were hysterical. Or they were down on their knees and praying. Fred wasn't even crying. As soon as I saw him, I knew something was wrong."

The police had arrived at the house a few minutes before the medics and two cops now barred the front door. McCann and Tasch were told they couldn't enter. No one could do anything for Carol, the cops said, and the house was now a crime scene, off-limits to everyone but the police. Tasch wanted to assure Matthew he'd done everything he could. He begged to go in, but the police, who were clearly shaken by what they had seen inside, refused. The best they could do to make Tasch feel useful was to let him stand guard and prevent anyone from entering. That was an easy task for Tasch. At six-feet-five and almost three hundred pounds, he filled up most of the doorway.

In the distance, Matthew's siren was wailing away, getting closer and closer as he pushed his ambulance to its top speed of seventy-five miles an hour. Tasch wouldn't tell him anything over the radio, and Matthew knew that wasn't good. If his mother were OK, Tasch would have said something. After what seemed like an eternity of driving, Matthew finally reached the house, jumped out of the ambulance, and ran past six parked police cars to his front door, only to be lifted off the ground by Tasch and carried about twenty feet to the end of the driveway.

No one had to tell Matthew that his mother was dead; he knew what it meant when medics were barred from a crime scene. A cop he knew came the closest to giving him the grim news, yet "Matthew . . ." was all he could get out before his voice drifted away.

Matthew's father was still standing in the driveway. His tie was neatly knotted. His breath was normal—not racing or gasping. "Dad, what's going on?" Matthew asked. "Where's Mom? Is anyone taking care of her?" Neulander's only response was to keep repeating, "Everything will be OK. Everything will be OK."

Matthew turned away from his father and walked about halfway down the block, away from the blinking lights and the cops and the medics and the detectives crawling all over his house. He walked until he was almost out of sight of his house. He needed to be by himself for a few minutes. "God, God, God," he muttered to himself. "What am I going to do? What am I going to do? I've lost my best friend." His father never called out to him or tried to persuade him to come back to the house.

Just as the rabbi was dialing 911, M'kor Shalom's assistant rabbi, Gary Mazo, arrived home from work. He took his dog for a walk, grabbed a beer, and changed into pajamas. He had just settled down in front of the TV for another episode of *NYPD Blue* when a good friend of Neulander's barged in. "Carol's dead," he blurted out. The visitor didn't know the details, only that she'd been killed.

Mazo dressed quickly and got into his car. Neulander's house was a mile away, past streets with tranquil names like Split Rock Drive, Lamp Post Lane, Gatehouse Road, Old Orchard Road. Highgate Lane was swarming with cops checking for prints, trolling the ground for weapons, and photographing everything, even some crumbled-up papers on the floor of Carol's Camry and the audiotape of Clive Cussler's *Inca Gold* that was sitting on the front seat of Neulander's Acura.

Mazo found Fred in Tasch's ambulance. The back door was open, the heat was blazing away, and the rabbi was sitting with his head in his hands. He was, Mazo recalled, "utterly, utterly distraught." Mazo tried to comfort him, even though he knew it was futile. That night, as members of his congregation gathered outside the Neulanders' house looking for solace, Mazo realized that nothing he did—*nothing,* despite all his rabbinic training and all the workshops he'd taken in grief counseling—could ease anyone's pain.

Later, around ten o'clock, Neulander called his daughter, Rebecca, who was at graduate school in Philadelphia. He told her that Carol had been in a bad accident and that two of his friends would be there shortly to drive her home to Cherry Hill. En route, the rabbi's friends told Rebecca that someone had broken into her parents' house. Suddenly, "everything clicked," Rebecca later recalled. She knew her mother was dead. "Why? Why? Why?" she screamed. She remained hysterical for the entire ride. Though both men were doctors, neither had brought any sedatives.

The rabbi, along with Matthew and Rebecca, were taken to the police station around one o'clock that morning for questioning. This is routine in such a situation. The detectives talked to Rebecca, then Matthew, and finally their father. While he awaited his turn, Neulander called Carol's oldest brother, Ed, whose wife answered the phone. Neulander told her what happened and she got frantic. She handed the phone to her husband, who was too stunned to fully absorb what Neulander was saying. The rabbi's next call was to Carol's other brother, Robert, and then to Carol's sister, Margaret. He said the same thing to each of them: "Somebody broke into the house and there was a scuffle. Carol didn't survive." He was calm enough—or controlled enough—to convey the news deliberately, almost matter-of-factly. No one who spoke to him that night heard him crying.

Carol's siblings and their spouses didn't go back to sleep, and in the morning, they all called their own children. One of Carol's nieces immediately walked into her nursery and held her eight-week-old son for a long time. A relative who was especially close to Carol phoned her own rabbi soon after she heard about the murder. "Is there anything . . ." the rabbi hesitantly asked, "anything amiss with anyone in your family?"

Around two in the morning, at the rabbi's request, Gary Mazo was finally allowed into Neulander's house to recite a prayer for Carol. Called a *vidui,* this is a traditional confession of sins when death is imminent. If the person is too ill to say it, or if she were unable to say it before she died, it is said for her. Mazo had barely crossed the threshold when he froze, riveted by the macabre scene. From the doorway, Carol's legs were barely visible and Mazo could see she was lying in a pool of blood. Black fingerprinting dust was everywhere. Shaken, Mazo backed away. The police agreed to place the body in a black bag and carry it to the front lawn, where Mazo would recite the prayer. Outside, Mazo knelt down next to the bag and said, on Carol's behalf, "Forgive me . . . for all my sins which I have sinned before You from the time of my birth until this time . . . If only my hands are clean and my heart pure. Protector of the bereaved and the helpless, watch over my loved ones. In Your hand, I commit my spirit; redeem it, oh God of mercy and truth." Completing the *vidui,* Mazo added a prayer of his own. "God, full of compassion . . . Let Carol find refuge in Your eternal presence and let her soul be bound up in the bond of everlasting life . . . May she rest in peace."

Nothing more could be done. Carol's body was taken away from the house where she had lived for twenty years.

Gary Mazo showed up at the Neulanders' again the next day at noon. There was already a funeral director in attendance, along with the director of the Jewish Community Center, who also happened to be a close friend of the rabbi's. Among the details they discussed was where to hold shiva, the seven-day period in which the deceased's family receives visitors seeking to pay their respects. Fred insisted that it take place at the home Carol loved: this was where she'd raised their children and where she and Fred had spent the best years of their marriage. This seemed reasonable enough— if not for the profusion of blood and brain matter splattered all over the living room. Besides, the place was a crime scene. Yet Neulander prevailed. After police permission was granted, maintenance men from the JCC quickly installed a new carpet, removed the soiled drapes, and repainted the room. By Thursday morning, it was ready for guests.

Almost a thousand people attended a hastily arranged memorial service for Carol at M'kor Shalom the night after the murder. The size of the crowd indicated not only people's fondness and respect for her but also their grief and rage at her murder. It was an offense against everything that Cherry Hill stood for—good schools, safe streets, a good middle-class life. This was a town that had gone through several permutations before reaching its current prosperity and respectability. Originally known as Delaware Township, seventeen hundred people lived here in 1900. The economy was entirely agricultural, except for the Blazing Rag Tavern (where cockfights went on in the back room). Even into the late 1930s, it was still a sleepy village with six thousand people. The postwar boom transformed the town, and by 1965, population reached forty-five thousand and major developments were everywhere, many of them named after people who'd lived here for genera-tions—Hinchman, Colwick, Erlton, Barlow, Hernwood. In those years, those early boom years, two thousand people would cram into the Latin Casino to hear Sammy Davis Jr. or Frank Sinatra, and the mob was hanging out at the Garden State Race Track on Route 70, and Muhammad Ali settled here briefly to take advan-tage of the seasoned trainers in Philadelphia, a city with a long and honorable boxing tradition. Despite belonging to the Nation of Islam, where he'd been taught that whites were "blue-eyed devils," Ali was a great neighbor in this suburb where whites outnumbered blacks more than fifteen to one. He'd invite kids, black and white, to play basketball with him and he'd sign autographs for them—which some of the kids sold the next day in school. Ali's ten-thou-sand-square-foot mansion became the most mythical house in town.

The people grieving for Carol at the service that night at M'kor Shalom were also mourning a different sort of loss: the loss of their own innocence, their certainty that life in Cherry Hill would always get better. At the funeral, they listened to Anita Hochman, the temple's cantor, sing, "*Makom she libi ohev . . .* the place that my heart holds dear, my feet will bring me there." Then Gary Mazo took over, delivering a sermon that was bitterly heart-felt. "We should not be here," he said. "This is not how our world is supposed to work." He tried to console and comfort his audi-ence, but all the while, Mazo kept thinking, "When do *we* get to grieve? When do *we* get to fall apart?" He had just turned thirty. Barely four years out of the seminary, he felt woefully ill-prepared for the job of assuring people twice his age that there was a pur-pose for everything under heaven.

On Thursday, the day of the funeral, Carol's brother Ed picked up his daughter, Diane, at the Philadelphia airport. As they walked through the terminal, he warned her not to glance at the newsstands—her aunt's picture was on the front page of every paper. Ed and his family were very private people. To them, this was a *family* tragedy, not a public spectacle. But overnight it had become a magnet for gawkers, cameramen, reporters—people who'd never met Carol. At M'kor Shalom, TV vans were parked in the lot; two thousand people were lined up outside, hoping to make it into the service. A reporter barely older than Ed's own kids whispered, "I'm so sorry for your loss. Give me a call me when you can." Then he stuffed a business card into Ed's jacket pocket. Ed threw it on the ground.

No one attending the funeral knew that roughly nine hours before Carol was killed, Fred had been visiting one of his girlfriends for some afternoon love. But more than a few people already had such deep suspicions about the rabbi that they whispered about a possible affair while they were waiting in line. "My God, maybe he didn't like her," said one person softly, "but why did he have to kill her? Why would a rabbi do anything like that? I can't believe it."

Inside the synagogue, people filed past Carol's coffin, which was shrouded with a black cloth with the Star of David embroidered in gold thread. Rabbi Seymour Prystowski, a good friend of the Neulanders, took the pulpit and spoke of Carol as "honest" and "forthright . . . a friend to everyone who knew her . . . She gave counsel to her husband . . . She was his anchor, his support." An exhausted Gary Mazo followed Prystowski and turned to Carol's children from the pulpit, reminding them how proud she had been of them, how much support she'd given him and his wife when he had come to M'kor Shalom, how much he'd enjoyed her Rosh

Hashanah meals. Mazo ended the service with a quote from Anne Frank, who, after hiding in an attic in Amsterdam for two years, was still convinced—despite all the evidence to the contrary—that "people are really good at heart," a sentiment that few people put stock in that day. Although tradition holds that at least one eulogy should be delivered by an immediate family member, Carol's husband and three children were too shattered to speak.

The coffin was carried to the hearse, which began its long crawl to the cemetery. A year later, according to the Jewish custom, the tombstone would be unveiled. It read:

CAROL NEULANDER
BELOVED WIFE, MOTHER AND SISTER
MAY 15, 1942–NOV. 1, 1994

The empty plot next to Carol was reserved for her husband, Fred.

2

"Everything Was Kosher"

"*Shiva* consoles and teaches and redirects," Neulander wrote when the seven-day mourning period for Carol was over. "*Shiva* bears the imprint of death and sorrow. It also bears the seed of life. We are mandated to go forth and to conduct ourselves . . . with greater compassion, decency, honesty and courage . . . [It] reminds us that each day is a gift and as its caretakers we must make of it something sacred and imbue it with God's holiness."

Neulander's words appeared in the first newsletter that M'kor Shalom published after Carol's death. His column read more like a lecture on the general virtues of *shiva* than like a husband's grieving for a murdered wife. An outsider perusing it would not have known that Neulander was referring to a personal loss until the very end. Only in the last two paragraphs did the rabbi mention "a horrible and ugly injustice" he had suffered (an odd euphemism for a homicide) and declare that his faith had not wavered. It couldn't waver. If he stopped relying on "Jewish truth," he wrote, his world would have "no meaning . . . In the valley of the shadow of death, I believe God is with me and I am less afraid." This was as personal as Neulander got.

He may have been trying to distance himself emotionally until he was ready to come to terms with Carol's death. Or, maybe, quite simply after more than twenty-five years in the pulpit, he couldn't suppress his rabbinic reflexes from kicking in, from restraining his persona as a "teacher," which is the Hebrew meaning of the word "rabbi."

Then again, his apparent stoicism may have simply reflected his upbringing. His parents were in their mid-thirties when he was born, older than most first-time parents, and their temperaments were more private and unemotional than that of other adults Fred knew in his youth. His father, Ernest, came to the United States from Hungary as a toddler, yet he remained very European in manner. That translated into parental strictness and emotional distance. Fred's mother, Sally, was more outgoing, but neither of them discussed their feelings or even their medical problems in front of their son. Fred's father taught him that strong men stood alone. They were patient and self-sufficient and didn't reveal disappointments or joys, much less weakness or pain. Years later, Fred described the effect that Ernest's parenting style had on him: he felt "banished to my private island of sentiments. It was terrible . . . Emotionally, I was as tightly wound as a golf ball." Not surprisingly, he chose a profession that fit well with his childhood training: there was certainly no shame in being, as a rabbi, calm and unflappable. Still, he came to realize over the years—or so he said—that it was "not only acceptable, but helpful to be seen as human . . . [as] vulnerable and fragile."

Within hours of Carol's murder, things began to unravel for her husband. He told the police when he was questioned that Tuesday night that Carol was "a terrific partner . . . a tremendous helpmate." He was "lucky" to be married to her. The two of them had never seen a marriage counselor. He'd known her since he was twenty, he said, and though they'd experienced the "normal friction . . . and disagreements" to be expected in any two-income family—raising their kids, for instance, or the lack of time he spent with her—the marriage was "great." No, they'd never needed counseling and there'd been no adultery on either side. The rabbi also asserted that Carol had no enemies and neither did he, aside from some anti-Semitic letters he'd received a dozen years before. "There's no ongoing hostility . . . ," he added. "I'm just bewildered by this."

When Neulander's interrogation began at 3:20 A.M., the police had already finished questioning two of his children. Rebecca's forty-minute interview centered on her story about "the bathroom man," as he would later be known. Exactly one week before the murder, Rebecca said, her mother had pulled into the driveway of her home while talking with her daughter on the car phone. Suddenly, a stranger approached the driver's window. Carol told Rebecca she'd have to interrupt their conversation to talk to the man.

"Who is it?" Rebecca asked.

"Daddy told me he was expecting a letter," Carol reported, "and I shouldn't be surprised if someone came over." Then the man asked to use the bathroom, a request that Carol relayed to Rebecca.

"Be careful," Rebecca had warned her mother. "You can stay on the phone if you want to. I wouldn't necessarily let him in." But Carol ended the call and let the man into the house. A few minutes later, she called Rebecca.

"Did he leave the envelope for Daddy?" Rebecca asked.

"Yeah," said Carol, "but it isn't sealed. The really strange thing is that it's empty."

Rebecca gave no further thought to the incident until the following Tuesday night, the night that would end with Carol's death. At around eight o'clock, when Carol was home from work, Rebecca called; mother and daughter chatted for nearly an hour. Near the end of the conversation, Rebecca heard some new voices on her mother's end of the line and realized she'd let someone into the house while they were talking.

"Who is it?" Rebecca asked. "Is it a neighbor?"

"It's the bathroom guy."

"From last week?"

"Yes."

"What's he doing there?"

Over the phone, Rebecca caught bits and pieces of her mother's remarks to the visitor: "He'll be home soon . . . Why don't you wait? . . ." It seemed that the man had come with a companion who was still sitting outside in his car, because Carol said, "Well, it's cold. Don't leave him outside. He can come in."

Rebecca, listening in, was nervous. She told her mother, "Keep talking to me while they're there." She didn't want Carol to be alone in the house with two strangers. But her mother seemed comfortable with these men. "No, no," she said. "It's fine. I'll talk to you later."

"OK. I'll talk with you soon." Rebecca hung up her phone.

She was the last family member to hear Carol Neulander's voice.

Under separate questioning by the police, both Rebecca and Matthew contradicted their father on key points. Rebecca's account of "the bathroom man" didn't square with the rabbi's statement that he never told Carol to expect a delivery on the previous Tuesday. Fred did say that his wife had told him about the first visit and what the man had left for him. The guy seemed "nutsy" to the rabbi, but as he told the detectives, the incident didn't upset him. "Carol passed it off," he said, "so I passed it off."

For his part, Matthew disputed his father's account of the Neulanders' marriage being "absolutely kosher" and very loving, with
little tension. Two nights before the murder, Matthew said, his parents stormed into the house around ten o'clock after spending the
day in northern New Jersey on a condolence call. Apparently, the
ride back home was anything but comforting. It was clear to
Matthew that both of them were upset.

"Your father has something to tell you," Carol told Matthew as
soon as she and her husband got inside.

The rabbi, who was standing right next to her, was silent, so
Carol relayed the news: he was leaving the next day.

"Oh, really?" Matthew assumed that his father had a business
trip planned. "Where are you going?"

"No," Carol corrected him. "He's leaving the house."

Matthew was stunned to hear this, he told the cops. Although
his parents bickered about small stuff, like who cleaned out the
dishwasher in the morning, there were "no fights, no violence, no
cross words . . . nothing more than basic disagreements over nothing." Now here was his mother crying, saying the marriage was
over, while his father was staying unusually quiet, other than agreeing that he didn't spend enough time with Carol or participate
with her in things she wanted to do. Overall, Matthew thought
Fred was acting "very much out of character."

"Are you getting a divorce?" Matthew asked his parents.

"Yes," said his mother. "I'm at my wit's end. Your father doesn't
love me anymore. He doesn't want me and he doesn't want our
relationship to work." Turning to Fred, she asked point-blank: "Do
you want to make it work?"

Fred shrugged.

"Do you want a divorce?"

"Yes," the rabbi responded. "It's over."

At this point, Matthew recalled, Carol raced down to the basement, grabbed some suitcases, and threw them at Fred, telling him to move out that very night.

Just then, Matthew's pager went off; he'd been dispatched on an ambulance call. He left the house right away, but en route to the house where there was a medical emergency, the dispatcher sent him a "recall" message, canceling the trip. Realizing that he was within minutes from the house of a close friend, Matthew decided to visit him. The young men spent about twenty minutes discussing the "bizarre" argument Matthew had just witnessed between his parents. "I'd never seen my parents argue like that," he later told the police. "It was surreal." He was afraid to go home and find out what they'd do next. But when he arrived at the house, Fred and Carol seemed to have calmed down and were talking in their bedroom. When she heard Matthew coming up the steps, Carol came out to the hallway and assured her son that the marriage wasn't over. She said that she and Fred both hoped to work things out and she apologized for fighting in front of him. Matthew, however, suspected she was just saying these things to make him feel better.

Husbands and wives argue, of course. It's a given of married life that people will bicker about little things, like who takes out the garbage, drives the kids to school, changes the empty roll of toilet paper. There are the more serious disputes, too, about sex or money or child-rearing, which can escalate into epic battles and sometimes end with suitcases being packed and lawyers summoned. But when one spouse is murdered forty-eight hours after the suitcases appear, all that's predictable is the assumption that the two events might be connected. For police, bad argument plus dead wife equals husband as probable suspect.

Thus, within hours of Carol Neulander's murder, the rabbi became suspect Number One. The interrogating detectives at the Cherry Hill station had heard the man's two children dispute his description of a perfect, loving marriage. They'd observed his amazing composure throughout the ordeal, even within moments after finding his wife's battered body. It was the rabbi's manner that most aroused police suspicion. How could any man, much less a clerical leader, who ordinarily personified moral goodness and sensitivity to others, be so apparently serene, so unmoved by the death of his wife, especially given the circumstances of a brutal murder?

Outside of Cherry Hill, detectives far more experienced with homicide cases were dismayed by the gentleness with which Neulander was treated that night. To a degree, it was understandable that the mayor herself showed up at Highgate Lane to pay her respects an hour after the murder—Fred Neulander was an esteemed community leader, as well as a clergyman. But as one Philadelphia detective and veteran homicide investigator commented, "That night was Fred's Waterloo. They were treating Neulander like he's a big deal. This the most critical time of the whole investigation and they're swooning over him! If Neulander did it, he was probably figuring that he's gonna get away with it if he gets through the first forty-eight hours. But Fred knew squat about how cops work. If I was handling it, I'd have him think real fast he's in *our* control. The longer he stayed in a warm ambulance outside his house, the longer he figured he was running the show. I'd have run him down to the station in half an hour so he's on our turf. He wants coffee? Fuck it: I get it for him. He needs to go to the bathroom? Fuck it: I go with him. I'd put him in one room and his daughter in another room and his son in another room and have them interrogated at the same time, then come out and compare notes with the other cops. And I'd go right back to Fred and bluff: 'We know you did it. And we know how you did it. You either come clean now or we get you anyway. It's that simple. We know what happened, and we're your worst nightmare.' I might even say we have the killer in another room. Or a neighbor saw what happened. You go right up to the line of being believable—and you try not to cross it. I'd want Fred to think that everything he's heard about cops is true: we're real smart and we can read minds. But the way the cops were working Carol's murder, *he* had the advantage. He was the rabbi. He was a pillar of the community. Everyone respected him. Everyone felt sorry for him. He intimidated the cops and they let him go. Talking with people like him is like playing chess: you bluff the shit out of them. That night was the first round. And Fred Neulander won it."

Hardly anyone saw Neulander cry over the next few days. That didn't surprise most of his acquaintances. They ascribed his calm demeanor to his macho personality and to the thirty years that he had professionally been consoling *other* people, lending them the comfort and strength of religious faith. He was playing a long-accustomed role, which did not include falling apart when people needed him. The role was compatible with the "tough-guy image" Neulander cultivated over the last decade or so, according to one rabbi who knew him well: "Fred never let people see his emotions. I would have expected to see more visible grief. But it was pretty consistent with Fred's personality that he kept so much inside of him."

It was also consistent with the lessons Fred's father taught him: a real man never complained or lost control of himself. A real man didn't show emotion, not to others, not even to himself.

Cherry Hill had never seen a *shiva* quite like the one for Carol Neulander. Every day, hundreds of people queued up outside the house, as if to go through a receiving line at a major event. Most visitors went directly to the family room at the rear of the house, although some gathered in the living room, where water stains on the walls left by the efforts to scrub Carol's blood and brains from view were still visible. One guest was stunned that people were "looking at the walls in the living room and seeing where there had been blood all over them. It was horrifically uncomfortable, just as it was discomforting and unusual that Rabbi Neulander was so insistent that *shiva* would take place in his home where his wife was murdered." A rabbi from Boston who had been a seminary classmate of Fred's but had rarely seen him in the intervening years drove down to pay his respects. This man noted Matthew and Benjamin's stunning resemblance to their father (all were short, solid, and muscular) and Rebecca's to her mother (both were thin, with black hair cut just above their shoulders). Rebecca also shared Carol's good-hearted nature. As the Boston rabbi was sitting alone with his grief in the Neulanders' living room, Rebecca walked over to console him, a gesture that struck the visitor and stayed with him for years. It was almost identical, he said, to what Carol would have done under the same circumstances.

Every morning and evening for seven days in accordance with the ritual of *shiva,* prayer services were held at the Neulanders' house. The practice reflects Judaism's concern for the bereaved: the synagogue comes to them during the mourning period. The *kaddish,* the mourner's prayer, is recited by those assembled twice each day, and in between these sessions, etiquette calls for visitors to refrain from questioning the immediate family. They are supposed to sit in silence, speaking only when spoken to, observing the Talmudic instruction, "Do not console your friend while his dead is before him." The need to perform the usual social graces is suspended during *shiva.* Instead of chitchat, mourners are expected—as God told the prophet Ezekiel—to "sigh in silence."

Neulander wasn't doing much sighing, however, nor did he seem to welcome silence. In fact, he seemed as upbeat as ever, almost like he was announcing that *nothing* could get him down, not even the murder of his wife. Carol's sister, Margaret, was shocked when the rabbi told her, "They'll never find who killed Carol. She worked at a bakery. It could have been the girlfriend or boyfriend of someone who worked there and they took off by now. They'll never find them." Didn't he *want* the cops to identify her murderer? It didn't sound like it. Fred seemed to be saying that this was a perfect crime—insoluble.

Day after day during *shiva,* Fred smiled as he introduced people to each other and plied them with soft drinks. He was an expansive and charming host, once even attempting a version of the how-many-Jews-does-it-take-to-change-a-lightbulb joke. (Example: "How many congregants does it take to change a lightbulb in a synagogue?" "*Change?* You want we should *change* the lightbulb? My grandmother donated that lightbulb!") When a bulb went out one night during *shiva,* everyone groaned, "Great! No one here can change a lightbulb. The room's full of Jews." Neulander quickly pointed to the one gentile in the room—Matthew's friend, Michael Tasch. "*He'll* know what to do," the rabbi laughed. Tasch changed the bulb, wondering how there could be so much joking—and so little solemnity at such a time.

But then, Jews are known for their ability to find humor in the most dire situations. Levity brings relief and its own version of comfort and solace. But while it wasn't unheard of for mourners to relieve their stress in this manner, Fred's jokes in particular seemed very much out of place. After all, the loss of his wife—the mother of his three children—hadn't exactly been expected. Or natural.

Some people who attended *shiva* at the Neulanders' thought Fred might be in shock, that his affability was reflexive. Others found his behavior disturbing. Matthew was mystified: How could his father joke around after what happened? Nothing could explain it. Neulander simply showed no sorrow. Maybe he didn't feel entitled to being comforted by others; maybe he was afraid to let the tears flow. It might have seemed to him like an impermissible act of self-indulgence. Even so, it was strange.

Even stranger was Neulander's reaction to a sensible idea from an old friend. One morning, Neulander got a visit from Joel Rowe. They'd been close for twenty years. The Rowe's lived a few blocks away. The two families sometimes went on vacations together, and their kids were so close they were almost like cousins. Sitting at the kitchen table with the rabbi, Rowe said he'd had a brainstorm in the middle of the night. "Fred," he started, "you know a lot of very affluent people. Why don't you ask some of them to each contribute ten thousand, twenty thousand dollars—you name it—and raise a reward to flush out the weasel who did this to Carol?"

Neulander leaned back in his chair and sighed for a minute. "Oh, Joel, Joel, Joel," he finally said, "it won't help. It won't bring her back. Why don't you just give me the money?"

For some time after Carol's murder, people in Cherry Hill were afraid a madman was loose in town. Salesmen called some of the Neulanders' neighbors, trying to sell them burglar alarms; parents picked up their kids at school instead of letting them walk home. And everyone was keeping their eyes out for a blue car—maybe an '84 or '85 Chevy Monte Carlo or Buick Riviera—that a neighbor thought he'd seen speeding away from the Neulanders' about twenty minutes before Fred got home that night.

The police questioned Fred and his kids a few more times, talked with neighbors and friends, drove about ninety minutes to northern New Jersey to interview Carol's siblings about her character and her marriage. For the moment, they were just fishing, doing the sort of preliminary guesswork that often paid off. They'd eliminated the possibility that Carol was killed during a robbery that went bad—she'd been too brutally beaten for that idea to hold up. A lot of people seemed to know that she often came home at night carrying a lot of cash from her bakery. But if robbery was the point, the perpetrator would have been carrying a gun in case he met with resistance from his victim: bullets were impersonal. But a beating—and Carol's had been as severe as any Cherry Hill cop had ever seen—was about as personal as it got. The fact that her purse was missing suggested burglary may have been a motive, but the physical damage she suffered indicated another kind of motive, maybe vengeance pursued by someone settling an old score. Her assailant may not have intended to kill her, the cops reasoned, but he might not have been able to stop once he started beating her.

About two weeks after the murder, detectives learned from phone records that Neulander had called a lady friend ninety minutes after returning home from the police station that night and again the next day. The second call was placed from the Philadelphia airport while waiting for his younger son's arrival from Michigan to attend his mother's funeral. By themselves, these calls didn't cast more suspicion on Neulander. There were bad marriages and indiscretion and infidelities in Cherry Hill, just like anywhere else, and there were plenty of people happily gossiping about them. You could hear the whisperings every day at Ponzio's, the most popular diner in town, or at the Springdale Deli, famed for its soup. Rumors had been going around about Fred Neulander's possible philandering at least since 1984, when Stacey, a twenty-eight-year-old living north of Philadelphia, got a call from a friend in Cherry Hill who had gone to Neulander for counseling. The woman told Stacey the rabbi fondled her. Stacey, who had admired Neulander ever since he'd taught her confirmation class at Temple Emanuel some fifteen years earlier, didn't believe her friend's story. She was talking about someone Stacey adored; to her, Fred Neulander was "this guy who was loaded with personality," so "cool" he let the girls in the confirmation class call him Fred. Not "Rabbi," but Fred! No one did that in those days. The story made no sense at all. But then Stacey began to hear similar things about Neulander from other people, and she gave the gossip a reluctant credence.

In time, everyone's question about Neulander wasn't whether he was a flirt or if he liked to fondle women who came to him for help, but whether he was actually scoring. What was odd was that he wasn't a great looker. He was short. His hair was tightly cropped. He dressed well, but in a conservative, Brooks Brothers sort of way. Women didn't swoon over him. Men didn't get jealous. Without the authority of the pulpit, he would have been just a regular guy. But his air of rabbinic wisdom and the power and authority that came with being a clergyman created a certain mystique. If a man in his position had a libido in frequent need of servicing, the potential for world-class philandering was there, no matter what he looked like.

To some outsiders, Neulander was better at intimidating people than invoking awe in them. "Fred was very dominating," said one man who had many friends who belonged to M'kor Shalom, although he was not a member himself. "He always tried to get his way. If you were smart, you didn't get into a conversation with him unless you planned to agree with him. He liked to throw his weight around. He had temper tantrums. He yelled. He bullied. A lot of people didn't like him, and a lot of people didn't trust him."

But determining the inner workings of any authority figure is no simple matter. It requires listening and watching carefully, without being seduced by the trappings of his power. In Neulander's case, it was nearly impossible. Over the years, he had fashioned an impermeable façade that let people see and hear only what he wanted them to. He was a cipher, a self-made mannequin. Whoever tried to know the "real" Neulander person ended up exceedingly frustrated.

3

"Sin Is Thrilling"

The people of Cherry Hill were no different from people anywhere else: they loved gossip, especially about how the mighty
have fallen. Clergymen gone wrong in a town this size qualified as
mighty enough. Over the years, there had been talk about one
rabbi who propositioned an attractive magazine writer; around the
same time, another temple was reeling from the news that its rabbi
had a "second family" in Israel. The news leaked out just before he
was to be honored at a testimonial dinner. His wife in Cherry Hill
was not happy to learn that he was a bigamist, but at least the town
had something juicy to talk about. Not that philandering religious
leaders were unknown in Cherry Hill's Christian community.
There was that Presbyterian minister who ran off with his secretary, and a Methodist cleric who was fired for preferring the sexual company of congregants.

"The gossip here scares the pants off of me," said one longtime resident of Cherry Hill. "These people have little sense that talking about others behind their backs can hurt. But *this* is how certain people amuse themselves around here. What else do they have to do, other than go to malls or buy fancy cars and second homes or send their wives and kids on long vacations in Europe."

In the 1950s, Abraham Heschel, one of the great rabbis of the twentieth century, explained gossip's appeal. It was really quite simple. "Sin is thrilling and full of excitement," he noted. "Is virtue thrilling? Are there many mystery novels that describe virtue? Are there many best-selling novels that portray adventures in goodness? . . . Ideals have a high mortality rate in our generation . . ."

Gossip was an easy way to believe you were superior to another person. It was especially fun when it was about clergymen, who were so mysterious that many people confused them with God. While *good* rabbis didn't portray themselves as representatives of God, that's how they were often seen, even by adults, who should know better, and definitely by children, who should be taught better.

Rumors about Fred Neulander's infidelities were so much a part of Cherry Hill's culture by the time of Carol's murder that detectives working the case couldn't have ignored them if they'd wanted to. Gary Mazo, M'kor Shalom's associate rabbi, heard about his boss's alleged liaisons during his first week on the job back in 1990. Two years later, Neulander installed a dead bolt on the inside of his office door. Mazo and Anita Hochman, the temple's cantor, found this questionable.

"Why do you need that, Fred?" they asked.

"Well, I need privacy," Neulander said, doing nothing to allay their suspicions. "Sometimes if I'm in a confidential conversation with a congregant, the wind blows the door open or a janitor comes in."

The rabbi's behavior provoked whispers on a weekly basis, since every Friday night he was in the habit of walking down from the *bima* during Shabbat services to greet his audience, especially the more attractive female members of the congregation. Often he'd ignore rows of people in his rush to kiss or hug a woman who had strategically positioned herself in an aisle seat. But there were also times when he singled out a male congregant with whom he had a special relationship, squeezing his shoulder or shaking his hand.

One of these men recalled the process by which he was "chosen" for specific rabbinic attention. He'd sought Neulander's counsel in the early 1990s because he feared that his job got in the way of being a good Jew. Neulander assured him that he needn't worry; he was not compromising his faith. After that conversation, the rabbi included this man in his meet-'n'-greet routine on Friday nights, stopping at his seat and patting him on the shoulder as if to say, "There, there. We've talked through your problem. We know all about it. We understand it. We have a bond, a secret, just between the two of us." The ploy had the intended effect of making the man feel special. For years, whenever he saw Neulander coming his way, he was honored to be among the trusted few, initiated into an almost covert alliance with this potent and charming spiritual leader. Still, it was pretty clear to almost everyone who attended Shabbat services that their rabbi's most fervent greetings were reserved for the good-looking, well-dressed women—although many congregants did their best to rationalize his behavior. One man who saw Neulander deep in conversation with one of these women after a Friday night service remembered telling himself, "Good for him. Who *wouldn't* want to be with women like these? Schmoozing with them is part of a rabbi's job—the good part."

Others were less inclined to deny the obvious signs of unseemliness and, in any case, found it disturbing that gossip swirled around their spiritual leader, deservedly or not. A few people were concerned enough to confront Neulander directly about the rumors. Early in the 1990s, an influential congregant sat Fred down and asked for an explanation; he didn't get one. Nothing to them, Neulander shrugged. A year or two later, Gary Mazo invited the rabbi to his home. He broached the subject at the kitchen table in the presence of his wife, herself a rabbi. They got the same runaround. In fact, Neulander joked about it. He, too, had heard these rumors and they were nonsense, just a bunch of silly women pretending that his hugs and his kisses were a come-on. In reality, *they* had come on to him. Naturally, he'd turned all of them away. He was a rabbi, not a playboy. If he really was the Casanova of South Jersey, Fred laughed, he'd be so tired from serving congregants in bed that he couldn't serve them from the *bima*.

Neulander was able to convince people that he was the innocent target of slander partly because he knew they wanted to believe him. A simple denial from him was sufficient to quell their doubts. After all, no one wanted a scandal. By hurting the rabbi, who was M'kor Shalom's heart and soul, it would hurt the entire congregation. And it would sully the names of the women who were linked—fairly or erroneously—with Neulander.

So the rabbi continued to lead M'kor Shalom and wander up and down the aisles of the sanctuary on Friday nights, doling out hugs and kisses to the prettiest congregants. And everyone kept talking.

PART TWO

THE GOOD YEARS

4

"Honey, You Can Still Back Out of This"

There was a time when Fred Neulander aroused no one's attention, despite his efforts to attract it. Although he made friends easily enough at Jamaica High School in Queens in the late 1950s, he was one of four thousand students spread out over three floors in a massive building that more closely resembled a cathedral than a school. Jamaica High had one of the city's more diverse curricula. Students could choose among five different languages, including Hebrew, or concentrate on music, art, business, even fashion design. After-school activities ran the gamut from the Problems of Democracy Club to a K-9 Club, although many kids preferred to spend their time hanging out in the candy stores along Union Turnpike or Hillside Avenue, or in friends' houses, playing the latest 45s. On weekends, everyone went to the Valencia, one of the most majestic theaters in all of New York City, where thirty-five hundred people sat under a ceiling painted with twinkling stars and drifting clouds, and a mural along the walls depicted a Spanish village. Out in the lobby, goldfish swam under a gurgling fountain. Manhattan was famous for its movie palaces, especially Radio City Music Hall on Sixth Avenue. Yet way out here in Queens, six miles away in distance and light-years away in sensibility, the Valencia could make the ornate cinemas of Manhattan seem pallid by comparison.

Because the Neulander family had moved to Queens from Albany, Fred entered Jamaica High as an outsider. But he quickly established himself socially. Years later, former classmates remembered him as "charming," "very sociable," "with a laserlike ability to make you feel important." Fred, people said, "could focus on you to the exclusion of everyone else." But he never made it into the most popular clique, which saw him as too pushy. Besides, he didn't live in the right neighborhood. The fathers of the kids in the "A-group" were doctors and lawyers and dentists, and lived in houses with yards and garages. Fred's father, who had sold insurance door-to-door in Albany, operated a dry-cleaning business. The family rented an apartment in a building indistinguishable from thousands of others in New York—it was square and grim and about as inspiring as a cinder block.

By junior year, Neulander hit his stride. He joined Arista, the club for the school's better students; he was co-captain of the swimming team and helped lead it to a 5–3 win for the season; he was assistant literary editor of the yearbook and vice president of student government. He was known for helping newcomers navigate the school's culture; when a cousin he'd never met transferred to Jamaica as a sophomore, Neulander tracked him down and gave him some pointers. And he dated a very popular Jewish girl who was sweet, smart, full of energy—and from a family that was more prosperous than his. They broke up after a year, but Fred wasn't lonely. As a senior, he kept company with a girl who was a year or two behind him. She happened to be a *shiksa,* which would have dismayed his parents. But then they probably didn't even know she existed.

One of Fred's closest friends in those days recalled wondering why he was never invited to the Neulanders' apartment. "Maybe," he guessed, "because my father was a lawyer and we lived in a nice house, and he lived in Kew Gardens. I always got the feeling that he was ashamed of his parents.

"When I was a senior," he continued, "the student government voted to give me an award. I ran into Fred and he took me aside. 'I wanted to do that for you,' he said. It was like he felt sorry for me or like I didn't really deserve the award. I'd known Fred for three years and I'd always thought that he was smart and very ambitious. Now I saw him as manipulative and very political."

His friend's opinion didn't matter much to Neulander: they never saw each other again after graduation. Neulander headed off to Hartford to attend Trinity College. The school was a notch or two down from the Ivy League, but if all went well, it would take Fred Neulander farther away from his past than the hundred miles that separated Hartford from Queens—farther than even he had imagined was possible.

The Trinity campus was designed eighty years before Neulander laid eyes on it by Frederick Law Olmsted, the most influential landscape architect America ever produced. Its quadrangles were bordered by dormitories with Gothic towers and thick, leaded glass that looked nothing like the brown-brick apartment buildings and the tiny storefronts back in Jamaica. Neulander loved his four years here. The place represented a world he'd seen only in photos in *Life* magazine. He had long talks with friends in oak-paneled common rooms and strolled through stone archways on his way to class. Unlike Queens, where the accents on the streets changed with every new wave of immigrants, the atmosphere of Trinity exuded manners and breeding and charm—what passes, in some circles, for the finer things in life. Still, Trinity wasn't Harvard or Yale. It remained a second-tier school with Ivy League pretensions, especially among upwardly mobile students like Neulander. These kids wanted to forget what they had come from: the candy stores and luncheonettes, the busy streets where kids played catch with an orange Spalding because everyone knew it was the ball with the biggest bounce for the smallest nickel. At Trinity, Fred discovered that he wanted something he'd never before wanted or needed—a life of comfort and affluence beyond the hard economic realities his father had never been able to escape.

Trinity, founded by Episcopalians in 1823 as a counterweight to Yale's domination by Congregationalists, was an odd place for a Jewish boy from Queens to inhabit. The overtly Episcopalian influence didn't last long at Trinity; by the end of the nineteenth century, its charter was amended so that Connecticut's Episcopal bishop no longer chaired its board of trustees. Yet when Neulander arrived there, the school still required students to attend chapel every day. Built in 1932, Trinity's chapel happened to be one of the finest structures of its kind on any college campus. Not only was it an outstanding example of perpendicular construction—a form of Gothic architecture that emphasized long, vertical lines intended to lift your eyes to heaven—but tile, brick, and stones imported from Mount Sinai and China's Great Wall had been used to build it. Lovely as it was, Jews might not have appreciated the chapel: until the early twentieth century, few of them enrolled at Trinity. But the immigration of millions of Jews at the turn of the century—urban Jews from Europe who respected learning and wanted their children to profit from it—changed Trinity's makeup, just as it changed the makeup of many institutions around the country. In 1904, just 2 percent of the student body was Jewish. By 1917, Jews comprised 15 percent of Trinity's undergraduate population—an eightfold increase in little more than a decade. The numbers didn't thrill the school's vast Christian majority, which included alumni and trustees as well as students. In 1918, the Student Senate warned the trustees that the Jewish onslaught was discouraging new Christian applicants. Since many of the aliens came from Russia, the Senate complained that "every . . . class now has a Russian socialistic expression of opinion." To minimize or eliminate further enrollment of this "undesirable element," the organization proposed that all students be required to live on campus, a tactic intended to discourage Jews from enrolling. (Most Jewish students were Hartford residents who commuted to campus.) The result was a new rule: students who were not American-born, or whose fathers were not, had to live in university housing for their freshman and sophomore years. But Trinity's president, to his credit, successfully opposed the trustees' decision, telling the college's board that the requirement was "not honest and rules out too many good students who would otherwise be with us."

When Neulander arrived at Trinity in 1959, the attitude toward Jews had improved—to a point. With at least half the students coming from WASPy private schools or from blue-blooded, monied families (or both), there were still spurts of anti-Semitism. One night, for instance, a few students were roughhousing in the hall of their dormitory. An upperclassman opened his door, saw who was making the racket, and snickered, "Shut up, you goddamn Jews."

But Fred seemed to experience no prejudicial treatment. In fact, at Trinity he achieved the popularity he'd sought in high school. "Everybody loved Fred," remembered one of his roommates. "He was so outgoing and friendly and popular that just about every fraternity put out a bid for him."

Trinity's frat houses were clustered along Vernon Avenue, which went up a hill. At the top of the hill, as well as at the top of the pecking order, was St. Anthony's, the wealthiest fraternity. Below it were several jock fraternities, then a few unaffected by social and religious distinctions, and finally one that was as working-class as anyone got at Trinity. Neulander ended up about halfway up the hill at Alpha Delta Phi.

His fraternity brothers were Jewish and Italian and WASP, and their small, fairly new house was only several hundred yards from Neulander's dorm. Most of them had a pretty sharp sense of humor: how else to explain the fraternity's page in the college's yearbook in 1963: "The mid-nineteenth century saw the rise of several great intellectual movements . . . Alpha Delta Phi, also a product of the zeitgeist of that age, has tried to maintain that tradition in its fine collection of wall-to-wall *Reader's Digest* and leather-bound printer's edition (with concordance) of the *Classic Comic Stories,* all of which can be found in the library of their house . . ."

Neulander had his own reputation when it came to humor. After buying a fifteen-year-old jalopy for seventy-five dollars, he drove around town in it with a handset from a telephone. At stoplights, he cranked down his window, waved the handset at the driver in the car next to him, and yelled, "Hey, there's a call for you." Anyone who thought college humor was dead just had to visit Trinity.

Neulander made Trinity's swimming team, as he had Jamaica High's. Of his performance on the lacrosse team, an old friend said, "Fred played energetically. What did a kid from Queens know about lacrosse? That was the sort of thing people played at clubs, the sort of clubs Fred wouldn't have been allowed to join anyway." It was his election as president of the Sophomore Dining Club that ranked among Neulander's greatest extracurricular triumphs, since the club was one of Trinity's oldest honor societies. But it was odd that as a Jew—and a future rabbi—Neulander never joined Hillel, the only campus organization that addressed the religious needs of Jewish students. Maybe establishing his academic and sports credentials was more important than reinforcing his faith. Maybe he didn't need his faith reinforced, because even here, on this classically WASP campus, he was confident enough about his religious identity that he didn't have to worship regularly with fellow Jews, or eat with them, or hear lectures about his heritage and the perils being faced by the State of Israel. Maybe, given all his other activities, he simply didn't have time for one more.

Despite the six generations of rabbis in Fred Neulander's family, he had never seriously considered joining their ranks. His original plan had been to major in astrophysics, go on for a Ph.D., and eventually become a college professor. But then he flunked Physics 101. Realizing that "I wasn't going to Stockholm," or anywhere near a Nobel Prize, he switched his major to religion. It was, after all, the "family business." Perhaps more important, he was encouraged to take that path by a charismatic professor, William Johnson.

Johnson, who became Neulander's mentor and friend, was described years later by one of Fred's roommates as "the sort of messianic figure who mesmerizes college kids." In the classroom, Johnson's ideas were inspirational; outside of it, he helped students get grants and scholarships. Many of them remembered having long, intricate conversations with Johnson in his office and coming away enthralled by the prospect of a life of the mind. Although he was only eight years older than Fred (the two of them arrived at Trinity the same year, 1959), Johnson had already earned two doctorates—one from Columbia and the other from Lund University in Sweden.

Fred took several courses with Johnson—two courses on the Bible, both Old and New Testaments, and one called "Christian Thought from Christ to the Twentieth Century." Johnson found Fred a bit rough around the edges—not especially cultured or well read. This was somewhat to be expected: Neulander was a product of Queens, not of a prep school, like many of his classmates. "Fred was smart, not brilliant," Johnson later remembered. "He did reasonably well because ideas were taken seriously at Trinity, and Fred liked that."

Early in his senior year, Neulander came to the professor's house to discuss his future. Johnson gave him a beer and sat him down in his living room, where Fred asked for advice on graduate programs in religion that would fulfill his new goal of becoming a college teacher in that field. He expected Johnson to rattle off a list of appropriate schools and then the two of them would design a secure future for him in academia, allowing him to mentor students as Johnson had mentored him. As it happened, Johnson had other ideas. The war in Vietnam was heating up, he noted, and would "cripple" the country by draining America's spiritual strength and material wealth. Johnson thought that the war could ruin university life. Although Washington was bankrolling a great deal of academic research, a considerable amount was increasingly underfinanced. As a result, scholarship in less "useful" fields was neglected. Anyone who could create a bigger bomb or design a better tank would do fine, Johnson told Neulander. But people who specialized in "softer" stuff that didn't make the world safe for democracy, like literature and philosophy, were in trouble.

From these developments, Johnson concluded, much to Fred's surprise, that he ought to become a rabbi, and then get a doctorate in Jewish studies. If the academic world suffered from less government funding, Rabbi Neulander would still be able to find a job. And if Johnson's prediction turned out to be wrong, a Ph.D. in Judaica would make him a very attractive candidate for a teaching position somewhere.

A few weeks later, Neulander applied to Hebrew Union College, the Reform movement's seminary in New York—but not really because he was interested in ministering to people's souls or because he had a "need to be needed," reasons that most students cite when explaining their choice of seminary training. Fred acted on Johnson's advice because it was a good career move. If his mentor was right, the rabbinate would give him a security blanket.

Once again, as he had in high school, Neulander was trying to maneuver his way into a place he didn't belong. Instead of seeking a place with the "in crowd," he now sought a profession rooted in tradition and faith and prayer and God because it promised job security. That was a reasonable motive for entering most careers. For the rabbinate, this was fairly unusual.

Most of Fred's friends knew nothing about his change of plan until the middle of his senior year. They were surprised to hear the news; they'd never thought of him as a rabbi or counselor. But his women friends were all for it. They felt that Fred, unlike most guys, treated them as equals and was interested in what they had to say. They believed that he was a natural for the rabbinate. One woman recalled almost forty years later that "Fred was kind and decent and bright—and he never wrote us off. So many guys didn't even think that we had brains. To them, we were just pretty faces. Fred didn't take us for granted. He wanted to know what we were thinking, which was more than a lot of other guys were doing in those days."

He was also, according to some former coeds, *almost* a catch: friendly, confident, always up for a challenging conversation; and after years on swimming teams, he had a powerful body. Yet he wasn't a dumb jock. The problem was his height. Not too many girls wanted to go out with a guy who came up to their chin. The truth was that he didn't date very much—until he met Carol Lidz on a blind date in 1962. Carol, a student at Mount Holyoke in South Hadley, Massachusetts, was a year younger than Fred and, at five-feet-three, three inches shorter. Her black hair was tossed back into a wave that neatly framed her face and her eyebrows were plucked into long, tapered parentheses set above her dark eyes. She was no beauty: her nose was too long for her face, though her smile was warm, if a bit tentative. But she was sweet and friendly and caring. By the middle of Neulander's senior year, the two of them were spending most of their weekends together, either at Trinity or Mount Holyoke, thirty-eight miles away. At Trinity, she spent the nights on a couch in Professor Johnson's living room.

Fred's mentor thought Carol was "perfect" for Neulander. "Carol made up for whatever rough edges were left on Fred," Johnson later said. "She was smarter than him, and certainly more sophisticated. All the travel she'd done in Europe probably had something to do with that. And clearly, they were both very much in love." One sign of Carol's seriousness about Neulander was to take several courses in religion at Mount Holyoke. She may have been a psychology major, but she still wanted to hold her own in discussions with Fred.

Carol had just about everything Neulander didn't: privilege, status, money, and siblings. There were four Lidz children: eight years separated Ed, the oldest, from Margaret, the youngest, with Robert and Carol falling in between. Carol was close to her brothers and especially tight with Margaret, who was three years her junior. Margaret's friends, who tended to fight and bicker with their own sisters, were impressed by the Lidz girls' intimacy, although one observed that Carol "always seemed like she was in a bad mood. But then again, so many of us were unhappy in those days. Maybe Carol was more up front than the rest of us." Or maybe Carol envied Margaret. The younger girl, after all, said someone who knew them both, was "stunning," "lovely," "elegant," and "statuesque," with "a more original bent of mind" than the plainer, more reserved Carol, a wallflower by comparison. Another Lidz family friend agreed with this assessment. Carol, she said, "never impressed me as Miss Creative."

The Lidzes grew up in a gracious colonial house at the end of a short cul de sac in Woodmere, one of Long Island's "Five Towns"— known collectively for their mostly nouveau riche, mostly Jewish residents, and their often gaudy and opulent taste. As one of Carol's brothers later described it, Woodmere was a "very protected community." The streets were safe, the schools were terrific, and the teenage social life was very active. Every Friday night after basketball or football games, a local diner, Bernie's, filled with kids. The girls sat at one table, the boys sat at another, and everyone eyed everyone else. "Your whole life," lamented a woman who spent her childhood there, "was about getting the guys' attention." On Saturday nights, there was usually a party at someone's house, with dancing to music by Elvis and Buddy Holly and the Platters and, a little later, four guys from Liverpool with very strange haircuts.

A tell-all book about the Five Towns cost its author, Rabbi Martin Siegel, his job at Temple Sinai, the Woodmere temple to which Carol's family belonged. Published in 1970, *Amen* portrayed the area as a lily-white haven for wealthy liberals. The author drew distinctions between the "old guard and the newcomers . . . The old guard are the . . . people with money but no stomach for flaunting it. They generally fall into two groups: the educated and the uneducated. The educated are the business executives and the professionals . . . The women dress simply and are active in various old-line charities; the children go to the best colleges; they themselves frequent the Philharmonic, the opera, and the theater. They also read books.

"The second element in this old guard are the garment manufacturers . . . As a group, they are not cultivated, but they are good, sensitive people to whom the Jewish virtues of charity and humanity have always meant a great deal.

". . . The group that moved here since the Second World War is the archetype of the Five Towners, those who have lost their Jewish humanity and haven't yet achieved their Anglo-Saxon polish . . . The emphasis in this group is on spending money, often more than they have."

Carol's family projected the elegance and refinement that placed it in the first group—old guard, old taste, old values, old money, even though their money was less than two generations old. It came from a button business that Carol's grandfather, who had emigrated to the United States from Poland, started in 1895. (The name Lidz was a truncation of the original family name, Lidzbarski, which derived from Lidzbark, their native town in Poland.) "When you entered their house," said one of Carol's high school friends, "you knew you were entering a world of quiet dignity. The best thing was that there was nothing snobby about them."

Carol's mother, Kitty, was thin and quiet, preferring solitary activities like knitting to the more sociable pastimes of golf or canasta. Her father, Maurice, was more outgoing, as his appointment as Woodmere's air raid warden during World War Two might suggest. Maurice attended the Manhattan high school run by the Ethical Culture Society, an organization popular with certain liberal New York Jews who were disenchanted with the supernaturalism of traditional religion and preferred Ethical Culture's emphasis on human worth. Once he moved his family to Woodmere, however, Maurice was an active Reform Jew, as involved in Temple Sinai as he was in the local United Fund. But his deepest interest was always his family. According to one of Temple Sinai's rabbis, "Every time we rode the train together into Manhattan, his face, which was kind and distinguished, would light up as he talked about how proud he was of his four kids."

Both Kitty and Maurice cared deeply for their children and were able to provide the best for them. Their house, one of only two on Ross Lane, sat on three quarters of an acre—enough land to ensure little threat from noisy neighbors or even noisier real estate developers. Maurice commissioned an architect to design the house during the war, and its formal dining room, separate breakfast room, five bedrooms, combination library and parlor, muted carpets, live-in cook (Hilda), and governess (nicknamed "Foodie" by the kids) imparted sufficient formality to impress even visitors of comparable affluence.

In school, Carol was cautious. Her hand didn't go up unless she was sure she knew the answer. "She wasn't a risk-taker," recalled a classmate. "But she wasn't the teacher's pet, either. She was a plugger and got A's in just about everything. And unlike a lot of other go-getters, she was very kind." At Hewlett High, Carol's quiet determination got her into such honors classes as "hislish"—a combination history-and-English class—and her thoughtfulness brought her legions of friends. The 1960 edition of *Patches,* Hewlett's yearbook, is typical of the genre, which never has a nasty word for anyone. In *Patches,* almost everyone "greets the world with a smile," is "easygoing," "casual," and "full of fun," or is "destined for success." But the entry for Carol Lidz seemed more genuine than most: "Always busy . . . Amazingly successful in all she attempts . . . Le Cercle Francais . . . Patches Specialty Section . . . Bulletin co-editor . . . Chairman of Sets and Scenery Committee of Jr. and Sr. plays . . . A wonderful person to be with."

Despite her accomplishments, Carol's ambitions were simpler than her classmates'. They wanted to become physicists or advertising executives. All Carol wanted was "to go around the world in eighty days." A close friend of Carol's from kindergarten through high school still saw her, decades later, as "the perfect girl with the perfect homework and the top grade. I can't imagine her as anything but 'good.' She may not have been the prettiest girl in her class, but she was content being who she was. When a lot of girls were getting nose jobs, Carol didn't. She was a very decent person, and that impressed all of us. A good many of us were very spoiled: our parents had a lot of money and we took advantage of it. They gave us stuff—nice cars, expensive clothing—because they felt guilty about not spending enough time with us. And a lot of us were pretty promiscuous: this was right near the end of the stifling fifties and we felt the changes in the air. Or we were just plain bored out there in the suburbs. But I can't imagine Carol playing around: she was such a *good* person, such a *decent* person. But also because no guy would look at her. She just wasn't sexy. She was like her mother—very thin and she carried herself with an air of insecurity. I have to laugh when I try to think of her with boyfriends during high school. She just didn't have any."

Carol's parents sent her to Camp Vega in south-central Maine for several summers. With its three hundred acres, art and dance studios, stables, and a small fleet of sailboats and canoes, Vega was (and remains) one of the most elite sleepover camps in the country. Later, between her junior and senior years of high school, Carol and her friend Libby flew to Switzerland for a six-week language immersion program. High in the mountains near the town of Champery, surrounded by chalets and cuckoo clocks, they played tennis and swam in an Olympic-size pool, toured museums and art galleries, and climbed about a quarter of the way up Mont Blanc, at 15,770 feet the highest mountain in the Alps. It was Carol's first trip abroad.

She was her usual reserved self that summer but still made friends with most of the girls in the program, thirty in all, who came from Latin America and South Africa, as well as Western Europe and the United States. At first, Carol and Libby were uncomfortable around the two German girls. World War Two had ended only fourteen years earlier, and Jewish kids who grew up on Long Island had been taught that *every* German was evil. But these two girls seemed so sweet and "normal," so much like everyone else in the program, that Carol and Libby warmed up to them. By the time the Americans returned home, they viewed Germans in a slightly different light.

By exposing Carol to a fancy camp in Maine and then to Alpine adventures, her parents had intended not to spoil her but to increase her self-confidence. Kitty and Maurice appreciated Carol's goodness, but they worried that she could be easily influenced by stronger, more forceful personalities.

Carol attended Mount Holyoke for similar reasons. The first all-women's college in the country, Holyoke was full of young women looking to marry the right fellow and spend their lives running volunteer organizations or holding teas at their local Junior League. The school could give Carol a first-class education, maybe even a career. It would also help her fit into her social niche.

Far more than Trinity, which Carol's boyfriend was attending, Mount Holyoke was very much an appendage of WASP culture. Some Christian students at Mount Holyoke, having absorbed the anti-Semitism prevalent in their own background, dropped friends once they learned they were Jewish. Sunday and Wednesday afternoons and evenings were reserved for "gracious living"—quasiformal dinners preceded by teas in common rooms furnished with pianos and hardbacked chairs and overstuffed sofas and slightly faded carpets, where students were subtly reminded that they weren't "women" but "young ladies." In this setting, the usual coed chitchat about boys, boys, boys was discouraged in favor of discussions on such burning issues as Kennedy versus Nixon, unilateral disarmament, bomb shelters, and the latest show on Broadway, about three hours away by train. Students dressed for these biweekly events in skirts and sweaters or blouses, and if a girl was brave enough to invite a "male companion" along—usually someone from Dartmouth or Yale or Harvard, the nearest schools with the right cachet—her date wore a jacket and tie and was on even better behavior than the young lady he accompanied.

Fred Neulander and Carol Lidz had more in common than their backgrounds might suggest. Both were smart, clever, hardworking, and popular. Once they started dating, they were as inseparable as the distance between Hartford and South Hadley permitted. Friends considered their relationship to be one of equals in which neither dominated, and it was obvious they enjoyed each other's company. Fred and Carol were "very happy and very loving toward each other," one friend said. "Carol was kind and decent and Fred was fun to be around. Both were witty. They came from the same gene pool: they were both short. But Fred compensated by having a more forceful personality than Carol. And by being built like a brick. You always knew that Fred was around: he had a pretty formidable presence. Carol was sweet and charming, but terribly quiet sometimes. And so slender that she seemed to disappear into thin air."

In June 1963, Fred and Carol braced themselves for a separation that could exacerbate their differences. Fred graduated from Trinity and went to Cincinnati for an intensive course in Hebrew that would prepare him for seminary in the fall, while Carol, who had just completed her junior year, spent that summer in Europe. Unlike some of her peers, she wasn't hitchhiking her way through France, Italy, Germany, England, Austria, Denmark, and Holland. Nor was she spending hours in Left Bank cafés for the price of one *café filtre* or attending recent plays by angry young men in London. Carol traveled in the more genteel style expected of "proper" young women, with monogrammed suitcases trailing behind her.

When Fred finished his Hebrew courses in Cincinnati, he moved back to his parents' apartment in Queens. After being away at college for four years, he soon realized that, besides helping him stay within his budget, there was a major advantage to living at home—he was being well fed by his mother, a "natural instinct," he wrote a friend, since mothers' "primary concern" was to keep their sons strong and healthy.

Fred was now studying at the seminary's branch on West Sixty-eighth Street in Manhattan, one block west of Central Park. Even amid the intense studies and the long hours, he continued courting Carol. By now, her parents realized that the two of them were serious about each other. They liked him—he was charming, affable, eager to please—and so did Carol's siblings. "When I first met Fred," one of them said, "I thought he was a nice guy. Everyone has an ego, and even then Fred had a bit of a swagger. But I had to think that a rabbi was more than a good person, and I wasn't worried we were going to have someone in the family who was a moral nag, that I had to watch my language and everything I did when I was around him. He was OK. The guy was a jock."

But Kitty and Maurice weren't thrilled with Fred's career choice. In the mid-1960s, a rabbi didn't have the professional status of, say, a doctor. Certainly the job was honorable, but two decades after the Holocaust, many Jews were conflicted about being Jewish. Often, they felt a collective shame for appearing passive in the face of escalating Nazi terror, yet remained afraid of seeming too assertive or visible lest they be singled out again. And what Jew was more visibly, more assertively Jewish than a rabbi?

Carol's parents were also concerned about Fred's future earning power. Recent graduates of Hebrew Union College, the seminary Fred was attending, were then making about ten thousand dollars a year. The select few who were among the most famous rabbis in the country—and had been leading their congregations for as long as three decades—made twenty-five thousand dollars at best. By contrast, recently licensed physicians and dentists could make twenty thousand early on; many in private practice earned more than thirty thousand. Engineers and landscape architects, professions with less prestige than rabbis, had a better chance of breaking the twenty-five-thousand-dollar ceiling at some point in their career. Fred's future in-laws, while respectful of his choice, were practical enough to wonder how well their daughter would manage. The pinched budget of a rabbi's wife would hardly allow Carol to live in the style to which she'd been accustomed, even if Fred somehow rose to the top of his field. And how stable was the rabbinate, anyway? American Jewry wasn't exactly a growth industry. There were still only 5.3 million Jews in the entire United States, barely up from 5 million in the early 1950s.

But nothing could deter Carol from marrying Fred. She was in love with him, and her parents finally accepted that. In the spring of 1965, a year after Carol's graduation from Mount Holyoke, the couple was formally engaged. Fred was ecstatic, crowing to a friend that he was marrying "*the* most wonderful young lady." A few months before the wedding, he took two of Carol's young nieces to the movies and told them how happy he was to be joining such a large, close family. Finally, he would experience everything he'd missed growing up as an only child in a cramped apartment in Queens. The kids thought he was "a great guy."

On December 26, 1965, Fred and Carol were married at the Inwood Country Club, about three miles east of Woodmere. The afternoon ceremony wowed Neulander's friends. "People from Queens didn't know people who belonged to country clubs," said one of Fred's high school buddies. Inwood was central to the culture of the Five Towns' older German Jewish families. Its shining moment had been hosting the 1923 U.S. Open, which twenty-one-year-old Bobby Jones won against Bobby Cruickshank. Despite the passage of four decades, Inwood had retained the aura of exclusivity dating from that match, and Fred was delighted to bask in it on his wedding day. Queens, he thought, was now behind him. He was in a different league, an unquestionably better league, surrounded by all the trappings of style and class. People who belonged to Inwood Country Club didn't go to laundromats to clean their clothes, and when they referred to Valencia, they meant the city in Spain, not the movie palace in Queens. At long last, Fred was one of them.

The bride's gown was accessorized by an exquisite long lace scarf. The bridesmaids were in hunter green. The groom, of course, donned a tuxedo. Ernest Neulander, Fred's father, was his best man—literally, Ernest insisted, as well as ceremonially. Fred's uncle Arthur, a distinguished rabbi and a leader of the Conservative Jewish movement, officiated. Decades later, Fred described the vows he exchanged with Carol as "sobering" because of their "promise of permanence." At the conclusion of the service, Fred's friends Isadore Fallek and Marc Newberg signed the *ketubah,* the Jewish wedding certificate. Some guests remembered the shrimp hors d'oeuvres served at the reception most clearly, since shrimp was a "rather odd choice for a rabbi-to-be." But Carol's siblings were struck by something else—the memory of their father turning to Carol, just before escorting her down the aisle, and saying, "You know, honey, you can still back out of this."

Carol paid no attention to her father's concern. Her wedding, she believed, was the fulfillment of a promise made three years before at a friend's wedding held at the St. Regis Hotel on Fifth Avenue. The men wore tails, the women wore gowns, and the bride cut a five-tier wedding cake. When it was time for Libby, the bride, to throw her bouquet into the crowd, she was so jittery that she had to close her eyes. She tossed it straight up and it came straight down, landing at her feet. On the second try, Libby threw the flowers forward. They sailed ten, fifteen, maybe twenty feet from the bandstand and then dropped into a cluster of six girls. And there was Carol Lidz, wearing a single strand of white pearls and a modest green silk dress that barely exposed her décolletage. The slightest hint of a pale pink slip showed as she stretched out her right arm as far as it would go. Under the chandeliers of the majestic St. Regis, Carol caught the bouquet. She smelled the fragrant flowers while the other girls joked about when she would be getting hitched. Even her parents, who were present, ribbed her; clearly, they said, this was a girl who *wanted* that bouquet. It was apparent that Carol wanted to marry sooner rather than later. She was a fairly conventional girl, and according to the conventions of the world she inhabited, marriage was her logical next step. But three years later, Libby would think it odd that Carol would choose to become a rabbi's wife. The two girls had attended Hebrew school together, where they'd hide in the rest rooms to avoid going to class, which they hated. Carol would even make jokes about their rabbi and *his* wife. Libby couldn't imagine Carol in the same role. Yet thirty-six months after that wedding at the St. Regis, Carol became Mrs. Fred Neulander; she was a rabbi's wife. Surely more improbable things had happened than Carol turning into a *rebbetzin,* but at the time Libby, who'd known Carol since kindergarten, couldn't think of a single one.

5

Trying On His "Rabbi Suit"

After a brief honeymoon in Bermuda, Fred and Carol began married life in Queens. "Our apartment," Fred scribbled to a mentor in Hartford, "is in a wild condition. But it's ours and we're delighted." Not far away was Flushing Meadows, where a huge pile of burning ashes—ninety feet high—had been leveled for the 1939 World's Fair. In *The Great Gatsby,* these ashes symbolically separated the affluent arrivistes of Long Island from the secretaries and shopkeepers who populated the neighboring New York boroughs of Brooklyn and Queens and struggled to make ends meet. Although Fred was still in Queens—his "wild apartment" was only a few blocks from his parents—it felt as if he had crossed that imaginary line that Fitzgerald wrote about in *Gatsby*. His apartment building was new and lavish. Its a driveway curved down to the main entrance, a doorman greeted people with a smile, and a golden swan with wings outspread graced the front lawn from its

perch atop a white fountain. The building had a name—The Eden
Rock—which seemed fitting for a young man studying to be a
rabbi. If it wasn't exactly the Eden that Fred was reading about in
his classes at the seminary, it was the next best thing.

It took Fred about forty-five minutes to get to the seminary in
Manhattan, and Carol's jobs—first as an administrative assistant at
the National Conference of Christians and Jews, then as a "social-
worker-in-training" at the Riverdale Children's Association—
were no closer. Yet despite their lengthy commutes, both were
thriving. Fred was on his way to the rabbinate, and Carol's work
inspired her so much that she applied to Columbia for a master's
degree in social work.

To his surprise, Fred was learning that being a rabbi was more
than just a variant on teaching that would bring him job security. It
was a calling, a way to breathe life into abstractions, to make them
real, and then to use them to benefit others. His studies at HUC
exhilarated him. He discovered in the rabbinate "a new dimension
. . . [which] offered satisfactions beyond study and teaching. I realized that a rabbi . . . is privy to the most intimate joys and sorrows
the human condition presents. He can make a difference in the
souls of his congregants, as well as in their minds . . . Rabbis can help
make the . . . darkness less frightening. The pulpit opened like a
flower before me."

His classes, he wrote to a mentor back in Hartford, were "stimulating, but not overbearing." They "challenged" and "excited" him.
This thrill stayed with him throughout his five years at the seminary; in his last year there he wrote that he was still "very excited."
He earned mostly A's and a few B's and was elected treasurer of
HUC's executive board. He led a Passover seder at Dartmouth College, left a conference in Washington about social action "armed
with information and methods to *do*—not only speak," and officiated at Rosh Hashanah and Yom Kippur services in a variety of set-
tings, from a Long Island hospital to a synagogue in a tiny New

Hampshire town along Lake Winnipesaukee called Laconia. It was there that Fred received his first lesson in humility, a quality that most young rabbis would do well to cultivate in themselves.

When Fred told the Laconia temple's directors that he couldn't lead certain prayers because he had no musical ability, they were most reassuring. Everything was fine, they said. They'd arranged for a Catholic family with four daughters—ages ten, twelve, fifteen, and seventeen—to sing Kol Nidre. The prayer, a plea to God to forgive unkept promises Jews made over the last year, is recited each Yom Kippur eve. A week before the service, Neulander met with this family. The girls and their mother wore identical white dresses with white hose and white patent leather shoes. Each outfit was accessorized with two white hair bows. Puffed sleeves billowed from the dresses, which were stiffly starched, and crinoline petticoats rustled with every movement. This picturesque female tableau almost rendered Neulander speechless, and when the girls' father said they'd been preparing Kol Nidre by listening to a recording of it by the legendary cantor Jan Peerce, Fred was momentarily stunned. Neulander was deeply familiar with Peerce's rendition, the gold standard of the prayer, but he was accustomed to hearing it performed by baritones or tenors—by professional cantors, that is, who were most decidedly Jewish. He couldn't imagine a family of gentiles, especially this family, on the *bima* in their virginal white crinolines singing prayers on the most solemn day of the Jewish year.

But there they were on Yom Kippur eve, the four young sisters and their mother, facing the congregation in matching ensembles. With Mom at the keyboard of an electric organ, the youthful quartet of sopranos and altos warbled Kol Nidre in an original harmony arranged by their father. Neulander was appalled. Far from sounding like a female variation on Jan Peerce, the girls' voices resembled an incongruous hybrid of the Carter Family and the Lennon Sisters and Aimee Semple McPherson. The Yom Kippur

service, he thought, was a disaster. Who needed these *shiksas*
singing the prayer that, to anti–Semites, effectively proved that a
Jew's word couldn't be trusted? To Neulander, the whole performance verged on heresy.

But when he looked at the congregation, he saw that people
were enthralled. They loved the music. They loved this Catholic
family. They loved the very idea that these people, their neighbors,
had listened again and again to the Jan Peerce LP and adapted it
themselves. For six months, the girls and their mother had practiced
rolling their tongues around the strange syllables of a language completely foreign to them—six months of singing *"Kol Nidre veh-eh-
sa-ray va-ha-ra-may, v'-ko-na-may, v'khee-noo-yay, v'-kee-noo-say oo-sh'-
voo-oht, deen'-dar-nah ood'-eesh'-ta ba'-nah . . ."* until they were as
close to saying it correctly as they would ever get. And now the
audience could see and hear what they'd accomplished over that
half year of hard work: perfecting a performance that constituted a
great gift to their Jewish friends, their fellow Laconians.

Fred Neulander had arrived in New Hampshire fully confident
that he, still a rabbi in training, but from an important seminary in
New York, had much to teach the Jews of Laconia, country folk
who needed guidance in the right way to worship. It took him
nearly thirty-five years to realize how patronizing his attitude had
been—to realize that his Yom Kippur eve in Laconia had been a
special night in which good Jews had come together to teach *him*
something. When he was in his fifties, Neulander looked back at
that night and perceived it quite differently. He had been "arrogant" and "presumptuous," he wrote. "The rabbi may guide, assist,
suggest. But beyond that, the rabbi must listen and respond as a
devoted partner in a sacred quest . . . I was taught that the more
everyone was touched by authentic Jewish values—no matter the
means—the more effective I felt. Learning to see and hear through
other's eyes and ears became a requisite for my rabbinate."

In September 1967, Neulander entered his last year at HUC expecting the worst. Juggling his position as president of the student body with his duties as student rabbi at a temple in Westchester along with working on his thesis would be, he predicted, "ulcerous." Even so, he was upbeat: "The more I experience, the more sure I am [about being a rabbi] and the harder I seem to work." And he always had an eye on tomorrow: "The contacts I make will be of invaluable help in the future." With that in mind, Fred did his best to impress his teachers and fellow students, and he apparently succeeded: just about everyone came away thinking highly of him. As one of his classmates put it, Fred was "bright," "polished," "well spoken," "A dream for American Jews! He was among the best that the seminary produced." Another student described him as "a competent guy, but not an intellectual. Did he have great insights? No. Few of us did. But the good thing about him was that he was always trying to see the good in people." This former seminarian recalled attending a conference in Washington with Neulander in 1965: "Civil rights leaders and union leaders and senators and even Arthur Goldberg, the Supreme Court justice, were there. One of our first classes when we got back was taught by a very strict Talmud teacher who asked, 'So? Where were you?' Fred was the only one brave enough to answer. With an almost little-boy enthusiasm, he said, 'We were in Washington for the conference.' The professor looked at Fred and, after a long pause, asked, '*Nu?* Did you study a page of Talmud?' Fred was deflated. We just about had to carry him out of the room."

In the face of professorial censure, the former classmate admired Neulander's courage. Rarely did anyone hear Fred doubt his aptitude for the rabbinate, although he did tell a friend during his fourth year at HUC that he was "ambivalent" about congregational life and the "frustrations" of dealing with congregants' "apathy."

"Don't let it get to you . . . ," his friend advised. "People are people and . . . some are dedicated and devoted just as others are frightfully disappointing . . . For the sake of awakening the nobility in others, the rabbi's duty . . . is to carry on without surrender."

So Neulander soldiered on in his generally uncomplaining way. He remained a straight arrow in his thinking and even in his attire. Most students, this being the 1960s, wore jeans or chinos; Neulander was one of the few who dressed routinely in tweed sport jackets and rep-striped ties. Some classmates thought he was as buttoned down as the shirts he wore. They noted his self-containment and his reluctance to reveal much about himself. His smile was a bit tight—tighter, people noticed, than Carol's—although one classmate attributed this to "the difference between someone who grew up in Woodmere and someone who grew up in Queens." His formality in dress and manner, said one HUC graduate, suggested that he "was a 'careerist.' " The term, this man explained, was used to refer to students who "were in the seminary less as a 'calling' than as a profession. It's like what William H. Whyte wrote in his best-seller, *The Organization Man,* which was about the conformity of people who were preparing to 'take the vows of organization life.' " In religious life, he continued, " 'careerists' were getting ready to worship the institution that had grown up around God, not to worship God. We always knew who were the 'careerists': they were the ones who wore suits and ties. They were the people trying on their 'rabbi suits.' "

6

The Price of Success

Fred completed his studies at HUC in June 1968 and immediately went on to Columbia for a doctorate in religion. He also worked as a rabbi for a small temple in Queens. The place was "warm and loving and terrific," Neulander later said, and the congregants—most of whom lived in a local housing project—"were the kind of people you would love to stay with."

Maybe so, but he didn't stay with them for long. Disappointed with Columbia, Fred transferred after one semester to Dropsie College in Philadelphia. He was especially excited about taking classes there with Theodor Gaster, one of the original translators of the Dead Sea Scrolls. Then he realized that commuting three days a week from Queens to Philadelphia was "insane" and would give him little time for Carol or for studying. So he gave up his work at the temple and moved with Carol to an apartment in Marlton, a town just east of Cherry Hill and a half hour's drive from Dropsie.

The temple in Queens may have been "terrific," but Fred was ready to move up the rabbinic ladder. The usual trajectory for an ambitious young man in his field began with a post as an assistant rabbi at a large synagogue, which would hopefully lead after a few years to a congregation of his own. For several months, Fred had been talking with a search committee at Temple Emanuel in Cherry Hill about becoming its assistant rabbi. He also spent hours discussing the job with the man about to vacate the position. In the course of these conversations, Fred learned that the town of Cherry Hill had much potential for growth—and he was gratified to hear that many congregants at Emanuel felt that the senior rabbi was too autocratic. Some were even thinking about starting a second synagogue. For an ambitious guy like Fred, the situation seemed promising indeed. "It was clear that a breakaway congregation was a real possibility," said a rabbi who knew the area well. "Fred was a go-getter. He may have seen this as the ticket to the future. Anyone who doesn't like the senior rabbi gravitates toward the assistant rabbi. If that happened, Fred would be in clover. He had the intelligence—and the ambition—to start a new temple."

When Neulander arrived at Temple Emanuel at the age of twenty-nine, quite a few of its members found him to be a breath of fresh air. The senior rabbi, Herman Yarrish, then in his early fifties, struck another rabbi in the area as a "martinet." He yelled at congregants during services if they wore *kippot*—in those days, skullcaps were considered antiquated by most Reform Jews—and he once demanded that a woman leave the sanctuary with her noisy two-year-old grandson before he'd allow worship to resume. The next day, the woman quit the temple.

Still, most people stayed at Emanuel because it was the only Reform temple in town. Why Yarrish stayed was more of a mystery, as he seemed frustrated and bored after two decades in the job. He'd occasionally leave his office in the middle of the day to attend to personal matters, including keeping an eye on his stock portfolio. But Yarrish also had his fans. Some members appreciated his efforts to get teenagers involved with civil rights, and he successfully encouraged a few to become rabbis or Jewish educators as adults. One man who attended Emanuel as a teenager in the 1950s described Yarrish decades later almost worshipfully: "He was highly educated. He was witty. He was handsome. He was a graceful man who stood for important things. He taught us the Reform way of reaching out to God through ethics and social justice. He brought to the Delaware Valley an admiration of the 'Kennedy type' before just about anyone had heard of Kennedy."

Yarrish, however, belonged to a generation of rabbis that believed they should be as distant as Moses and as imposing as Sinai and that their authority should be unquestioned. Fred Neulander's style was the precise opposite: young and loose and informal and full of energy. He was especially well liked by congregants in their twenties and thirties who felt that he was truly able to *hear* what they were saying. Fred was close to them in age and sensibility. He shared their social and historical touchstones: the banality of Eisenhower, the frisson of Kennedy, the challenge of civil rights, the horrors of Vietnam, the assassinations of JFK, RFK, and Martin Luther King. Perhaps most important, he had a preternatural knack for making whomever he was with feel like the most important person in the world. It was a skill that took considerable empathy and charm, not to mention a smidgen of pretense, and Fred was a master at projecting it.

As for Carol, she was considered quiet and modest and not quite ready for life as Mrs. Rabbi—always on picture-perfect display. Fred had spent five years learning how to be a rabbi; no such education was available in the art of being a rabbi's wife. Not long after Fred and Carol got to Cherry Hill, they were invited to a Sunday brunch at the home of a member of the temple's executive board. No business would be discussed, the Neulanders were told, but with the whole board present, Fred and Carol knew they'd be on display. After the young couple had arrived and filled their plates at the buffet, they sat on opposite sides of the room, making small talk with Emanuel's secular leaders—and being judged by them. Suddenly, Carol went pale and from across the room, Fred saw her sit straight up. Sensing that something was wrong, he came over to her and whispered, "Are you OK?"

"No! We have to get out of here. *Now*."

"Honey, we've been here less than an hour. We can't leave unless you don't feel well. Are you getting sick?"

"*No*," Carol said firmly. "We just have to get out of here."

Fred tried to joke: "Did I lose my job already? Did you reveal one of my secrets?"

Carol smiled lightly, then whispered, "Look at my shoes."

Fred glanced down and saw that Carol, who was usually an impeccable dresser, had arrived at this all-important social event wearing one black shoe and one blue one. Fred, who could never have made that mistake—he owned only two pairs of shoes, cordovan loafers for work and tan bucks for leisure—felt oddly smug for a moment, until Carol gave him a withering look that said "Get me out of here."

But the torture continued for another hour. Carol sat with her legs tucked way under her, while Fred, trying to act like a thoughtful husband, served her dessert and tea. At the first appropriate moment, they said good-bye and walked quickly to the car, giggling so much that Fred had to lean on the fender to keep his balance. They laughed all the way home, especially when Carol threw one of her mismatched shoes out the window.

This was not the kind of life Carol had expected: back in high school, she'd talked about going round the world in eighty days. Now she was on show for middle-class Jewish suburbanites in South Jersey. This was a long way from circling the globe at record speed—and an even longer way from the life of relative privacy she had once planned for herself.

Fred's arrival at Emanuel was a textbook example of what happens when you're in the right place at the right time. Dissatisfaction with Rabbi Yarrish among certain influential members was rising and would soon be exacerbated by the contrasting presence of his new associate, who stopped studying for his doctorate soon after moving to Cherry Hill. Where Yarrish was distant and detached, Neulander offered warmth and comfort. Within two years, he had assembled his own circle of admirers and became especially popular among teenagers. In warm weather, he took students in his confirmation classes outdoors, across the street from the temple, where they sat on the grass near the Cooper River. They thought he was hip and cool, sort of an older version of them. His attire was more informal than it had been at seminary—he often wore jeans or chinos—and sometimes his young wife with the cute pixie haircut drove over and sat listening to the discussion while holding the Neulanders' baby, Rebecca. The kids learned more from Fred than from any other teacher. He was always referring to current events, to other religions, even to rock 'n' roll. Besides, he made them laugh. They'd dreaded confirmation classes before; now they were studying from someone who was bringing *life* into their classroom.

The students were even coming to Friday night services because they wanted to hear what the young rabbi would say. His sermons were so stirring, so theatrical, that they felt he was talking directly to them. He gave them a vision of Judaism that was young and vigorous, which in turn gave them a new vision of themselves as Jews.

Neulander's lessons were so appealing that even truant students were truant no more. Two girls who had routinely been cutting confirmation classes taught by Fred's predecessor still remembered many years later the new rabbi's effect on their behavior. Before his arrival at Emanuel, they'd wave good-bye to their parents after being dropped off at the temple, then run to the motel next door to buy soda and doughnuts from vending machines, using the money they were supposed to donate to charity. Thus fortified, the girls spent the next two hours hanging out by the river, until their parents picked them up from "class." Then Fred Neulander showed up at Emanuel, and everything was different. "We loved him," said one of those girls some three decades after the fact. "He was the only reason we stayed in confirmation class or went to temple or had anything to do with being Jewish. He made everything come alive. He was funny and smart and he knew how to talk to us. It was like having an older brother, but one we liked. He made being Jewish fun."

Meanwhile, Neulander found himself admiring aspects of Yarrish, writing to a friend that "he's good to work with. Fair, straightforward, and always teaching me." Fred knew he was "fortunate" to be at Temple Emanuel, where there were "challenges on many levels." But he also realized that the temple was too insular for his tastes: "This is not as community-oriented a place as I would like." Moreover, he didn't like playing second fiddle. An assistant rabbi was essentially an internship that, in Fred's opinion, should last no more than two or three years—when the intern would become a rabbi in his own right. Instead, Neulander remembered in the early 1990s, "I had to check everything with Yarrish." The senior rabbi retained all the power and it was obvious that Neulander's job was to agree with him. "In such a situation," he explained later, "you can't use all your capacity. For my own personal ego needs and my professional needs, I had to get out."

Neulander wanted to lead a congregation with a less formal, more egalitarian bent. He wanted to break down the barriers between the rabbi and the lay membership. He thought that services should feature more Hebrew and that people should be able to wear *kippot* if they wished. Being "modern," one of the keystones of the Reform movement, had spawned a Judaism that was so cerebral that it offered little spiritual nourishment. Neulander's intention was to change that, to give people a keener idea of their faith and its traditions.

To accomplish this, Fred had to flee what he called Reform's "minimalism." It attracted, he noted acerbically, "people who wanted to be attached to Judaism, but didn't want to do a hell of a lot. They wanted a sense of Jewish identity—and Reform Judaism was doing just that: providing a *sense* of Jewish identity. Reform Jews needed to discover that there was a certain value in tradition, that we weren't just adrift and improvising as we went along." Neulander's opportunity to incorporate his ideas into practice would come along sooner than he expected, but first he'd have to do a bit of wandering, literally, through the same wasteland the Jews of the Old Testament had wandered for forty years—the Sinai Desert. Fortunately for the young rabbi, his sojourn would be considerably shorter.

For ten days in February 1974, the Neulanders and two other Cherry Hill couples toured Israel. The trip, organized by the United Jewish Appeal, was intended to show support for a country whose sense of invincibility had been shattered by the devastating Yom Kippur war in October 1973. Once in Israel, the group split up according to gender. The wives made the rounds of schools and *kibbutzim* and their husbands flew deep into the Sinai on an Israeli military plane, then boarded a bus to meet with Israeli soldiers stationed at an army base in the desert. En route, they reached a checkpoint that was too narrow for their bus to make the necessary U-turn. United Nations soldiers from Peru who were manning the checkpoint waved them through, instructing the driver to turn around farther ahead. The driver overshot the mark and landed the bus in enemy territory. At that point, Egyptian soldiers came on board, blindfolding the passengers and taking them to a courthouse in the dusty town of Ismalia, right next to the Suez Canal. There, the fourteen Israelis and twenty-six Americans were questioned one by one. The first few interrogations went on at length, but once the Egyptians realized they didn't have a busload of spies on their hands, they relaxed. After ten hours or so, the hostages were released.

The worst part of the whole experience, Neulander told a Cherry Hill newspaper, was "not knowing what's going to happen to you . . . Being under the control of someone else is pretty frightening."

By contrast, the rest of the trip was low on drama. Neulander even managed to do some personal business with Sam Lear, who was also on the tour. The two men discussed a project of great mutual interest: starting a new Reform temple in Cherry Hill. Fred, as usual, was driven by ambition and restlessness, but he needed a well-connected businessman like Lear as a partner. Lear sat on the board of Camden County's Jewish Federation and had had several recent conversations with friends, brainstorming about what they wanted in a temple—for starters, fewer Bible stories, more Hebrew, and especially a focus on ethics. They wanted a leader who would help them explore the relationship of Judaism to real life. Someone who saw beyond merely ritual observance. They were convinced that Rabbi Yarrish was not that person. The problem was that Yarrish, they feared, would not be easy to get rid of. "We were afraid Yarrish was *never* going to leave," said someone who participated in one of those meetings, held at Sam Lear's house the previous fall. "We could wait for him to retire, which might happen in another ten or twenty years. Or we could leave Emanuel and head off on our own."

Luckily, the leader they sought was right in their own backyard. Fred Neulander was their kind of guy, and the feeling was mutual: their kind of Judaism happened to be his as well. Since the marriage had already been arranged, Neulander and Lear used their time in Israel to hash out the details of the new temple-to-be, starting with its name. Neulander wanted *shalom* in there, not surprisingly. The founders of other breakaway temples often used that word, as if putting "peace" in the name eased the rupture with the "mother" synagogue. Lear agreed. M'kor Shalom—"A Source of Peace"—was chosen without a fuss. Once again, Neulander benefited from his knack for being in the right place at the right time.

The second half of 1974 turned out to be the beginning of a new life for Fred and Carol. The first sign was their move to a larger house in Wexford Leas, a new development just a few blocks from their former home. Wexford Leas, according to the ad copy, offered "the luxury of unlimited living space." The typical residence featured a "beautifully proportioned living room" and a "formal dining room with deep-pile Wedgwood-blue carpeting." There were "loads of extras," too, "even a gas barbecue." The price was $75,900, not a small sum in those days.

The move was another example of fortunate timing. With Carol pregnant with their third child, their growing family desperately needed more space. Soon the Neulanders formed close friendships with three neighboring couples, all with children roughly the same age as their own. M'kor Shalom had become a reality, and within a year or two of its inception it was suddenly *the* hip temple in town, attracting new members so quickly that it would soon outgrow the farmhouse where services were held. A realtor friend of Fred's offered the congregation a building in an industrial park along the eastern edge of Cherry Hill. The place, barely a quarter mile from the New Jersey Turnpike, was absolutely undistinguished. It didn't inhabit its site as much as squat on it: its windows were narrow slits, and the brick façade lacked a single embellishment to break up the monotony. It didn't help that a looming metal warehouse restricted what was already a crummy view. The structure, in other words, wasn't exactly *Architectural Digest* material.

But it didn't seem to matter all that much. The *idea* of the temple was more important than its physical appearance. The membership was increasingly drawn from the cream of Cherry Hill: top lawyers, surgeons, developers, psychiatrists. Congregants made a point of volunteering in soup kitchens and literacy programs nearby in Camden, the ruined city from which many of them had fled a decade or more before. (Whitman's line about Camden, "In a dream, I saw a city invincible," was by now a parody at best, as anyone familiar with its thousands of vacant buildings, 60 percent high school dropout rate, and addicts roaming the streets could testify.) M'kor Shalom's new cantor, Anita Hochman, was already known for her folksy, guitar-strumming sing-alongs, which transformed routine worship services into the next best thing to a cozy session around a campfire. And at the center of it all was Fred Neulander, constantly in motion, exuding his charisma, wowing people with sermons full of dry humor, intriguingly arcane words, a kaleidoscope of quotes from the Torah and the kabbala and the latest from the evening news. He was showman, scholar, counselor, and pal, and he reminded no one of Herman Yarrish. Rabbi Neulander was so deeply consumed by synagogue life that any energy left over for his wife and three children was nothing short of miraculous. Actually, some people wondered if their rabbi had a life beyond the temple. Not that anyone suggested that he minimize his involvement, even a little. After all, they'd joined M'kor Shalom because of Fred Neulander, and they wanted to get as much of him as they could get. By all accounts, he did not shortchange them.

Neulander rarely revealed his interior life, certainly not to congregants. His sense of privacy precluded that. But in the early 1980s, a series of poems that he wrote alluded to loneliness, a restlessness, even a crippling unworthiness. Everything he had worked for, everything he had achieved was a sham. Even as he was almost single-handedly creating the largest Reform temple in South Jersey, *nothing* was satisfying him, not even

> *. . . the words of praise, the acknowledgment*
> *That lifted spirits and made me soar.*

No "prizes" and "accolade[s]" pleased Neulander anymore. To him, they were like "empty noise in the quiet of the night."

An "edgy tightness" woke him before dawn; he was "weary before my day begins."

> *I am the enemy. I, the victim. I, the achiever . . .*
> *I choke on the victories*
> *For I fail to be sure that they—or I—am real.*

Neulander was struggling for some kind of authenticity, for an assurance that his existence was legitimate and valid. But how could that be? He had never met the standards and expectations of the man who meant the most to him, his father. After Ernest's recent death, he would never have the satisfaction of doing so. Fred had left the bedside of his ailing father with "anger," drawn to be there

> *. . . yet seek[ing] to leave impatiently.*
> *Humiliated by the unworthiness of being his succeeding*
> *Generation.*

That was the private Neulander—terrified and angry. Even the title of one of Neulander's poems, "Pelf and Self," hinted at his emptiness. A tempting title for Neulander to use, given his penchant for obscure words. "Pelf" referred to money and riches, and generally conveyed the idea of something ill-gotten. The poem ostensibly condemned the quest for material gain because it can insulate us from our feelings. But it could just as easily have been that Neulander perceived his swift success to be ill-gotten, ill-deserved.

Within a year of its founding, about 150 families joined M'kor Shalom; that number more than tripled over the next five years. Although the temple was outgrowing its building in the industrial park, some members wanted to remain there and close the membership. They liked M'kor Shalom's relative intimacy. Its rather small membership distinguished it from other Reform temples in the area. But Neulander and his allies prevailed, and the temple stayed open to all Jews.

Architects drew up plans for the expansion and M'kor Shalom published a snazzy brochure with the renderings. Then, right out of the blue, a Conservative synagogue came along with a proposal. It had recently built a $4 million, fifty-thousand-square-foot building, but it couldn't pay the mortgage: new membership was way below projections. Was M'kor Shalom interested in buying the building? The offer was too good to turn down. The building hovered near the epicenter of Jewish life—the Jewish Community Center, Jewish social service agencies, a Jewish nursing home, and several other temples were no more than a mile or two away. Even better, it had been designed from the ground up to be a *real* temple, with meeting rooms and classrooms and reception rooms and a chapel and a library and a sanctuary whose peaked, wooden ceiling echoed the wooden roofs of old synagogues in Eastern Europe. From the outside, in fact, the building suggested the low skyline of a Jewish village in eighteenth-century Poland, where the rooflines worked their way upward toward the center of the village and the heart of its Jewish worship—the *shul*.

The building wasn't perfect, however. Its orange metal roof and white, stuccoed walls would never have been found on synagogues in Poland. But orange metal and white stucco were commonly used for a certain fast food chain with a fair number of franchises in South Jersey. That's why some locals called the place "Taco Bell."

By the early 1990s, about nine hundred families belonged to M'kor Shalom. It was the largest Reform temple in South Jersey. Its popularity was largely due to its charismatic rabbi. People joined because Neulander was there. He inspired people. He excited people. When he spoke, people listened. When he taught, they paid attention, whether he was teaching a class or counseling individual congregants. This was not quite a cult of personality, but an appreciation that this was a man to be reckoned with, and esteemed, and admired.

The founders of M'kor Shalom had originally envisioned a congregation defined as much by its lay leadership as by its clerical staff. But in reality, it was Neulander's baby, a reflection of his personality; without him, its identity would be lost. His Friday night sermons alone were a major attraction. They invariably began with the invitation, "Let us study . . . ," followed by dazzling riffs on current events and Jewish history or the Torah portion of the week, and sprinkled with ideas and quotes that looped and twisted around each other. Just when his audience began to think he'd lost his way, he would pull all of his themes together into one coherent and impressive conclusion. The sermons were invariably inspiring, with Neulander teaching them something important about what it meant to be a Jew. The sermons were also reassuring; no matter how lost Neulander seemed while delivering them, he always found a way to bring them together.

Often, the style of these sermons was conversational rather than preachy. Neulander might raise an issue of current social or political importance—civil rights, intermarriage, women as rabbis, the

Middle East—and throw it back to the congregants for their opinions. He was a showoff, but a charming one. He had a tendency to let his sermons drag on for too long; members teased him about it, knowing he'd do the same thing the very next week. He sprinkled his oratory with obscure words—a memorable one was "struthian," which turned out to mean "ostrich-like." People called these "Neulanderisms," and many of them appeared nowhere in the dictionary for the simple reason that Neulander made them up impromptu during the sermon. He found it irresistible to use weird words in private, as well, sometimes grabbing a dictionary to challenge friends about how to pronounce obscure words or to prove that he was using them correctly. When Neulander did this, his friends would mutter, "Oh, Jesus, Fred. Cut it out."

But Neulander didn't charm everyone, and more than a few people considered him a charlatan. One lawyer who visited M'kor Shalom about twelve times, usually to attend bar or bat mitzvahs, distrusted Neulander from the moment she saw him. "Going to M'kor Shalom was like watching the Phil Donahue show," she said. "Neulander was always in motion. You had to keep swiveling your head to keep up with him. He was here, he was there, he was all over the place. I knew that he was the latest sensation in Cherry Hill, but I couldn't figure out *why*. He was always using words that no one understood. It seemed like he just wanted to impress people. And whenever I saw him at a reception after a bar mitzvah service, he had an arm around some good-looking woman. It was really weird. I had the feeling that something wasn't right with him, that he was trying to be someone he wasn't."

Another visitor attended M'kor Shalom for one service and never returned. "I got the wrong vibes," he said. "For me, the most powerful insights in religion come from each individual. What went on at M'kor Shalom was exactly the opposite. I saw Neulander making a blatant attempt to cast a spell on people. He was good at making soothing tones and uttering meaningless words. A lot of rabbis are showmen, and in a lot of ways, they need to be. But Neulander didn't sound genuine or real or committed. He sounded like a guy who was full of himself."

By the early 1990s, some longtime congregants began to feel that Neulander was changing, and not for the better. There were objections to the amount of Hebrew he used in the prayer book he wrote for the temple and to his growing enthusiasm for more tradition. And his angry displays were becoming disturbingly frequent. He yelled at meetings, either over the phone or in his office. Or he subjected them to "the Neulander stare"—"a glare that would melt people," according to someone who'd been on the other end of it more than once. "He was very stern, very intimidating. Sometimes, he invited members of the congregation into his study and sat them down like children and berated them until they sort of crawled out the door."

His sermons, too, were criticized. Over time, they bored some people. They'd seen or heard it already. The tone, the gestures, the rhythms, even the sentences: clearly, he was recycling the material, word for word, almost by rote, as if he no longer cared about what he was saying. His best sermons had always been full of passionate conviction; they seemed to emanate from a place deep inside him. Now he seemed to be going through the motions. Even when some of the old fire returned, people weren't sure what was igniting it. Neulander was certainly passionate, for example, throughout a tirade in the early 1990s against homosexuality that stunned his listeners, who felt it could have come from a right-wing, Orthodox rabbi. So many people complained about the sermon that Neulander had to apologize for it in the temple newsletter. The apology was accepted, but congregants remained uneasy. If their rabbi was so quick to disavow a point of view he'd seemed adamant about, what did he really believe in?

Yet Neulander still possessed some of his magic. He was endearing and caring when he wanted to be, sometimes well beyond the expected. When the daughter of a member family died on the same day that Neulander's father passed away, he asked the girl's bereaved parents if they'd delay her funeral for twenty-four hours. It went against Jewish tradition to do so, he cautioned, but he wanted to be able to give the eulogy himself, and he had to do the same for his father beforehand. The parents were grateful. "*That* was Fred at his best," the girl's father later said. "*That* was the Fred we admired."

Rabbi Neulander's prominence and visibility made him (and by extension his family) a public figure. This took its toll on Carol, who'd never desired the spotlight. She had never really taken to the role of the rabbi's wife, even though it was a privileged one. She disliked the exposure, and disliked even more the assumption that she was no more than an appendage to her husband, expected to attend every sisterhood meeting and worship service, all the while setting the right spiritual example. Tradition called for a rabbi's wife to model a high standard of moral conduct for other women to follow, as the rabbi himself was supposed to do for the entire congregation. And like him, she was subject to constant scrutiny— which made both of them easy targets for gossip. But while the rabbi held, in essence, an elected office with power and perks, his wife did not. He had been chosen for his wisdom, erudition, training, experience, and general leadership qualities, while she was there by the accident of marriage. This setup led many rabbis' wives to feel isolated and alone, without the automatic respect enjoyed by their husbands and with less freedom of behavior accorded to other wives. As one rabbi's wife from Philadelphia came to realize soon after her marriage in 1985, it "wasn't all bat mitzvahs and honey cake. It was meetings and fierce politics, late-night phone calls and constant ambushes in local restaurants and supermarkets. I got used to having my privacy exposed; I got used to sharing my husband. What floored me was realizing I had mar-

ried a man *and* a community. Our lives were tightly woven into the
life of the congregation. I saw a baby battle cancer, a family crumble under a father's cocaine abuse, a young mother commit suicide.
All these people needed my husband to make Jewish sense out of
their chaos." It took this woman another fifteen years to appreciate the opportunities open to a woman in her position. She was
asked to speak about the weekly Torah portion to the local Hadas-
sah meeting; lectured to other groups on Israeli writers; welcomed
visiting scholars; had her work published in a Jewish magazine;
launched a women's group. In the end, she said, she was privileged
to lead "a life of extraordinary heart and mind and spirit," something she never anticipated when first married, and had "no clue
that this might be the role my soul was yearning for."

But Carol Neulander continued to find that having a rabbi for
a husband was a confining experience. While most spouses of
Reform rabbis—75 percent, according to a survey by the Central
Conference of American Rabbis—nearly always worshipped at
their husbands' temples, Carol was rarely seen there. She was also
unconventional because of the business she started. In the late
1970s, she began to bake cakes for a friend who was a caterer.
Some family members—a niece, for instance—were amused: Aunt
Carol barely knew how to boil water when she got married, since
she'd grown up with a live-in maid. Now her kitchen was full of
hundreds of eggs and fifty-pound bags of coconut, the ceiling was
splattered with chocolate icing, and flour dust was over everything.
Soon a local restaurant featured her cakes on its menu, and friends
came over to help her out. It was almost like a sorority party. Their
arms and hair were white with flour, their hands sticky with
dough, and they teased each other mercilessly. One summer was
forever remembered as "The Summer of the Carrot Cakes"
because that was all Carol made. It was all great fun—just a lark—
until the health department warned Carol that her kitchen wasn't
up to commercial baking standards. Then it became a business.

In any case, the Neulanders' house had become too small to accommodate the growing demand for Carol's creations, sold under the name of Classic Cakes. So the health department verdict was actually a boon. It forced Carol to move sooner rather than later into more spacious surroundings. She opened a retail shop that had a professional kitchen in the back, and she did well. The next year, she expanded to a second location. By then, Classic Cakes was grossing seven figures a year and had more than sixty employees on its payroll. Carol, however, still thought of herself as an amateur, bringing home cash almost every night, sometimes as much as fifteen thousand or even twenty thousand dollars, dumping it on the dining room table to be counted. Occasionally, she'd just leave it in her purse, infuriating her daughter, Rebecca, who yelled, "Mom, you gotta be more careful."

Rebecca thought Carol's attitude was disturbingly casual, especially when envelopes stuffed with cash would fall out of her mother's purse, spilling currency all over the floor. There was also the fact that Carol ran the place like it was a social service agency, employing ex-cons and junkies and alcoholics. "It was like an orphanage," Rebecca observed. "Once, she caught a guy doing coke in the bathroom and fired him."

But Carol was content. She loved giving free pastries to her kids' friends when they stopped by, or treating her son's ambulance squad to a chocolate cheesecake that weighed nearly ten pounds. ("The best friggin' cake I ever had," remembered one medic.) She went out of her way to accommodate her customers, even the ones she didn't know, staying open on Friday nights past closing time if someone was running late to pick up their challah for Shabbat dinner. When she sold the company in the early 1990s and became a salaried employee, Carol no longer made the rules. Nonetheless, she got around them if necessary—like the time an elderly couple, en route to Florida to attend a grandchild's graduation, ordered two cakes at the last minute. Not to worry, Carol reassured them; she baked the cakes herself at home that night.

The bakery gave Carol a life outside her home. But more important, it also gave her the satisfaction that she needed—and wasn't getting—from Fred. At his fiftieth birthday party in 1992, Neulander referred publicly to Carol as "my listener, my guide, my support, my honest and fair critic." But in truth, M'kor Shalom was his life—he *was* M'kor Shalom. There was no room in there for Carol, so she constructed a separate life for herself, centered on her cakes and her kids. He had the temple; she had a business and a family. That was the problem, not just for M'kor Shalom but also for Fred and Carol: the man had become the synagogue and the synagogue had become the man, and it would take a convulsion of the first order to pry them apart.

PART THREE

THE WOMEN

7

"Know Before Whom You Stand"

Four months after Carol's murder, a fifty-one-year-old woman came to the Cherry Hill police with a tale about a Fred Neulander. In late 1993, she said, she ran a personal ad in a local paper: "Single white female, pretty, green eyes, well built. Wishes to meet . . . white male." A man responded, suggesting they meet around lunchtime at Olga's, a massive diner on Route 73 with slabs of chrome along its front façade, a throwback to the 1950s. After a few minutes of small talk in Olga's, he asked her what she liked to do. Thinking he was inquiring into her interests, she started rattling them off. Then he cut her off. "No," he said brusquely. "What do you like to do in bed?"

My God, she thought, it's too soon to inquire about *that*.

He reached across their table and handed her a business card by way of introduction. The woman, glancing at it, was taken aback. The card said "Rabbi Neulander."

"Oh," she said. "You're a rabbi?"

"Yes."

"Where?"

"Here in Cherry Hill."

He assured her he was a powerful man in the community, with a large congregation and a seat on the board of the Jewish Community Center.

"Well, why are you here?" she asked. "I bet you can meet a lot of women at your synagogue."

Oh no, he answered. *That* would ruin his reputation. Then he asked her to check into a nearby Red Roof Motel with him.

"I don't think so," she said, anxious to get away from him. He was moving too fast; she preferred a man who at least put up a pretense of romance. "My daughter gets out of school in a little while and I have to go home and be with her."

Outside the diner, they separated. She walked briskly to her car, hoping he didn't see her pull away. "He gave me the creeps," she told the detectives.

If this was indeed Neulander, he'd chosen a risky place for a tryst. Olga's was less than a mile from M'kor Shalom. Any number of congregants could have spotted their leader in there with this "pretty, well-built" stranger. There was also the fact that one of Neulander's closest friends, a realtor, happened to work next door to the diner and occasionally enjoyed lunch there. But the rabbi seemed to have reached a point in his life where he hungered for risk. After twenty-five years of officiating at bar mitzvahs and weddings and funerals, of leading worship services week in and week out, of teaching classes sometimes twice a week, he was intent on pursuing his own pleasures, not just enhancing the lives of others.

If he had been caught in Olga's, Neulander would have had to do some fast, clever talking, spinning out a convincing story about who the woman was and why he was with her—she was considering joining the congregation, perhaps, or she had suffered some trauma and he was counseling her—and he'd sacrificed his own lunch break because, well, that's what a good rabbi does. Whatever fiction he came up with would turn into gospel, accepted by the flock as further proof of the exemplary wisdom and compassion of their leader.

Despite the speculation that had been swirling around for years about the rabbi's extramarital predilections, no one at M'kor Shalom had grasped the reality: Neulander had become a chronic philanderer. Adultery was already a compulsion for him that washed away everything that had gone wrong in his marriage. Carol had gotten a bit dowdy over the years, especially in comparison to the well-kept women Fred was drawn to at the temple. The bakery absorbed too much of her time, and besides, hearing about the decorations on the birthday cake du jour wasn't his idea of a turn-on. Also, alas, Carol, wasn't quite the intellectual partner he fancied—not that she was dumb, but she seemed more absorbed in baked goods or in the kids than in the Talmud or the Mishnah, which, like any rabbi, Fred opened with some regularity.

His adultery obscured other frustrations as well—not making as much money as his friends, "the docs," as he once referred to them enviously, while complaining to a lady friend about his own measly salary of $111,000 a year. "The docs," however, lacked some of Neulander's perks, like living in a mortgage-free house assessed at over $225,000.

For a man who had long been addicted to playing the game of seduction, sexual and otherwise, and accustomed to winning it with ease, infidelity offered an immediate fix. It also fed his outsized appetite for power and control. If he scheduled a tryst on a Tuesday afternoon, he didn't have to wait until his regular Friday night stroll through the pews during Shabbat services to get his ego gratified—or to enjoy physical contact with the good-looking women in the sanctuary who were happy to receive his hugs. He could still work a crowd like no one else, and he still took every opportunity to commandeer center stage, swooning people into their faith, and also swooning a chosen few of them—his mistress of the moment—into his arms, secretly, of course, in their homes or even his study.

Neulander wasn't aware that his weekly Shabbat stroll had turned into a running joke for some observers, who watched with bemused fascination, curious to see just which thin, dark-haired, stylishly middle-aged woman would be the flattered recipient of his attention this week. Considering that more than a few ladies showed up at Friday nights apparently fresh from their hair salons, there was something of a competition for the rabbi's roving eyes, especially between those who were newly divorced, widowed, or in a chronic state of conjugal unhappiness.

This dizzying conflation of prayers and primping turned Shabbat, for some women, into a combination of *Lamp unto My Feet* and *The Dating Game,* practically erasing the line between the sacred and profane while keeping the rumor mill churning out new tidbits about the playboy rabbi. Still, as one Friday night regular said, "At M'kor, there were all kinds of rumors that he was with this woman or that woman or another woman. But nothing was ever confirmed."

Confirmed or not, the gossip about Neulander was so consistent for so long that one congregant didn't hesitate to tell her friend, a woman in her fifties who had just lost her husband, "When Rabbi Neulander comes to your house to comfort you, be careful. He'll make a pass at you." The president of the temple didn't need confirmation to ask Neulander if there was any basis to the rumors. Neulander, of course, dismissed them. Nor did Gary Mazo, when he invited Fred to his house that night to raise the same question, and when he received the same shrugging denial. People tend to believe what they want to believe. Even after years of rumors about their rabbi, officials of M'kor Shalom certainly wanted to believe him, or at least to avoid the spectacular scandal that not believing him would inevitably cause. So Neulander kept his job, carrying on with his Friday night sanctuary stroll, kissing this woman or that woman and giving little heed to the consequences. What was being burnished into the memory of congregants was the sight of a presumably smart rabbi behaving, as they would soon discover, foolishly and tragically, substituting his own moral compass for the words engraved on the ark in every temple—*Dah Lifnei Mi Atah Omed* ("Know Before Whom You Stand").

Fred Neulander met Elaine Soncini in mid-December 1992, the night her husband, Ken Garland, died of leukemia. A friend of Soncini's had recommended that Neulander officiate at the funeral. Garland, a Jew averse to the trappings of organized religion, didn't belong to a synagogue, and, anyway, his wife wasn't Jewish.

"I want to help you," Neulander told Soncini when he entered Garland's hospital room. "Let me comfort you."

Soncini didn't want comfort. She wanted her husband to live.

"Why don't you tell your boss—God—to come through those doors and tell me what's going on?" she said.

"God isn't a bellhop, but maybe I'm his messenger," responded Neulander.

He had a calming effect on Soncini. She felt safe with him. She told him that she'd been sleeping on a mattress on the floor of Ken's hospital room so that he wouldn't be alone. Neulander hugged her, saying she was the bravest woman he'd ever met.

Garland's son from a previous marriage was holding his father's hand as Soncini, her voice breaking, sang a Cole Porter song— "their" song—to her husband:

Do I love you? Do I?

Doesn't one and one make two?

Cole Porter wrote Garland's kind of music: gentle, intelligent, old-fashioned. Garland had started out playing trumpet in the late 1940s, touring the country with a couple of bands, then going to

Chicago to join a group that was just forming after acquiring all the arrangements of Artie Shaw, the great clarinetist who had recently retired. The orchestra was getting ready to hit the road when its rehearsal hall burned down. Everything—all the arrangements, all the instruments—literally went up in smoke. Garland was reduced to working at a loading dock at a department store until earning enough for bus fare to New York. Flipping through the Yellow Pages in Manhattan, he saw an ad for a radio school; six months later, he was spinning records at a small station in Manchester, New Hampshire. After that, he made the rounds of New England at stations in Maine and Rhode Island, playing *his* music wherever he went: the full, rich, gentlemanly sound of the big bands—Glenn Miller, Tommy Dorsey, Benny Goodman—all of which, of course, had long since disbanded.

Garland had his eye on New York, like almost every other disc jockey. He finally got a job there in the early 1960s with a wake-up show on WADO. A year later, WADO changed its format, so Garland went over to WINS, one of the flagships of early rock 'n' roll. Garland couldn't wait to get out of there, and when a slot opened up in Philadelphia where he could play his Big Band music, he grabbed it. For the next twenty-eight years, he was on the air at six, playing Frank Sinatra and Sarah Vaughan and Judy Garland and Nat "King" Cole, easing Philadelphians into a new day with his friendly baritone and his sweet music that made life just a little bit more gentle.

In October 1993, when he was sixty-five, Garland told listeners that he had chronic leukemia and would retire at the end of the month. On his farewell program a few weeks later, he played his favorite songs, stuff like Bunny Berigan's "I Can't Get Started" and Rosemary Clooney's "Oh, What a Beautiful Morning." But he'd started the show in pain and it got worse as the morning went on. Halfway through the program, Elaine took him to the hospital. On the way, they turned on the radio. His friends in the studio were singing "Happy Trails," his sign-off song for his Friday shows. Six weeks later, Garland died. Soncini, who was nineteen years his junior, was with him until the end. Neulander delivered the eulogy at the funeral home, which was packed with the best people from newspapers, TV, and radio in Philadelphia. Neulander was in his element: this crowd would appreciate his eloquence and his erudition. "A precious husband has been torn from his beloved," he began. "A father has been torn from the embrace of his children . . . There are poets who will never reach what could be said. There are musicians who could compose and it would be inadequate. There are philosophers who could never catch the soul . . ."

Garland, he said, had done for his wife and children what these poets and musicians and philosophers could never have done: touched their souls and stirred their hearts. Now it was his family's turn to live out the last, unfinished chapter of Garland's life. The eulogy was pure melodrama in the inimitable Neulander style. The coda about living Garland's last chapter especially impressed Elaine. But she had the last word: she came forward to sing "their" song for the last time, adding at the end, "I love you, Ken. On this earth and thereafter."

The next day, Neulander called Soncini to make sure she was OK; later that week, he invited her out to lunch. Soncini suggested he come to her house instead of meeting at a restaurant. He arrived around noon the following Monday. Over whitefish salad in her dining room, they discussed poetry and their respective careers. Neulander reminded Elaine of her husband because he was "so smart and so knowledgeable." After lunch, they continued talking in the living room. It was all so relaxing and they felt so good with each other that when Neulander was getting ready to leave, he asked Elaine if he could kiss her. She consented. He kissed her on the mouth, like a lover, and kissed her again like that before he got to the door, once more with her permission. When he asked if he could come back soon, she agreed. Three days later, they became what prosecutors would later call "intimate."

Within a few weeks, Neulander's visits to Soncini's house had increased from once every couple of weeks to every single week-day, from around noon until just after two. Sometimes, he returned again in the evenings; on those nights, Carol thought he was still doing rabbi's work at M'kor Shalom. Soncini kept the garage open; Neulander shut the door once he was safely inside.

Their lovemaking left her breathless: "It was heart-stopping, goose bumps, take off your clothes in the hallway and go right upstairs without saying a word. It was a wonderful, powerful attraction."

Then a sixth day, Sunday, was added to their routine, and finally a seventh—Saturday, the Jewish Sabbath. There was no rest for this rabbi, not even on the day of rest. Jews "are special people who have set aside a special day for God," Rabbi Neulander wrote in M'kor Shalom's prayer book. The day brings "the presence of God" and "helps us make our home a sanctuary warmed by reverence, adorned by tradition, with family bonds that are strong and enduring, based on truth, trust, and faithfulness." So much for that.

Seven days a week and counting: the lovers could simply not get enough of each other. Fred was supremely crafty. Carol assumed that when he left the house at five-thirty on Saturday and Sunday mornings, he was going to the gym—after all, he was dressed in his sweats and was careful to be back in ninety minutes or so, just about the right amount of time for a decent workout. Or when Fred's schedule got overcrowded with bar mitzvahs or weddings and funeral services, he'd flip the dead bolt on his office door at M'kor Shalom and he and Elaine would have sex on the couch.

At forty-six, Soncini was six years younger than Neulander. She was also more extroverted than Carol. Elaine was an entertainer, a "personality"—a voice people knew, a smile they saw on bill-boards, a local celebrity who once made *Philadelphia Magazine*'s list of "People to Watch." "Soncini might . . . have the best delivery on the air right now," *Philadelphia* declared in the mid-1970s. "That and some good looks might easily push her into the local TV mar-ket this year."

The "TV market" never happened, but compared to Elaine, Carol seemed invisible, a wallflower. Despite the cachet that bou-tique baking acquired around the time Carol got into business—Famous Amos and Mrs. Fields were red-hot novelties—Fred thought nothing could be more dull than what Carol did—spend all day in a place where the biggest kick was watching the dough rise.

Elaine believed that God had sent Fred to comfort her after Ken died. She adored him, and he adored her: the glossy black hair that fell to her shoulders, the fullness and grace of her body, the dresses that so nicely accentuated her curves. She was three inches taller than he, unfortunately, but he could live with that. To Elaine, they were "best friends." Fred's term was "soul mates." She was, he said, "the most special person" in his life. They talked about every-thing: religion, God, philosophy. He wrote poetry about her; "beautiful" poetry, she later said. She helped him with his sermons, clarifying his points and sharpening his rhetoric. As far as they were concerned, they were a team, a secret team. They looked out for each other.

There was the time when Elaine was sick and couldn't go to work, and Fred let himself into her house with his key in the mid-dle of the afternoon just to see how she was doing. On another occasion, her car phone rang as she was driving to the radio station early in the morning. The caller was Fred. It had snowed overnight and road conditions were dangerous; he was worried about her safety. "You're not going to work, are you?" he asked Elaine pro-tectively. She had no choice, she said. He stayed on the phone until she had reached a main thoroughfare that had been plowed.

Elaine, for her part, helped Fred financially—he was always complaining about money. She made a good living and showered him with gifts—sport jackets, shoes, a tuxedo, a large-screen TV for his family room, a bust of Moses, a Mont Blanc pen, a Wittnauer watch, furniture for his office. Acknowledging some of the less personal gifts on M'kor Shalom letterhead was his idea and could potentially benefit both of them. By calling these "donations," he could provide himself with a cover that explained why he was the recipient of such largesse, and Elaine, if she chose, could use the letters to write off the "contributions" to the temple on her taxes. If nothing else, the strategy was another demonstration of Neulander's considerable skill at deception.

As it turned out, Elaine's salary was only one source of her income. Fred discovered this by accident one day almost six months after Ken died when he saw a letter on her desk from her lawyer that took his breath away. "Oh boy, look at *that*," he whistled. Ken had left her almost $1.5 million, a fortune for a rabbi chronically short of cash.

When the lovers had to be apart physically, they were still connected by telephone; they sometimes talked eight or ten times a day. The calls continued even when Fred was home with his wife. He'd use a cordless phone, carrying it into the backyard or a closet, just about anywhere to make sure that Carol couldn't hear him. If Soncini was on a date, something she rarely did but sometimes accepted just to enjoy not being furtive, Neulander would call her answering machine compulsively, leaving one message after another. When he'd finally reach her, he'd say that he'd had a horrible night because he couldn't stop thinking about her being with someone else. Once, while she was on a blind date with a plastic surgeon, he recorded a cryptic message: "Look for the blue rose on the windshield." Hearing this when she arrived home, she went outside. There *was* a rose on her windshield. Neulander had left it there while Elaine was out with the surgeon to remind her of him.

When Soncini took a short vacation at the New Jersey shore with her sister and niece, Neulander phoned at least twice a day. Once Soncini's sister answered the phone; she was treated to a bit of rabbinic wisdom. "Life sucks," Fred told her. "Sometimes things aren't the way we want them to be."

The affair was barely three months old when Neulander told Soncini he loved her. She satisfied him, he said, as Carol never had. Although his wife was a "wonderful mother" and a "good person," he felt more like her brother than her husband. He was miserable, he told her, and he planned to end his marriage. Soncini was delighted. If they got married, they could do what "regular" people did: dine out publicly, attend Shabbat services as a couple, travel together. In short, their sneaking around would end.

8

"When God Closes a Door, He Opens a Window"

In early 1993, the leaders of M'kor Shalom encouraged Neulander to go on sabbatical for four months. His recent behavior perplexed them. He seemed preoccupied, was spending less time in the temple, and was throwing more of his responsibilities onto his assistant rabbi, Gary Mazo, who was officiating at most of the bar and bat mitzvahs. He also seemed restless. About a year before, he'd informally told some board members that local Republican leaders had asked him to run for the state senate. He was seriously contemplating the offer and wanted the temple's directors to know that, if elected, he hoped to remain as senior rabbi of M'kor Shalom. The leaders immediately vetoed the proposal. On an official level, they worried that having a rabbi in the state house would jeopardize the division of church and state; on a practical level, they feared that the temple would be picketed when Neulander weighed in on such controversial issues as abortion or gun control. Given the lukewarm reception he received from the temple's leaders, Neulander opted to stay with the career he had: state senators earned only thirty-five thousand dollars, slightly more than a third of his salary at M'kor Shalom, and he literally couldn't afford to make the leap into politics.

The temple's board believed that Neulander needed a new perspective, new energy. It was understandable that he was burned out. In twenty years, he'd founded the temple, increased membership to nine hundred families, and counseled congregants during some of their worst crises, yet he rarely took a vacation. The board told him to recharge his batteries for four months.

Rabbis on sabbatical usually seek spiritual enrichment. Many go to Israel to study or write or confer with other rabbis, or simply to breathe the holy air and reconnect with the physical roots of Judaism. Neulander mentioned that he was thinking of writing a book about being a rabbi. Maybe he'd take a literature course, too. He never mentioned Israel. He wanted to stay in Cherry Hill.

What Neulander actually did during those four months, aside from growing a ponytail, was apparent to no one. He came into his office, checked the mail, and otherwise divorced himself from the life of the temple, which, of course, was one purpose of the sabbatical. And that made his new grandiosity, evident from the moment he returned from the sabbatical—just in time for Purim—even more mysterious.

Purim joyfully celebrates the salvation of the Jews from a massacre in fifth-century Persia. On Purim, everyone, even the rabbi, wears costumes to an elaborate party; all are considered equal, and equally subject to mockery. Some people even get drunk. Traditionally, people dress as characters from the Book of Esther, the Biblical account of Purim, but at M'kor Shalom, as at most contemporary temples, there was a great variety of costumes, ranging from Minnie Mouse to Popeye and even Yassir Arafat. Rabbi Neulander's costume was most unusual—because it wasn't a costume at all. He attended the festivities in jeans and a T-shirt that exposed the thick muscles on his arms and the broad contours of his chest. Some congregants were understandably confused. They were also impressed.

"Say, Fred," said one congregant admiringly, "you're in *very* good shape."

"Thanks," he said. "I work out a lot—lift weights, play racquetball. I take care of myself."

Neulander's comment did not sit well with the listener. It was decidedly unlike the rabbinic ideal—the Jewish ideal—of humility. There was nothing wrong with a toned and muscular body; quite the contrary. But flaunting it, and the effort expended in building it, was offensive. Especially from a member of the clergy, who in this case was M'kor Shalom's senior rabbi.

This egregious bicep display would prove to be a harbinger of behavior to follow. A few months later, one of Neulander's friends, a doctor, arrived home from M'kor Shalom enraged. He called another member to vent.

"Fred's gotta be losing his marbles," the doctor sputtered.

"Why?"

"His ego's getting too big. We've known each other for twenty years. We've always called each other by our first names. I run into him tonight in temple and he says, like out of the blue, 'Don't you think you should start calling me *Rabbi*?' And I say, 'Yeah, sure. And from now on, you start calling me *Doctor*.'"

Neulander pulled the same thing in one of his classes. Entering the room, he looked around at his students—all adults—and began to scold them. "You know," he groused, "there was a time when people stood up when a rabbi walked into the room."

No one rose, but the students wondered about Neulander. One quality they'd admired in him was that he had invariably shown that he was as human—and as fallible—as his congregants. Now his vanity was almost insufferable.

The temple's board met with Neulander. The sabbatical hadn't worked. Neulander was not pulling his load, his new temperament was grating, and Gary Mazo was still being overworked. "What do *you* want, Fred?" the board asked Neulander. He didn't know.

A rabbi-turned-psychologist named James Bleiberg developed a theory in the 1990s—call it "passages of a rabbi's life"—that aptly describes the trajectory of Neulander's career. Bleiberg thought that most rabbis are fairly content until they reach middle age. At that point, Bleiberg wrote in his doctoral dissertation, they start resenting their "emotional distance from others." They feel that their congregants, and even their own families, don't know who they are—their "most authentic selves." They "long to feel accepted as individuals." As a result, they may distance themselves from the rabbinate, while moving closer to their spouse or children, or they may counsel congregants to help them in dimensions of their lives not addressed satisfactorily by religion. Sometimes they attempt to prove that they're as "ordinary" as everyone else by swearing or telling dirty jokes. In extreme cases, said Bleiberg, they might pursue sexual liaisons with congregants "in a vain hope of reducing their sense of isolation." Eventually, they "descend into burnout, abandon the field, or find themselves forced out because of their misbehavior."

Fred Neulander achieved quite a lot by the time he entered his fifties. He'd built M'kor Shalom into the largest temple in South Jersey; he had many friends, some dating all the way back to high school; his charisma and his empathy were legend; he had three fine children and a wife who was a successful businessperson. Now, perhaps, he was trying to figure out who *he* was. The ponytail he'd worn briefly was one way, experimenting with his identity, pushing it in a vaguely hip direction, growing it while on sabbatical, then cutting it off when those four months ended; the Purim costume was another, allowing him to pose as a macho man; and then, of course, there were the women he flirted with or bedded, women who satisfied, but only to a point, a neediness—and a riskiness—in this renowned senior Rabbi.

Even as she plunked down five thousand dollars to M'kor Shalom for a stained glass window in the sanctuary as a memorial to her husband, Elaine Soncini was lending new meaning to the words "grieving" and "mourning" and "widow." Ken Garland's gripes about organized religion surely would have been exacerbated if he'd known what his wife was up to with the rabbi who officiated at his funeral. For Elaine was not only Fred's mistress; she had decided, six months into the affair, to be his convert as well. A lapsed Catholic, Elaine seemed convinced that if she became a Jew, she could save Ken's soul. This idea of redemption by proxy (not to mention the notion of embracing the faith that Ken had come to disdain) had never occurred to her during Ken's lifetime. But then, she wasn't acquainted with Fred Neulander during Ken's lifetime.

In any case, Judaism didn't work like that—no amount of repentance on Elaine's part could affect the quality of Ken's afterlife; every Jew's ultimate fate was determined by how he lived, not by someone's intervention on his behalf. And Jews, unlike Catholics, aren't big on repentance. They believe that what matters to God is ethical behavior on earth, not apologizing for someone else's bad behavior.

But Soncini had other reasons for converting besides Ken's postmortem comfort. She thought that it would draw her closer to people at M'kor Shalom, where she was already a regular at Friday night services. It would also draw her closer to Neulander. If you're going to become the rabbi's second wife, as Elaine fantasized, you'd also need to be a Jew, at the very least.

So Elaine took Gary Mazo's conversion classes for four and a half months, and in March 1994 she was interviewed by a panel composed of Mazo, Neulander, and two synagogue members. The panel's purpose was to determine the candidate's level of knowledge about Judaism and to assess her motive to convert: Did she seek conversion for herself? Or to please someone else? When Elaine passed on both counts, the panel escorted her to the *mikvah*, a ritual bath, at a nearby Orthodox synagogue. When she emerged from her immersion, she was a Jew.

Apparently, Fred found the whole process erotic—not exactly the most appropriate rabbinic response to a conversion—and while Elaine was taking a post-*mikvah* shower, he dismissed the three panelists. Go back to the temple, he told them; he'd be along shortly. As usual, Neulander called the shots, and they returned to M'kor Shalom, uncomfortable that Fred was alone with a naked woman in the next room, and attempting to disregard their worst suspicions.

At that week's Friday night service, Soncini was presented to the assembled congregants as a new member of the Jewish family. The audience included Elaine's father, stepmother, sister, brother and sister-in law, a nephew and a niece, and friends from the advertising and broadcasting industries. As part of this induction ceremony, M'kor Shalom traditionally gave new converts a volume of the prayer book Neulander had written. The book was duly presented to Elaine, although hers bore an inscription from the rabbi of a personal nature that other converts' copies lacked: "FN to EL—I hope this exalts you as you to me." The convert also assumes a Hebrew name, usually one that he or she has selected. But Elaine's was chosen by Fred. It was Shulamit, a reference to the eponymous Biblical character, a young woman who slept with the elderly King David to keep him warm. Completing the symbolic symmetry, Fred's own Hebrew name was Shraga, Hebrew for "ruler" or "leader"—a term which was often applied to King David.

Well before that Friday night, of course, this modern-day Shulamit had been keeping her David warm. Privately, they already considered the Song of Songs, the famously erotic Old Testament psalm, to be *theirs*—the story of their passion. Through the naming ceremony, their romantic connection was strengthened by a Biblical connection, known only to them. While Elaine's relatives and friends in the audience that night could only admire the strength of her convictions that brought her to Judaism, the secret lovers could only admire the power of the mutual desires that had brought them to this special moment.

The lovers shared another secret: right about this time, Soncini told Fred that she would end the affair if he wasn't divorced by the end of the year. Skulking around with a married man wasn't enough for her. She wanted a future as Mrs. Fred Neulander. She wanted permanence. As she later said to the grand jury, she certainly "didn't want to be somebody's French fries anymore."

"Hang in there," Neulander assured Elaine at the time. "We'll be together. Just hang in there."

Yet he also said, more than once, that rabbis don't get divorced; it would shatter everyone's illusions about him, get him fired from the temple, ruin his career. He begged Soncini to accept the situation as it stood. He would fall apart, he said, if she left him. "Hang in there," he repeated. "Something's going to happen. We'll be together by your birthday."

Soncini would turn forty-eight on December 17, 1994. Seven weeks before Elaine's birthday, Carol Neulander was dead.

Soon after returning home from the police station on the night Carol was killed, Fred called Elaine. He was too exhausted to talk for more than a few minutes, but he called her again the next day from the Philadelphia airport; his son Benjamin was coming in from Michigan for the funeral. When Elaine asked if he was frightened, he answered, enigmatically, "No, I just don't want to lose my children."

Within a few days of Carol's murder, investigators received several anonymous tips about Neulander's affair with Soncini. Staking out her house with a surveillance van, they videotaped one of the rabbi's usual visits to her: pulling into Elaine's garage, shutting the garage door, emerging a few hours later a happy man. After monitoring Elaine for a few more weeks, they summoned her for questioning. She checked in with Fred by phone immediately afterward, telling him she'd followed his advice and denied their affair. Neulander was her rabbi, she explained to the detectives. He'd taught her Hebrew. They were friends, that's all.

But the following day, panicked, Elaine contacted her lawyer. She admitted the truth to him and volunteered to submit to another police interrogation. This time, she not only acknowledged the affair but also recounted two disturbing things that Neulander had said to her. During the summer, a couple of months before Carol died, he confided that he'd been dreaming of violence visited upon his wife; he also had a premonition that the coming autumn would be "tumultuous." Then, within weeks of the murder, he mused to Elaine as casually as if he were talking about the weather, "I wish . . . I wish Carol was gone." He raised his hands, exclaiming, "Poof! She could just vanish. *Just like that.* Maybe her car could just go into the river."

To which Elaine could only reply, "You better not be thinking what I think you're thinking."

A day or so after the conclusion of *shiva* for Carol, the grieving widower asked his mistress to meet him at his office at M'kor Shalom. When she arrived, he handed her a piece of paper on which he'd written the letters *NYY*. Fred pointed to each letter in turn.

> N: "*Do I think God is punishing me? No.*"
> Y: "*Will I marry you? Yes.*"
> Y: "*As soon as appropriately possible. Yes.*"

At any other point during their two-year-old relationship, marriage would have been Elaine's dearest dream come true—the culmination of her secret affair with Fred. But the dream had turned nightmarish—just a few weeks before, Carol was killed, and here was Carol's husband calmly proposing to her. Elaine didn't know what to say; a week later, the two of them were together again in Elaine's bedroom. Afterward, Fred told her, "I *told* you to trust me. When God closes a door, He opens a window."

The day Soncini leveled with the police about Neulander, they returned the favor: she wasn't his only girlfriend. The rabbi was possibly involved with three other women, all of whom they identified. That night, Elaine called Neulander, rattling off the names the cops gave her. She was furious, too furious to believe any of Neulander's explanations:

"They know about Debby."

"Oh, her. I just bought some jewelry at her store."

"And they know about Rachel."

"Rachel? I only performed her conversion."

"And they know about Anne."

"Anne? She was Carol's associate. Nothing more than that."

Soncini didn't know the truth, but she figured that if the names were there, something was going on. It appeared that her tireless lover had an appetite for sex that even she hadn't suspected.

Although Soncini didn't recognize the names of these women, she probably knew their faces; all were members of M'kor Shalom. Anne was single, about five-five, with long brown hair and a stylish, somewhat coquettish way of dressing. Debby, a divorcée, was five-four, almost Neulander's height; a fairly private person, she wasn't very involved in temple activities. Rachel stood a few inches taller than Neulander and was the slimmest and the most reluctant of his girlfriends. She'd never committed adultery before and didn't really want to now.

"You better get yourself a lawyer, Fred," Soncini frostily told Neulander the night she got back from the police station.

"What do you mean?"

"I told them all about us. I told them *everything.*"

Neulander, seeing the situation seeping beyond his control, told Soncini he would get a lawyer for her from northern New Jersey who would "work with" his own lawyer. But Elaine guessed that hiring any lawyer Neulander recommended meant paying for someone to inform the rabbi of everything she told the police.

Elaine, Debby, Rachel, Anne . . . a lot of women for one man to handle, especially a man who spent a great deal of energy trying to convince the cops he was happy with his wife. Four wives too many, actually, for a rabbi who taught a seminar at his temple called "Fidelity and Marriage," in which he stressed that marriage was a sacrament of cosmic significance. Conjugal life, he lectured, was more important than studying Torah; according to an old Jewish proverb, it was the only way to live. "Whoever spends his days without a wife has no joy, no blessing and no good . . ."

Reform Judaism had struggled with defining itself—and the role of its rabbis—from its beginnings in the early nineteenth century among restless German Jews. Wanting to be part of the modernity that was sweeping Europe, they rejected the faith they knew as old and rigid and quaint, an antique from another time. They sought to create a new, updated Judaism that relied on logic, not tradition. The first Reform Jews observed the Sabbath on Sunday at services accompanied by organ music; they used little Hebrew and rarely referred to God. By the turn of the twentieth century, dinners held in Reform temples in the United States often featured shellfish, and there was even a Reform rabbi in Boston calling for Judaism and Christianity to merge. As late as the 1950s, some Reform rabbis were still opposing bar mitzvahs, arguing that the ritual conferred the religious responsibilities of adults on thirteen-year-olds who did not necessarily *desire* those responsibilities. Students at Hebrew Union College, the Reform seminary in New York, complained about taking courses on Torah and Jewish law—they wanted to be therapists sorting out neuroses, not rabbis monitoring souls.

The revolt so alarmed some Jews that, in 1962, a controversial book called *The Failure of the American Rabbi* was published. The author, S. Michael Gelber, a professor of religion at New York University, despaired that Reform rabbis were "being frittered away." "Our world is crying for spiritual guidance and moral instruction and prayer . . . And our rabbis? What are they doing in the face of this demand? They are busy, busy, busy. Dances, book reviews, bulletins, interfaith meetings, drama groups and teenage outings . . . The demands on their schedule have made them . . . into the heads of community centers . . ."

In seminaries, too, the issue was hotly debated. What was the *right* way for rabbis to act? In the early 1960s, Rabbi Abraham Feldman, one of Neulander's mentors while he was at Trinity, told students at the Reform movement's seminary in Cincinnati that "our outward appearance, our manners, . . . the way in which we behave and conduct ourselves . . . make a lasting impression . . . You want to indicate . . . that there is a point beyond which you may not go—that beyond such point is sacred terrain . . . Guard your private life not only against invasion by others, but against scandal . . ."

Similarly, a rabbi from Detroit told seminary students, "What we do and [what] everybody knows about gets us in the headlines. But what we do and nobody knows will get us into heaven." Years later, a rabbi who attended Hebrew Union College the same time as Neulander still recalled the spiritual leader of the largest Reform temple in Los Angeles bluntly telling seminary students, "The best advice I can give you is to keep your zippers up—literally and figuratively. That's really all you need to know."

But newly minted young rabbis had their own vision. They'd rather be "human" and "authentic" than "rabbinic." They spent years learning Talmud and Torah, but they thought of themselves as fallible human beings and regular guys. The problem was that many people didn't want a regular guy to lead them. A rabbi was supposed to be the conscience of his congregation, not exactly a job for a "regular guy." This gulf between what young Reform rabbis and their congregants thought a spiritual leader should be caused pain on both sides. As Jack Bloom, a former rabbi in Connecticut, realized, no matter what he did, he was always *the rabbi*. He wore shorts on weekends, played tennis, drank with friends, was open with others about his self-doubt and personal confusion. He was, in short, as "real" as he could be. After six years in the pulpit, he discovered he was still living "behind a glass wall."

"I don't know how it happened," he later reflected. "There was a sense of loneliness that increased with time. People always treated me as something else than what I was. The sense of apartness increased with time, a kind of loneliness in the middle of the crowd. I discovered how powerful the rabbi is. I also discovered that he is always an outsider. He is never a part of the town in which he lives." Eventually, Bloom left the rabbinate and became a psychologist.

Rabbi Fred Neulander also wanted to be a "regular guy." By the early 1990s, he was fed up with giving his life to his congregation, working as many as twelve hours a day, often six days a week. He had no life beyond the synagogue.

Regular guys like sex, conjugal and otherwise. Besides, an affair (or two or three) released him from the sanctimony and restrictions of rabbinic life. He could be his true self—*not* Rabbi Neulander, who had time and compassion for everyone in need, but just Fred, a regular guy with regular needs of his own. Neulander sought a new life, a private life behind bolted doors—a life of motel rooms, of lady friends' boudoirs, of his own office at M'kor Shalom. In these surroundings, he commanded attention as fully as he did in the sanctuary on Friday nights. The difference lay merely in the size of his audience.

9

"Why Didn't You Run Her Off the Road?"

Fred Neulander's affair with Elaine Soncini was about three months old when he began seeing Rachel Stone. Both women had more in common than clandestine meetings with Neulander: both were gentiles worshipping at M'kor Shalom. Both were taking Gary Mazo's class for converts. And both had the same "mentor" for all things Jewish—Fred Neulander.

Elaine and Rachel belonged to a secret sorority: women who have affairs with their clergymen. Typically, these women are grappling with a crisis, a loss, or a period of despair in their lives. They seek solace from a religious authority figure—priest, minister, rabbi—who then takes sexual advantage of their emotional fragility. In studying such men, Richard Irons, a psychiatrist at the Menninger Clinic in Kansas, and Katherine Roberts, an Episcopal priest in Atlanta, distinguished six types. "The Naïve Prince," they wrote, is newly ordained and feels invincible; "The Wounded Warrior" has affairs to relieve professional and social pressures; "The Self-Serving Martyr" is in midcareer and resents the sacrifices he has made for his congregation; "The False Lover" hungers for adventure, fame, and fortune and preys on a series of women; "The Wild Card" is mentally ill and has performed erratically in his personal and professional life—and the "Dark King," whose profile matches Fred Neulander, uses his charm and charisma to convince congregants that he has "special abilities." In essays published in 1995 in *Restoring the Soul of a Church: Healing Congregations Wounded by Clergy Sexual Misconduct,* Irons and Roberts said Dark Kings had "a pathological need to control and dominate," and their careers were almost unstoppably successful. They used sexual exploitation to express their "power, superiority, and dominance." Dark Kings, continued Irons and Roberts, "may be . . . Dr. Jekyll/Mr. Hyde figures" who, from time to time, act very much out of character. Or they "may appear refined" and have many friends who "attest to their virtues and good moral character . . . When allegations against them are found to be true, they are discovered to be in abject spiritual poverty."

The reverence M'kor Shalom heaped on Neulander, the way he dominated the temple, his growing disregard for what congregants thought of him—all this made him a Dark King. Fred's uncle, Arthur Neulander, was a famous Conservative rabbi who made a deep impression on Fred as a boy; it's ironic that Arthur once gave a sermon about the "two opposing natures in each individual" that Robert Louis Stevenson addressed in *Dr. Jekyll and Mr. Hyde.* All of us, Arthur Neulander preached, struggle like Jekyll "between the beastly and the spiritual . . . By means of a mysterious potion, the kindly, friendly, helping Dr. Jekyll . . . [was] slowly, painfully transformed into the terrifying, abhorrent Hyde . . . Finally, the beast in Hyde overpowers the man in Jekyll."

Yet Arthur refused to accept Stevenson's grim view of human

nature. Our "angry passions," he insisted, "must be overpowered by the better nature within us . . . No matter how hopeless our outlook, the ideal must always be sought . . . In all our misfortunes, all our persecutions and trials, we have ever been aware of our higher calling, our one great purpose: to glorify God, to make humanity more divine . . ." Uncle Arthur never lost his faith in people's ability to vanquish their demons. He died in 1988; six years later, half of South Jersey would know that his own nephew either lacked that ability, or chose not to exercise it.

Rachel Stone, the "other" other woman, was in great shape—slim with "nice legs" (in Neulander's words), and long, straight black hair that reached just below her shoulders. She trained horses and jogged daily. Friends called her "decent," "adorable," "caring," "vivacious." She wasn't promiscuous. Just needy.

Rachel met Neulander in 1986 at the Omni-Fit Gym, right down the street from M'kor Shalom, when she was thirty-four. She'd been married for three years, she told Fred. Neither she nor her husband belonged to a synagogue. Neulander graciously said that if they ever needed a rabbi, they should call him.

Rachel occasionally saw Neulander around the gym, but she didn't take him up on his offer until 1992. Three years earlier, she and her husband, Larry, had adopted a baby girl. They wanted to raise her as a Jew, and Rachel, convinced that having parents of the same faith would make her daughter's life easier, decided to convert.

Although Larry had yet to meet Neulander personally, he'd attended a few services at M'kor Shalom and had found the rabbi impressive. Neulander was unlike any rabbi he'd encountered: learned and intense, yet somehow informal and accessible. Larry felt drawn to him.

The Stones met with Neulander, who agreed to sponsor Rachel for conversion. In the fall of 1992, she began Mazo's course—the same one that Elaine Soncini took about a year later. The rabbi's sponsorship meant that candidates for conversion would meet with him a few times during the process. During these sessions, Rachel confided in Fred about her marital difficulties, which had intensified recently because Larry began spending four days a week in New York for his work. She was also terrified about losing her daughter; the biological mother had spent most of the first year of the adoption trying to get the girl back and she hadn't given up.

With Larry gone so much, Rachel would later tell the police, and with her daughter's future uncertain, she was "at the lowest part of my life. I just thought the rabbi could not do wrong and that he knew what he was doing. I was in his office one day and he started getting close to me, consoling me, hugging me and kissing me. I cried and he hugged me, kissed me. He was very easy to talk with, and he made me feel so comfortable and that he was there for me. I thought he had no motive for doing these things: he kissed everybody. He wasn't a standoff kind of person. He was a very 'touchy' person. If you went to his synagogue, you would see that he kissed every single person around. But he kissed me differently. And he locked the door in his office when he did it. I knew it was inappropriate. But you know, here he is: he's a rabbi! What did I know? I'm a non-Jew. I trusted him."

Rachel told Neulander things about her marriage, her daughter, her sex life that she'd never told anyone. He was her counselor, her confidant, her healer, her pal. Everything she wasn't, he was. She was weak; he was strong. She was confused, bewildered, befuddled; he was wise. Most important, he was literally *there,* while Larry was not.

Not long after Rachel began attending Mazo's classes, Fred took her on a leisurely drive to Medford, a suburb about fifteen miles east of Cherry Hill. It was all quite innocent; they were just two friends chatting away. On another occasion, they played racquetball together at the gym to which they both belonged. Nothing wrong here, either. This time the two friends were getting some exercise.

In February 1993, after three months of palling around, Neulander made his move. Knowing that Larry was, as usual, out of town, he called Rachel, suggesting he stop by for a visit. He drove the three-quarters of a mile from his office to her gated development, identified himself to the guard, and proceeded to her home. He took a quick right, then a left at the four-foot stone pagoda that graced the front yard of the house at the corner. Another twenty feet down the street and he came abreast of Rachel's house. Her lawn was closely clipped and adorned by three fir trees; the brass-handled front door was inlaid with gold-stenciled glass; and the fieldstone-and-stucco façade was more reminiscent of the better neighborhoods in Los Angeles than in South Jersey. But the rabbi didn't dwell on the look of the place. He headed straight for the garage, wasting no time pulling his car inside and—as was his habit at Elaine's—closing the door behind him. Rachel greeted her guest, then took him on a guided tour of her home, a normal thing to do with a first-time visitor. Less predictably, when the hostess showed her guest the downstairs bedroom that her twenty-one-year-old stepson used when he was around, they lingered for quite a while. That's where the innocent friendship between mentor and acolyte became something else entirely.

Popular fiction about lust in the pulpit has long hewn to the Adam and Eve model of an honorable male being seduced into dishonorable behavior by a wily female predator. In a 1910 novel titled *A Circuit Rider,* one character—the wife of a Methodist preacher—bitterly observed, "When we hear of a minister who has disgraced himself with some female members of his flock, my sympathies are all with the preacher. I know exactly what has happened. Some sad-faced lady who has been 'awakened' from a silent, cold, backslidden state by his sermons goes to see him in his studies . . . This lady is . . . very modest, really and truly modest. He is a little on his guard till he discovers this. First, she tells him she is unhappy at

home . . . He sees her reduced to tears over her would-be transgressions, and before she considers what he is about he has kissed
the 'dear child.' That is the way it happens nine times out of ten, a
good man damned and lost by some frail angel of the church."

Four decades later, a young minister in Agnes Turnbull's *The
Bishop's Mantle* muses, "Every . . . clergyman had to recognize this
menace. A few . . . had escaped by a hair's breadth. A few here and
there had not even escaped. There were always the neurotic women
who flocked not only to the psychiatrists but also in almost equal
numbers to ministers, pouring out their heart's confessions and
their fancied ills; there were those pitiable ones in whose minds religion and sex had become confused and intermingled; there were
those who quite starkly fell in love with a clergyman and wanted
love from him in return. Yes, a man of God had to be constantly on
his guard in connection with this problem of women."

But the fictional cliché of the passive cleric whose naïve good
intentions allow calculating women to lead him into sinful acts
hardly fit Rabbi Fred Neulander. As Rachel Stone told the police,
he knew exactly what he was doing.

Neulander's affair with Rachel lasted a year and a half, despite
numerous attempts by her to break it up. The rabbi was very persist-
ent at rebuffing her efforts, even though his hunger for her was relatively mild. Their trysts occurred just once a week, usually around
nine o'clock on Tuesday or Wednesday mornings. This was nothing
like his daily liaison with Elaine at the height of their romance. And
it wasn't unusual for Neulander to experience erection problems
with Rachel (or, for that matter, with Carol, who told her sister that
he was receiving treatment for impotence). He blamed his difficulties on the medication he was taking for high blood pressure.

Fred rarely discussed personal matters with Rachel; that sort of
talk was reserved for his A-list mistress, Ms. Soncini. All he said
about his own marriage was that he and Carol lived very separate

lives, connected only by their kids, and that divorce for a rabbi was out of the question, no matter how bad things were. If Rachel had known anything about Judaism, of course, she would have found this statement laughable. Rabbis were no different from the lay population; Jewish divorce law from the very beginning had been liberal, bordering on lax, as far as men were concerned. Deuteronomy, for instance, let a man divorce his wife if he found her "obnoxious." This was later interpreted so broadly that it applied to wives who happened to be bad cooks or were less attractive to their husbands than were other women. Nothing in Jewish law or tradition prevented a rabbi or any other husband from dumping his wife, nor were there professions in which there were career consequences for divorce. But for a philanderer of Neulander's caliber, a cover story for staying in a bad marriage was essential—and this one served him well with his non-Jewish girlfriends.

There was, however, a small kernel of truth to the story. Divorce was unlikely to separate a rabbi from his pulpit, but it could affect public perception of a man assumed to be morally superior to others. Special. Different. More holy. And in some ways, rabbis did function as guardians of matrimony. A rabbi's marital problems weren't entirely his business, especially if they led to a split with his wife. Some congregants took their leader's conjugal failure personally; they'd invested him with integrity beyond the norm, placed him on an ethical pedestal, and were loath to accept him as an ordinary person with ordinary problems all too familiar to them. He was, after all, their counselor, the man they turned to for wisdom and compassion. When he was revealed to be a mere mortal, the disappointment could be intense.

One Connecticut rabbi, who was on his third marriage at the turn of the twenty-first century, was only too aware that "there is more negativity attached to a rabbi getting divorced than people imagine. My first divorce was absolutely crushing: in addition to my wife having an affair with my best friend [a man who was also this rabbi's lawyer and the president of his temple], people began asking me what right I had to be a rabbi. In fact, the day I decided to divorce my wife, I officiated at a wedding. In my brief sermon, I said that marriage was like the covenant between God and the Jewish people: both require exceptional love and commitment and patience. As the couple headed off to their reception, I drove to my lawyer's to initiate my divorce.

"Then I had a fairly brief marriage while working at another temple. The president of that congregation took me aside and said, 'schmuck! Next time live with her for a while before you get married.' I've now been married to the same woman for more than twenty years, yet some people think I'm too immoral to be their rabbi." In the early 1990s, he flew out to Los Angeles for a job interview. "I mentioned that I'd been divorced and they said, 'Who cares? This is California.' They gave me a contract to sign on the spot. I said I'd think about it." When he called to accept the offer a few days later, it was rescinded; in the interim, synagogue officials had learned he'd been divorced more than once.

So Neulander had some reason to worry that members of M'kor Shalom would stop respecting him if he divorced Carol. And if the divorce was especially messy and his adulteries were somehow revealed, he could even be fired. When you're in your fifties, it's not easy to land another job as a senior rabbi. Fred would do just about anything to preserve the professional status quo.

By June, Rachel had completed her conversion to Judaism, and her marriage was getting worse. Neulander advised her to see a psychologist in a nearby town, someone who, she later said, seemed to get "a lot of referrals" from the rabbi. Fred didn't tell her that the psychologist just happened to be one of his best friends, and Rachel didn't tell the therapist that she happened to be sleeping with the rabbi—although the sessions went on for a year. Her failure to disclose that little detail may explain why the treatment proved useless, neither improving her marriage nor ending her adultery. It didn't even help Rachel stand up to Fred and insist he be more of a gentleman. On three occasions, the lovers checked into a motel near M'kor Shalom, and each time it was Rachel who paid for the room.

Whenever Fred called Rachel at home and got her answering machine, he didn't speak into it; he tapped out his messages according to a prearranged code. But Rachel wasn't always the one who intercepted these Morse-like signals. Sometimes her husband, Larry, heard them in the course of checking the tape. He shrugged the whole thing off to some pesky kid playing around—until the day he heard Rabbi Neulander's voice telling a secretary he was on the phone. When the secretary left the room, the tapping resumed. The whole sequence was captured on Rachel's machine. Larry was suspicious, although he thought he must be paranoid: his rabbi *schtupping* his wife? Rabbis didn't do that sort of thing. But he continued to suspect that something was going on.

Rachel finally managed to end her relationship with Neulander. At first, he flirted with her at every opportunity, often cornering her in the temple's gift shop, where she worked as a volunteer, and loudly admiring her figure, her outfit, whatever he could think of. Rachel used every bit of strength she had to resist him, until even Fred could no longer deny that the affair was over, roughly six months before Carol's murder.

When the homicide detectives showed up at Rachel's house to question her, Carol had been dead for two weeks. Rachel denied everything at that first interview, just as Elaine Soncini had, but she was frightened. That night, Rachel attended a Bible class at the temple. Before it began, she went up to the teacher, Rabbi Neulander, and asked for a private meeting after the class about a rather urgent matter. Rachel described the police visit.

"Did you tell them about us?"

"No," she assured him.

"That's good. But be careful what you say on the phone. It might be tapped."

A couple of weeks later, Fred found out that the police were beginning a second round of interviews. He phoned Rachel at the Cherry Hill Racquet Club. "You know," he said, "they're going back and talking with some of the same people they did the first time. Have they seen you again?"

Rachel, standing near a noisy aerobics class, could barely hear him. "No," she almost shouted. "They haven't called me."

"Well, good. But if they do, you'll tell them the same thing, right?"

"Yes. Yes. Of course."

"And don't forget: Be careful. The phones might be tapped."

Neulander was pleased that Rachel was obeying his orders and stonewalling the police. Still, he was worried. If the cops somehow linked her and other women to him, what else would they try to connect him to? As he well knew by now, a spouse is always the first suspect when there's a murder, and weeks of prevaricating by him and his mistresses was anything but in his favor.

Rachel, too, was worried—about something else. She couldn't forget what the rabbi had told her a few months prior to the murder. While the two of them were enjoying the bolted-door privacy of his study at M'kor Shalom, Rachel mentioned that on her way to the temple, she'd passed Carol, who was driving in the opposite direction.

"Well," Fred had coolly responded, "why didn't you run her off the road?"

Courtesy of the Lidz family

A young Carol Neulander at summer camp in Kents Hill, Maine.

Photo from Jamaica High School Yearbook, 1959

Fred Neulander excelled at sports and served as co-captain of
the Jamaica High School swim team.

FRED NEULANDER
137-21 83 Avenue, Jamaica 23
Vice President of G.O.
Literary Editor of Yearbook
Captain of the Swimming Team
Co-Manager of Red 'n' Blue
Junior Arista

Jamaica High School (Queens, New York) yearbook photo, 1959.

Carol catches the bouquet at a friend's wedding in 1962.
Three years later, she would marry Fred.

Courtesy of the Lidz family

The Neulander family in the early 1990s *(clockwise from top left):* Benjamin, Matthew, Fred, Carol, and Rebecca.

© Courier-Post

204 Highgate Lane, Cherry Hill, New Jersey—the Neulanders' home the day after Carol's murder. "I, I, ah, just came home and my wife is on the floor and there's blood all over," Neulander told the 911 dispatcher.

Photo by Tina Markoe Kinslow. © Courier-Post

Until Neulander's conviction, a space was reserved for him next to Carol at the Crescent Burial Park, Pennsauken, New Jersey.

Photo by Ron Karafin. © Courier-Post

Confessed killers Len Jenoff *(left)* and Paul Michael Daniels.

earth are defined by my Transgressions of Nov 1, 1994, and That's a shame.

I could "SAVE" FIFTY children From a Burning School - Bus Accident and yet I will forever be known as the "Rabbi's HITMAN" and murderer.

This Tribulation is so very painful for both myself and for Martin. Martin deserves so much Better.

I don't expect to be portrayed AS A "Boy Scout", but I'm also <u>NO</u> TED BUNDY OR Timothy McVeigh.

I would give my life if I could turn back the clock to pre Nov 1-94.

Shalom -

Unlike Neulander, who never showed remorse, Jenoff expressed eternal guilt and shame both in the courtroom and in this letter he wrote to the author.

Photo by Craig Terkowitz

Rebecca Neulander's testimony about the "bathroom man" helped convict her father.

Photo by Paris L. Gray. © Courier-Post

Photo by Tina Markoe Kinslow. © *Courier-Post.*

"I would give my right arm to hold my mother's hand and let her know I was there," said Matthew Neulander about the night his mother was murdered.

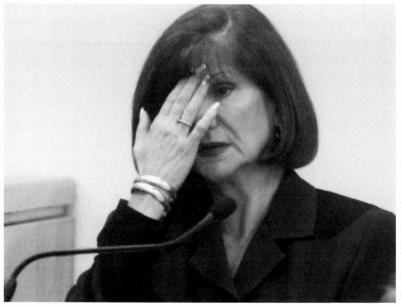

Photo by Avi Steinhardt. © *Courier-Post*

Elaine Soncini, Fred's girlfriend who had wanted to become "Mrs. Fred Neulander," testifying at Neulander's first trial.

Photo by Tina Markoe Kinslow. © Courier-Post.

Prosecutor Jim Lynch suggested that Neulander was "overwhelmed by lust, greed, arrogance, and betrayal."

Photo by Craig Terkowitz

In an eerie coincidence, in the same year that he had his wife killed, Neulander wrote an article about the media coverage of the O. J. Simpson case. In it he chastised people obsessed with the case, calling them "voyeurs, eager to fill . . . [their] days with gory details or fanciful theories . . . How shallow our lives must be if another's travails and machinations filled our world."

new jersey
doc **department of corrections**
Commissioner
Devon Brown

Inmate Search - Details

SBI Number:	000375614C
Sentenced as:	Neulander, Fred
Race:	White
Ethnicity:	White
Sex:	Male
Hair Color:	Gray
Eye Color:	Gray
Height:	5ft'6in"
Weight:	195 lbs.
Birth Date:	August 14, 1941
Admission Date:	January 16, 2003
Current Facility:	NJSP
Current Max Release Date:	N/A
Current Parole Eligibility Date:	June 20, 2030

Current Prison Sentence

Number of Counts	Offense	Offense Date	Sentence Date	County of Commitment	Commitment Order	Mandatory Minimum Term	Maximum Term
1 count of	2C:11-3A Murder /1	November 1, 1994	January 16, 2003	Camden	I-1993-06-00	30 Years	LIFE

Incarceration History		Aliases
Date In-Custody	Date Out-of-Custody	No Aliases Available
January 16, 2003	Currently In Custody	

[previous] [back to list] [next]
[modify search] [new search]

The New Jersey Department of Corrections updates this information on a biweekly basis to ensure that it is complete and accurate as possible. This information, however, may change quickly. In addition, it is noted that offenders on Work Release, Furlough, or in a Halfway House are visible to the public and these types of releases are not necessarily reflected in their profile. Therefore, the information on this may not reflect the true current location, status, release date, or other information regarding an offender.

The New Jersey Department of Corrections Database was last updated on February 1, 2003.

For questions concerning any offender information available on this WebPage, please contact:

New Jersey State Prison
PO Box 861
Trenton, NJ 08625
(609) 633-7890

Guilty. Fred Neulander, the first rabbi in America
ever convicted of capital murder.

PART FOUR

THE TROUBLES

10

"My Heart Tells Me You're Not Telling the Truth"

Limericks are a strange way to tip off the police about a truly awful crime: no one takes them very seriously and it's the rare English professor (and usually not a respected one) who considers them "literature." Invariably, limericks are written by really bad poets who just want to make someone smile. They were never intended—as were those that started coming to the Camden County Police in early 1995—to help detectives solve a murder case.

Limericks, some people say, were invented in the 1700s by Irish soldiers returning from France to their hometown of Limerick. They ad-libbed five-line verses in an *a-a-b-b-a* rhyme scheme about the inhabitants of other villages, each verse ending in the same refrain, "Will you come up to Limerick?" According to *The Oxford Companion to the English Language,* this bastardized style of poetry has barely changed in three hundred years. Its "simple form and easy, swinging rhythm makes it particularly suitable for humorous or scurrilous use and for taboo subjects." By definition, a limerick isn't meant to be taken seriously—especially, by detectives trying to solve a murder. But in February 1995, a series of them began arriving anonymously at the Camden County prosecutor's office. The author's identity remains anonymous, but whoever wrote them seemed intent on linking Fred and Elaine to the case. The author also possessed inside information. Although some of those details were never released to the public, it was credible enough to convince detectives to take them slightly more seriously than the usual mailings from frustrated housewives who thought they were Miss Marple.

Each limerick was signed "Yair"—Hebrew for "He gives light." But who was giving it, and why, and where'd they get their information? With each submission, the mystery deepened for the police.

Although pleasant to all he greets,
There's more to the rabbi than eye meets.
He loves to philander,
The more all the grander,
Ask those with whom he's been 'tween the sheets.

But as he likes chasing new dresses,
He also a great temper possesses.
Though he hides it quite well,
Those who know him can tell,
The anger will boil if one presses.

The limerick writer now turned to Elaine Soncini, who was never mentioned by name. Instead, she was "Lumen," Latin for "light." And "light" just happened to be the translation of the Old French word "Elaine." Using this pseudonym, the writer maintained that Neulander . . .

. . . [I]s also enamored of fame,
And some of those who play in the game.
See, for Lumen he fell,
Some around him could tell,
And his wife knew. Was all quite a shame.

Another limerick followed two days later, suggesting that

The rabbi's marriage was in trouble.
For quite some time, burst was the bubble.
He wanted a divorce.
But she wouldn't, of course.
Now his woes have doubled by double.

Before the day fateful for his mate,
Rabbi called Lumen at daily rate.
Many months there were calls,
Many trysts behind walls,
While back home his poor wife she did wait.

Just hours after the burying,
With Lumen on he was carrying.
He called her next morning.
'Fore dawn was e'en borning,
Did they talk so soon 'bout marrying?

Were then two of them in collusion?
Or could it all be an illusion?
One thing is for certain,
There's no final curtain,
Just why is there so much confusion?

"Yair" knew that Fred and Elaine were involved with each other and even that Fred called her when he returned from the police station the night Carol was killed—a detail that would not be released publicly until six years later at the rabbi's trial. "Yair's" hypothesis was that Fred was a fraud and Elaine was a slut. They'd fallen for each other, and together, they'd killed Carol.

Fred called Elaine as often as usual in the weeks immediately following Carol's murder, but she was pulling back. She didn't know what to believe about him anymore. He'd always sworn that he'd had one brief affair prior to theirs, and that that ended ten years before. Now police were telling her that he'd seen three other women since then in addition to her, one of these at the very moment he was insisting that she was his one true love. She was also haunted by some of his comments that now seemed cast in an ominous light: "It'll be a tumultuous fall." "Poof! Maybe Carol could just vanish. *Just like that.*" Elaine couldn't shake the thought that Fred had something to do with his wife's death. So she had her reasons to tell Fred in early December to stop calling. But she kept one reason to herself: there was a new man in her life—a Cherry Hill policeman working on the Neulander case. Larry Leaf had been assigned to stake out suspects, which involved trailing Fred or Elaine in his Pontiac Firebird, or just sitting unobtrusively in their vicinity and waiting for one of them to go somewhere. This kind of surveillance was tedious and rarely resulted in a breakthrough, but it was the sort of boilerplate police work Leaf was paid to do. For a good part of the day, he just sat in his Firebird with his eye on Fred or Elaine's front door on the chance that they'd emerge and do something incriminating.

When Elaine admitted the affair, Leaf's job changed almost overnight from staking her out to protecting her; her lawyer was now insisting that the police ensure her safety from Fred. Officers assigned to guard a witness usually remain outside her house on the street. But Elaine didn't want to draw her neighbors' attention, and suggested that Leaf and his partner, John Breitling, come inside. They'd arrive around six o'clock, and set the alarm not long after that for four in the morning, which is when she began getting ready for her early morning radio show. If they were lucky, they'd get a few hours of sleep and all of them would leave the house at five-fifteen, with Leaf and Breitling following Elaine to the station in Philadelphia. On a couple of nights, they escorted her to a local high school, where she was rehearsing for a Christmas show; once, they attended the show itself. Most of the time, they just sat around Elaine's kitchen table and talked. All the while, Elaine—who tended to ask of Leaf more personal questions than of Breitling—wondered if Leaf had ever fallen for someone he was supposed to be guarding.

Elaine's police protection ended on Saturday, December 6. Although this was the same day she ended her relationship with Neulander, she seemed to be in no danger, and at midnight Leaf and Breitling returned to the station. As the two men prepared to go off duty, Leaf told his partner he'd be stopping at Elaine's house once more. He had a Christmas gift for her.

"That is *not* a good idea," Breitling said. Cops shouldn't get too familiar with people they were guarding, and he was a bit disgusted that Leaf seemed to be doing just that. "I don't want to know what's going on with you and Soncini."

Leaf took a toy Santa and a bottle of liquor to Elaine's, arriving about twelve forty-five. They talked for an hour. Leaf told her she was "neat," and Soncini spoke sadly about her mother, who was in a nursing home in Philadelphia with Alzheimer's. When he left just before two in the morning, he asked if he could call on her soon. "Yes," she said. "I'd like that."

Elaine's birthday fell on the following Saturday. It was to be on that date, Neulander had promised months ago, that he would free himself from his marriage in order to be with her. Instead, the rabbi sent her a birthday card with a photo of a cat that looked exactly like Priscilla, Elaine's pet feline for seventeen years. But after everything that had happened since November 1, the gesture—and the promise—meant little to Elaine. She and Leaf drove to Atlantic City on the night of her birthday and strolled on the boardwalk for a chilly hour and a half, doing their best not to think about Fred and the strange circumstances that had brought them together. When Elaine visited her mother in the nursing home the next weekend, Larry went with her. They celebrated Christmas quietly. On New Year's Eve, they attended a party at Leaf's ex-sister-in-law's house, after which they spent their first night together, at Leaf's house. Throughout this period, the new lovers avoided the subject of the Neulander case: if the rabbi were ever tried for Carol's murder, the defense could claim that any pillow talk had corrupted Elaine's testimony. But in early January, she was summoned for a third round of questioning—this time accompanied by her lawyer—and Leaf began to "go crazy with myself." He knew that they shouldn't be seeing each other at this juncture.

"You're not out of this thing yet," he told Elaine. "I thought you were and you're not and we have to stop this. When you get your shit together, when you get everything taken care of, then we can be together. Not now."

Three days later, his resolve crumbled. Larry was miserable, Elaine was miserable, and when he called her he blurted out, "We have to see each other." First, though, he had to know two things. Did she have anything to do with Carol's murder? Could Neulander hurt her in any way, physically or by impugning her word? Her answer on all counts was no. Soon, they were back together, despite Larry's better judgment. He tried to be a good cop nonetheless, responding to Elaine's occasional comments about the rabbi ("He's a nasty guy" or "He's interfering with us") by hushing her up: "We're not talking about that." Meanwhile, Neulander kept phoning Elaine at work, even though she invariably hung up on him after saying "I told you to stop calling." It got so bad that her lawyer had to intervene, instructing Neulander's attorney to forbid his client from contacting Elaine.

But Neulander wouldn't—or couldn't—stop badgering her. He sent Soncini letters full of passion and regret in which he begged her to come back. "Angry" because she had cut him off, he couldn't "remain passive for an indeterminate amount of time." Losing all contact with her was "unimaginable." Theirs had been "a gift from God," he wrote, a "treasure." He would "always" love her, and she "of course . . . [would] always love" him. However "devastated and depressed" they both might be at the moment, they couldn't squander that love. In one letter, Fred pointed out that his African violets were blooming, "despite being really cold during the last month . . . An organism—when threatened or deprived— responds by marshalling its resources and sending forth whatever it needs to ensure survival. I sense that is what I need to do . . ."

Apparently, he also needed to convince Elaine of his innocence. If she doubted that, it contradicted "all that I've ever worked for . . . [which was] connected to life and hope. The thought of my being a murderer or an instigator is repugnant with how I've conducted myself all my life . . ." He claimed to be "weeping" for the "injustices" she was suffering. He prayed that both of them would "find the spiritual strength to endure and get beyond this" and hoped she would "never forget who you are . . ."

Early in January, when he had resumed dating Elaine, Larry Leaf was alone in an office at the prosecutor's office, flipping quickly through the Neulander files for a look at statements she had made to investigators. As a patrolman, especially a patrolman who was dating someone who'd briefly been a suspect, this was not his domain. But as he said later, "I needed to see what she had to say and whether I was in more trouble than I thought I was."

It became clear, by the end of the month, that he was. That's when he told his superiors not only that he'd rifled through the case files but also that he and Elaine were engaged. Although Leaf had spent twenty-four years as a police officer, he was soon fired.

By this time, Soncini's priority was to persuade detectives that she had nothing to do with the murder. She cooperated fully with them, even agreeing to try to entrap Neulander by phone. This would be their first conversation in more than a month; its timing coincided with negotiations over the rabbi's severance package from M'kor Shalom, when detectives felt he would be under pressure and in need of support. Elaine's job was to assure Fred that she was still his friend and to hint that she might again be his lover—if, that is, he was able to erase her doubt about his innocence in that small matter of Carol's murder.

According to a police transcript of their conversation, Neulander admitted that "long-term prospects at the synagogue do not look good" when Elaine asked about his professional future. "A lot has happened. A lot has been forced upon me . . ."

"What do they know about me?" Soncini asked.

"No names. They know no names . . ."

"Where would you go?"

"It all depends on how much is revealed. Or how ugly it gets . . ."

"I'm worried about you . . . I wish they could find whoever did this to your poor wife . . ."

Neulander laughed: "At this point, I'm not even sure that would solve one problem."

"I wish we had told police about the affair from the very beginning . . ." Elaine said. "I've somehow been brought into a situation I know nothing about. I feel like I'm being attacked from all angles. And there are women who are talking to reporters about this stuff and that's got to unsettle you because that's your personal life. You know, you're talking to a friend that loves you. I've been battered and beaten just like you have. Don't you feel like you have been battered?"

"Absolutely . . . Now you know why I don't pick up the phone."

"I know," said Elaine consolingly. "I'm sure you're paranoid . . . Now you don't have to worry. You're talking to a friend . . ."

"You're the only person I can trust . . . ," Fred agreed.

They discussed leaving Cherry Hill and starting a life together somewhere else—but that would only be possible, Elaine explained, if she was convinced that he had nothing to do with his wife's death. "If there is a future," she said, "I want to trust you. I want to believe in you . . . Somebody's been murdered and I can't get that out of my head . . . I need to know for us, for our life together . . ."

Neulander hesitated. "I've been warned about recordings."

"Well, then you don't trust me . . . I'm sorry. I don't mean to keep bringing it up . . . Just my heart tells me you're not telling the truth . . . Let's just say good-bye."

"What!" Fred blurted. "Do you believe I had something to do with this?"

"I believe we can handle it," Elaine said soothingly. "I just believe we can handle it . . . All I can think of is that you did this for me."

"No, no," Neulander said firmly. "You're out of your mind if you think I had anything to do with it . . . Taking life for any reason . . . I couldn't have."

"I know what you said," she reminded him. " 'Trust me. Trust me. We're going to be together.' You said something was going to happen by December. What did you expect me to believe? All of a sudden this woman gets killed? What did you think I was going to think? Help me there. Help me!"

"Oh, my God," Neulander shouted, apparently concluding that she was connecting what he had said to Carol's murder. *"Oh my God!"*

Elaine wasn't sure what to think about his impassioned denials. Even at the height of their affair, she had never quite believed Fred would leave his wife. "When you're married and having an affair," she had told herself, "that's already a lie. The marriage is a lie. The person is a lie. So everything else could be a lie, too."

But she hadn't lied to herself about loving Neulander. He'd *seemed* so caring, so kind, so considerate. It was all, she now saw, an illusion. "The person I loved didn't exist," she later told investigators. The real Neulander was "controlling" and "manipulative." And she still didn't know if Carol died because of her. "How do I live," Elaine thought, "knowing *I* could be the possible motive?"

11

"Come Back, Shulamit"

Fred Neulander and his three children spent Thanksgiving 1994 at Carol's sister's house in northern New Jersey. Since only three weeks had passed since the tragedy, family members naturally ascribed Fred's disorientation—he had to be told several times, for example, that a baby born to one of his nieces two months before was a boy, not a girl—to extreme shock and grief.

Taking a long walk between turkey and dessert had become a Lidz-Neulander Thanksgiving tradition, with the purpose of freeing up space in everyone's stomach for goodies from Carol's bakery. This year's expedition was understandably subdued, and once they returned, no one was in the mood for the cheesecake and baba au rhum Fred had brought from the business that Carol had proudly nurtured from scratch. Aside from a few crumbs, the cakes remained intact.

In December, based on a list drawn up by Rabbi Neulander and his lawyers, thirty-five thousand dollars was collected from some of the wealthier residents of Cherry Hill and offered as a reward for information leading to Carol's killer, or killers. Fred had seen to it that Rachel and Larry Stone were on the list—and had asked Gary Mazo to solicit this particular donation in person.

Mazo arrived at the Stones' house with no idea that Mrs. Stone had been sleeping with his boss, or that she had told her husband about the affair a few days before. "Needless to say," Mazo wryly commented later, "I didn't get a very positive response from them. I felt like a complete fool when I found out from the police that Fred had been romantically involved with her."

Unlike Gary Mazo, some of Neulander's best friends had never heard a whisper about his affairs. In early 1995, a couple that had been very close to Fred and Carol invited the rabbi over for a talk. "Fred," they said, "you have to think about dating, maybe not now, but eventually."

Neulander heaved a long sigh. "I can't do that," he finally said.

"Are you concerned about what the community might think?" the friends asked. "Look, Fred, it's not good to be alone. Maybe you can date someone on the sly?"

Neulander was pleased that his friends, for the most part, were rallying around him, but at the same time, he was getting frightened. Rumors about his extramarital life and the circumstances surrounding Carol's murder were relentless, some people he'd known for decades weren't returning his calls, and detectives kept dragging him down to the station for more questions:

Did you and Carol ever discuss divorce?

No, but we saw a marriage counselor twelve years ago.

Did you discuss divorce the Sunday before the murder when you traveled with Carol to see her relatives?

No.

That's not what we've heard.

Well, she complained that we didn't spend enough time together and asked if I wanted a divorce. I said no.

Did you instruct a man to leave an envelope at your house the night of the murder?

No.

Did you tell him to leave an envelope the Tuesday before the murder?

No.

His nights were getting longer and his days were getting quieter. Obviously, the cops were trying to link him to the murder. He hated the long hours of questioning at the prosecutor's office and the disrespectful attitude of his interrogators. He'd devoted his life to God. He'd consoled other people in tragedy and blessed them in joy. But to the detectives, he was just another mug shot. Their theory about the case was pretty simple: Neulander, assumed the lead detectives, wanted to end a crummy marriage and had ruled out divorce as too risky—it might cost him his career, or at least his share of the half million dollars in investments he and Carol held jointly. But the rabbi's alibi—a couple of dozen people saw him at M'kor Shalom at the time of the killing—meant that he'd had at least one other person do the dirty work. Which was good from the standpoint of the police: the more people involved with a crime, the greater the chance that someone would talk. At the moment, however, investigators had no weapon, no suspected hit man, and no confession. Hunches and gossip weren't sufficient to file a homicide charge against a husband for killing his wife, even if he was a proven philanderer.

The fallout from all this had an almost immediate impact on two of Neulander's girlfriends: Debby sold her shop that was a mile from M'kor Shalom and moved to Pennsylvania in an attempt to escape the gossip. The husband of Rachel Stone had taken to standing near the rabbi during the *oneg Shabbat* reception that followed the Friday night service, stare straight at him, sometimes muttering under his breath, "I'm gonna kill that son of a bitch." On one of these occasions, Larry's muttering so distressed two other congregants that they planted themselves between the deceived husband and his nemesis lest they come to blows. In the end, there were only unpleasant words, all from the husband, but the incident underscored the mounting tensions at M'kor Shalom. How could it have been otherwise, given the increasingly more fantastic gossip—such as the story about the local politician racing into the Neulanders' in the wake of the murder to retrieve a videotape of the rabbi having sex with her.

M'kor Shalom's board of directors was meeting once and some-times twice a week to decide Neulander's fate. The rumors were only part of the problems. Reporters were laying siege to the tem-ple, some even attending Friday night services so that they could distribute their business cards to anyone who would take them and, hopefully, later give them a quote. Most alarming, Neulander him-self was behaving as if nothing untoward were happening. He taught his classes, counseled congregants, led the worship service, even went ahead with the class on ethics he'd been scheduled to teach before Carol's death. Early in the course, he featured the topic of murder and capital punishment. "Everyone there got chills," said one student. "Hearing him talk about this so soon after Carol was killed—just the fact that he could even mention it—gave us goose bumps. We wanted to get out of there as soon as possible."

To convince the cops he was innocent, Neulander proposed to his lawyer that he take a lie detector test. It was administered in early December in Fairfax, Virginia—about 160 miles south of Cherry Hill—by Paul Minor, who'd been the top polygrapher for the FBI and the Army's Criminal Investigation Command.

After the usual preliminary questions (*What's your name? What's your age? Where do you live?*), Minor asked Neulander if he killed his wife. He said no and the machine was satisfied. But when the rabbi was asked, "Did you have your wife killed?" the polygraph "went off the charts," according to someone familiar with the results. The same questions were asked at a later point during the exam. Neulander's response was identical: two no's. Again, the polygraph's needles swung wildly at the second "no."

In 1996, when the *Philadelphia Inquirer* reported about the ambiguous polygraph test, one of Fred's lawyers attributed his client's performance to tranquilizers that had been prescribed after the murder. "There's no doubt in my mind he had nothing to do with [the crime]," the attorney insisted. "He was terrified [during the polygraph test]. He was in active grief and he was taking medication."

But the president of the American Polygraph Association, Steve Bartlett, said medication wouldn't significantly alter the results, and that the emotions of a subject are always considered when interpreting them because taking the test scares *everyone,* innocent or not. Certain drugs, Bartlett acknowledged, might dampen or exaggerate responses, but they wouldn't affect someone's overall reactions. "Drugs won't change the outcome of the examination so it's the opposite of what it should be," Bartlett stated. "If somebody tells you they were on drugs and therefore it was a bad test—well, that's crap!"

Crap or not, there would be no legal consequences for Neulander. If he were ever charged with killing Carol, a polygraph taken in Virginia couldn't be used as evidence. In New Jersey, the test results could be admitted in a criminal case only if both sides allowed it—and Fred's lawyers weren't stupid enough to do that.

In early January, Neulander had written Soncini that she wouldn't hear from him until Valentine's Day—"unless the situation dramatically changes as we would wish." He omitted saying that he would stay away from her office. A few weeks after promising not to write to her, the rabbi dropped off an umbrella with a receptionist at WPEN, explaining that Soncini had mistakenly left it with him. In truth, he'd just bought it for her at Nan Duskin, an upscale ladies' shop, knowing that she'd seen it and admired it.

Just as he'd promised, Fred called Elaine on Valentine's Day, but she refused to talk to him. Two days later, he followed up with a letter. He hoped—despite mounting evidence to the contrary—that she still had feelings for him.

> *Dear Elaine,*
>
> *When you didn't take my call two days ago, I assumed that was your wish. I'm hopeful that it was on counsel's advice and not anything else. As I assumed, and later confirmed, the police lied and misrepresented and dissembled . . .*
>
> *I've been working to assure you that our situation is not compromised. I know how isolated and frightened I am; I assume the same for you . . .*
>
> *By way of apology—I hurt for the pain I caused as the situation unfolded for you. That is my deepest feeling. The murder investigation will unfold at its own pace. I wish it could be resolved soon.*
>
> *. . . We knew it would be a difficult time. I had no idea how viciously difficult . . . I've been working to assure that your and my situation is not compromised . . . Everything I know to do is being done to protect us. It's obvious that we have to write or speak.*
>
> *I hope to hear from you.*
>
> *Fred*

Neulander was reiterating his usual theme: he and Elaine were star-crossed lovers longing to be together but kept apart by others—police, lawyers, friends who thought they knew what was best for them. For more than two years, they'd shared something precious and rare. They couldn't let that slip away. He still loved her; she *had* to still love him.

Soncini was oblivious to Fred's pleading; she found certain passages of his letter disturbing. She wondered if he was so frustrated by her rejections that he planned to implicate her in the murder, even if by doing so he implicated himself. In his letter, he said they had to write or talk to each other. But *what* would they write about? *What* would they speak about? From *what* was she being protected? Soncini wasn't sure—but she didn't like the conclusions someone could draw from what he had written. That's why she passed his letters along to the police.

Neulander didn't sign "love" in his closing to any of his letters to Soncini. One farewell was the lengthy and fairly formal "Thank for your honesty now and your hope for the yet-to-be." Another was neutral: "I hope to hear from you." A third had the traditional Hebrew word of parting: *Shalom*. A fourth was "Shalom, Shulamit." "Shulamit" was the Hebrew name Soncini adopted when she converted to Judaism, a name Neulander handpicked for her. In the Song of Songs, Shulamit yearns for her lover to

> . . . *kiss me with the kisses of . . . [your] mouth!*
> *For your love is better than wine . . .*

Her lover's hands are "like gold" and his "mouth is full of sweetness" and Shulamit "glows like the dawn" and is "as pure as the sun." When she turns away from her maids, who are singing her praises, they cry out, just as Neulander was crying out for Soncini, who had turned away from him:

> *Come back, come back, O Shulamit,*
> *Come back, that we may gaze at you.*

For now, Neulander had no one to gaze at. He was alone, maybe more alone than he had ever been.

12

"Couldn't He Have Just Gone to a Cathouse in Camden?"

To isolate Neulander from M'kor Shalom, investigators gave a board member at the temple the names of his girlfriends. Three board members met with Neulander and the rabbi confirmed the information from the police. Obviously, this was not the same man who'd said his marriage was "kosher" the night Carol was killed.

The board originally wanted an indefinite leave of absence for Fred. In a letter that Sheila Goodman, the temple's president, sent congregants in late February, she said Neulander needed time for "counseling and to be with his family" and that he would "not be responsible for services, life-cycle events, counseling, meeting attendance, or teaching." The letter said nothing about the extramarital liaisons.

So a few days later, people were shocked—despite what local gossips were saying about Neulander—when tabloids along the

East Coast featured screaming headlines about the rabbi's scandalous personal life and his current position at the top of the suspects list in Carol's murder. The papers didn't mention his girlfriends by name, but that was a small favor, considering the damage done otherwise.

The *New York Post* went with "SEX, MURDER—AND THE RABBI WITH A CHEATING HEART." The *Trentonian* (New Jersey) chose "CHEATING RABBI SUSPECT IN WIFE HIT" and followed the headline with a story whose lead paragraph staggered congregants at M'kor Shalom:

> *The wife of a prominent and apparently amorous rabbi might have been murdered by hired killers . . . With news reports suggesting the woman's murder is a tale of salacious sex, religion and conspiracy, [Camden County Prosecutor Edward F.] Borden . . . attempted to stifle what he called "exaggeration" without flatly denying the talk of love affairs and hitmen.*

The dignity with which the temple's members had been trying to conduct synagogue business was shattered. People were furious: their own rabbi had conned them. "This showed us all as fools," said one congregant, shaking his head. "This was a *shanda* [Yiddish for "scandal"]. It disgraced the Jewish community before the rest of the world."

"How dare he stand on that pulpit year after year," demanded another member, "telling me what was right and wrong and him not knowing the difference. What are we supposed to tell our children?"

Neulander offered his resignation to the temple's board, without accepting any responsibility for his actions. Infuriated, the board dispatched two of its members to the rabbi's house to negotiate the wording of the letter. While they were there, the other directors tried to figure out how to handle Neulander's resignation at the meeting of the entire congregation, scheduled four days later. It had originally been called to present Neulander's open-ended sabbatical. Now the board had to explain why the temple was losing its rabbi. The tabloids had already muddied the waters, and the board preferred not to confirm what they were saying about Neulander's affairs. But some directors were so mad at the rabbi that they were considering forgoing the high moral ground and telling congregants the true reasons for Neulander's departure.

One board member spent a sleepless night after this meeting, and the next morning, he called Sheila Goodman. "This is the wrong way to go about this," he told the board's president. "Saying Fred had affairs will make every woman in the temple the target of ugly rumors." Goodman agreed, and the next night—Friday—a slightly calmer board met after the Shabbat service and determined that no reason would be given.

In the Middle Ages, Jews who committed adultery were instructed to sit in an icy river for the same amount of time that had elapsed between meeting the women they'd seduced and actually having sex with them. If the punishment took place in the summer, an anthill was substituted for the river. This medieval form of repentance was a good deal more lenient than the Old Testament law requiring adulterers to be stoned to death. Given the historical context, Neulander had nothing to complain about. He walked away from M'kor Shalom with a settlement that amounted to half his annual salary.

At the end of February, the congregation-wide meeting was held for what would presumably be a discussion of the rabbi's leave of absence. But when Sheila Goodman rose to address the audience of eight hundred, she said, "Our original purpose has changed. Rabbi Neulander has tendered his resignation." People gasped; some cried. Goodman went on to read aloud a letter from Neulander in which he called himself a victim of "the media frenzy [which] has revealed information I'm not proud of and behavior that brings no honor to me and hurts M'kor Shalom." He wrote that he was forced to resign because of "misinformation" leaked by the police. He begged congregants not to press for further details. Almost as an afterthought, he assured them that he had "no involvement in my wife's death."

People were angry—at the board, at the rabbi, at the press. Some pleaded for the same understanding toward Neulander that he had taught them to have toward everyone else. Others felt that there'd be no due process, that he'd been dismissed without a fair hearing by the board. "Why does it have to be a done deal?" one person demanded. Another said, "During Rabbi Neulander's worst crisis, do not turn him out of our family." A third insisted, "There's a missing piece of the puzzle. Explain why it was appropriate to accept the resignation so quickly."

But the majority of those present were silent, trying to absorb the news. They'd admired Neulander, or at least been intrigued by him. Some loved him. Others feared him. A rabbi ends up being all things to all people: father figure, God's representative on earth, divine wrath itself. People were disappointed, betrayed, angry—at Fred and at themselves. How could he do this to them? How could they have been so stupid, so blind, so clueless that they didn't see who the guy was? Most devastated of all was the handful of congregants who had been so taken with Neulander that they called him a "prophet." Without him, why should they even belong to M'kor Shalom? It would become just another temple in the broad suburban landscape of New Jersey.

But the board wasn't yielding: Neulander had submitted his resignation, and they had accepted it. He was *not* returning. And no, he had *not* been pressured to leave. M'kor Shalom could not heal if it was saddled with the millstone of its own rabbi. The health of the congregation, said Goodman, was more important than any one person, even the man who had created it and nurtured it from the very beginning. Questions about Neulander had to stop, Goodman insisted. He had relinquished his position as rabbi and it was no longer the temple's job to dig deeper into the matter.

"Do not ask your synagogue to . . . probe for knowledge of things that are no longer relevant," begged Goodman. "We love our rabbi. We support our rabbi. But our rabbi feels he can no longer be our rabbi."

As the confrontation between the board and the membership continued, some people were aware of an agitated young man at the back of the room, pacing back and forth and cursing under his breath. It was Matthew Neulander, the rabbi's older son. After a while, Matthew came forward and approached Marc Cutler, a former synagogue president with access to a microphone. "I want to speak," Matthew told him. Cutler was worried about Matthew's intentions. "Think about your father," he whispered. "You're upset. You don't want to say things that would embarrass him."

Matthew, staring him down, stepped toward the microphone. As *Philadelphia* magazine later summed up the moment: "You could have heard a handkerchief drop." People's eyes riveted on the young man, whom some had known since his infancy. Nearly everyone had seen him four months earlier before at his mother's funeral. Now the rabbi's twenty-two-year-old son stood before them, thanking everyone who had been kind to his father—but also wondering aloud if the congregation *really* understood the man who had just resigned, or, for that matter, anything he had taught them over the years.

"What's going on here is a tragedy," Matthew said, anger rising in his voice. "Dad's behavior was an indiscretion. It was beneath the way a rabbi should act, and he feels terrible that we should have to suffer for it. But just think of what Dad did for you. Just keep that in a special place in your hearts. For twenty-one years, he gave his life to this place . . . Every nuance, every program has his personal touch on it. The real tragedy is that all this will go to waste if he didn't teach any of you compassion and forgiveness. He's just a human being. He never claimed to be anything else. And he's really hurting right now."

Matthew was right: his father was human, with human flaws and weaknesses, as well as the human tendencies to cover them up. But Neulander's profession placed him on terrain that was different from everyone else's. As a man, he inhabited their world, but as a rabbi he operated at a slight remove from them. He was aware that this would be the case from the moment he'd decided to enter the seminary. And he had agreed, back then, to follow certain ethics that others could ignore or make light of. A mentor from his college days in Hartford, Rabbi Abraham Feldman, told students at the Reform seminary in the early 1960s that the marriage of a rabbi had to reflect the blessing recited at Jewish weddings: *ahavoh v'achovah v'shalom v're'us* ("love and comradeship, peace and friendship"). "The people," Feldman said, "like to see it that way, and they have a right to."

Few people who were at M'kor Shalom the morning that Neulander's resignation was announced knew that "love and comradeship, peace and friendship" had been lacking in his marriage. In time, M'kor Shalom's members would realize that the union of Fred and Carol Neulander was neither as they would "like to see it" nor as they had "a right" to see it.

What Matthew didn't say was that not long after the murder, he'd asked his father, point-blank, if he had anything to do with it. Without a pause, Neulander told this son who raced home in his ambulance on that awful night, "Absolutely not." But every day, Matthew learned more things about his father's betrayals of his mother, which made it harder to live in the same house with him. Things came to a head when Matthew told Fred he was thinking about hiring a lawyer in case the police called him down for more testimony. OK, said the rabbi, but *he* had to choose the lawyer. Matthew rightfully worried that an attorney handpicked by his father would not keep his client's confidences to himself, and Fred blew up. He threatened his son: if Matthew didn't do it *his* way, he'd stop paying his tuition at medical school. In the end, Matthew hired his own lawyer. He also moved into a rented apartment a few miles from his father's house. Yet, after all this, the rabbi continued to pay for Matthew's medical school, partly from guilt, partly because he did not want to renege on the promise he'd made years ago to Matthew to help him out.

As the most painful meeting in M'kor Shalom's history wound down, Cantor Anita Hochman gently strummed her guitar and sang of the peace that everyone in the room could use at that moment:

> *May we be blessed as we go on our way.*
> *May we be guided in peace.*
> *May we be blessed with health and joy.*
> *May this be our blessing. Amen.*

For many years, the congregation would be haunted by the idea that their leader could be described by these ominous verses in the Book of Proverbs:

> *He that commits adultery . . . lacks understanding;*
> *Whoever does it will destroy his own soul.*
> *Wounds and dishonor shall he get.*
> *And his reproach shall not be wiped away.*

Fred Neulander's reproach was just beginning. And the gossip about his infidelities would soon pale beside what people were saying about his possible involvement with Carol's murder.

Board members could not control the rumors, but they were determined to keep the names of Fred's girlfriends secret. A few years before, when a rabbi in San Francisco resigned after news of his philandering surfaced, four women who had filed complaints against him for harassment appeared at a temple meeting to testify about his behavior. "Harlots," people screamed. "Jezebels. Whores. Liars." M'kor Shalom's efforts to protect the identities of Neulander's consorts reflected something they'd learned from the disgraced rabbi himself: words alone can wreck careers and marriages and honor and trust. "Death and life," the Book of Proverbs (18:21) confirms, "are in the power of the tongue."

Fred Neulander had said as much in September 1994, writing in his column for the temple's newsletter about the O. J. Simpson case, which was then in its fourth month. People obsessed with the case, he wrote, were "voyeurs, eager to fill . . . [their] days with gory details or fanciful theories. A tragedy became a soap opera spectacle. How shallow our lives must be if another's travails and machinations filled our world." The nonstop talk about O.J., in Cherry Hill and throughout the country only served to exacerbate the tragedy. "A life is lost . . . [Simpson] continues to exist, but . . . in the shadow of innuendo and horrid speculation," Neulander's column continued. "The situation is horrific enough without our adding to its ugliness . . . We diminish ourselves and our world when we lose ourselves to the . . . antics of a true tragedy." The rabbi implored his readers not to participate in such "antics," asking instead that they fill their lives "with creation's beauty." Lift your eyes, he begged, and look at the wonder around you. In hindsight, that column would have an eerie resonance; it might just as well have been autobiographical. Like O.J., Fred had sunk from stardom—the celebrity rabbi—to being a suspected murderer.

A few days before the temple meeting, Neulander got his last call from Soncini. Detectives were worried that Neulander had somehow concluded from her previous call that she and the rabbi still had a future. Now, they told her, she had to tell him she was dating someone else. That, plus the strain of his resignation, might force him to blurt out something incriminating.

Neulander did not take the news from Soncini well. "Oh, my God!" he cried out. "I gave up my synagogue for you."

Now that Neulander and M'kor Shalom had gone their separate ways, Carol's family also wanted him out of their lives—even though it went against their grain. The Lidzes had treated him like a brother ever since Carol had become his wife, inviting him to all their gatherings and not only because he was Carol's husband. They generally liked him as a person and enjoyed his company. But when his infidelities were exposed, and all the lying that went with them, Fred's in-laws felt betrayed and mocked. It was bad enough, said Ed, one of Carol's brothers, that Fred had "demeaned her by his behavior. Now we hear he's spreading stories about Carol being frigid and they had an 'arrangement.' Couldn't he have just gone to a cathouse in Camden?"

In the early spring of 1995, Ed called Neulander to tell him it would be best if he didn't officiate at his daughter's wedding that spring. Neulander exploded. He instructed his children to boycott the affair in his defense—but they went anyway.

There was a plethora of theories about who killed Carol. Most of them involved Fred. Maybe Neulander, while on a trip to Israel, hired a killer affiliated with the Arab terrorist group Hezbollah. Except that Arab terrorists don't do favors for American Zionists.

Maybe Neulander had connections with the Russian Mafia, which flew a killer in from the former Soviet Union. Except that Russia was ten thousand miles away, and surely there were hit men somewhere nearer to New Jersey.

The limerick writer, naturally, had his own theory. His last poem, written two days after the congregation-wide meeting where Neulander's resignation was announced, attacked Soncini for ditching the rabbi and taking up with Larry Leaf:

> *Lumen is always looking for more.*
> *In the old days, you'd call her a whore.*
> *We know she will tarry,*
> *With Tom, Dick or Larry,*
> *She's a Jezebel right to the core.*

> *While professing love for the rabbi,*
> *Engaged she is now to the cop guy*
> *Who has information*
> *On investigation,*
> *Appears now she has her alibi.*

> *Perhaps it was Lumen herself, who*
> *Wielded the weapon that death do.*
> *Where was she when the blood*
> *On the rug it did flood?*
> *Was it all part of a witches brew?*

You had to hand it to the anonymous poet for his command of information that no ordinary citizen knew. "Yair" was aware of Fred's calls to Elaine around the time of the murder, for example, and of Elaine's romance with Larry Leaf and even whether Carol Neulander really refused to give her husband a divorce. "Yair" also revealed that Elaine dumped Fred for a guy she'd known for barely a month. Whether these details made Soncini, as the last limerick insisted, a "Jezebel" or a "whore" was arguable.

Judaism teaches that man has two opposing inclinations—the *yetzer hatov,* or "good," and the *yetzer hara,* or "evil." Both are essential to life: the *yetzer hatov* emanates from reason and reflection, while the *yetzer hara* corresponds to untamed natural appetites, like ambition or sex. Left unchecked, the *yetzer hara* leads to avarice, vanity, vindictiveness. Yet if the *yetzer hara* were denied altogether, we would never marry, or beget children, or advance in our careers. So the *yetzer hatov*—good—has to constantly monitor the *yetzer hara,* and channel its energies toward virtue. Neulander had clearly succumbed to the power of the *yetzer hara,* and now he had no office to go to, no congregants to inspire or counsel or con. He was a rabbi in name only, and without the "emeritus" title that is usually conferred on those who retire honorably from leading a temple. And he was still the man who wrote these words for M'kor Shalom's prayer book . . .

> *We live at any moment with our total past;*
> *We hate with all our past hatreds,*
> *And we love with all our past loves . . .*
> *That is why it is so important to be careful about what we*
>   *do each day.*
> *What we do will stay with us forever.*

13

"If You Divorce Your Wife, Fred, You'd Lose a Popularity Contest by a Landslide"

Every town has a few crooks who could have walked right out of *Guys and Dolls*—someone charming, maybe a bit eccentric, who stays just enough on the right side of the law to seem almost law-abiding. Cherry Hill had a couple of these guys, like "Cherry Hill Fats," a three-hundred-pound swindler who made a few million bucks a year in the mid-1960s but was so mammoth he couldn't squeeze into his shower. Or Myron "Peppy" Levin, who was convicted in the 1970s for fraud, tax evasion, and conspiracy to commit arson but for whom everyone in town seemed to have a soft spot. Peppy's most ambitious scheme was a silver-smelting operation that grossed about $100 million a year, moving stacks of coins in and out of New Jersey in old hearses and chartered jets. Levin laundered his money by investing in mundane enterprises—including linen-supply stores and liquor marts and novelty products, like sunglasses with built-in transistor radios—and earned enough to drive around in stretch Cadillacs and take luxury vacations in the Virgin Islands. Not bad for a sharp-nosed, fast-talking kid raised in a Jewish-Italian ghetto in Camden who was known to his friends as the cheapest guy in town. "Peppy doesn't put out a penny unless he absolutely has to," said one of them. "If he owes you five cents, he'll try to figure out a way to pay you four."

Levin was a folk figure in Cherry Hill, but his cops-and-robbers days had ended about twenty years before—the last time he was behind bars—when he swore to his kids that his days of crime were over. From here on in, he'd have "nothing to do with people who could possibly put me back in prison. No way." And he kept his word. "When I make a promise," he said, "it's a promise." By the 1980s, he was in the billboard business—the legal end of it—and while it was a struggle sometimes, it was also a way into the "good, clean, balanced life" he now wanted for himself.

In that spirit, Peppy became a regular at Gold's Gym on Old Cuthbert Road in Cherry Hill, playing racquetball almost every day and getting pretty good at it. One morning, another regular, an attorney by trade, invited the ex-con to join him and another man in a game. Pretty soon, that other man was Peppy's regular racquetball partner. He also became a friend.

In April of 1995, Levin told investigators all about his new gym buddy—whose name was Fred Neulander. The cops knew about Peppy's past, but they also knew he'd been straight for almost two decades, so they listened to his stories.

According to Levin, he and Neulander hit it off that first morning, and within a few weeks, they were playing together regularly. Once a month or so, they met for lunch, usually at an Italian restaurant. Peppy was a dinner guest at the Neulanders' home a few times and reciprocated by inviting Fred and Carol to his sixty-ninth birthday party, held on October 10, 1994—three weeks before Carol was killed.

In the locker rooms at the gym, Peppy reported, Fred behaved like any other guy. He cursed, complained about money and his family and his job, and never mentioned the prophets or the Bible or Jewish ethics or anything else that would identify him as a clergyman. At Gold's, he was just a man who kept in shape and who happened to be earning his living in the rabbi business. He even gave out the names of his girlfriends. Most of the guys who heard him shook their heads and thought, "What a crazy rabbi! All those women! The guy's gotta be *meshugener.*"

It sounded almost like Neulander was back in high school, attempting to swagger around like the rest of the guys but not quite pulling it off. As in Queens, there were people at the gym who wrote him off as some nerd trying too hard to fit in, trying to make them forget who he was when he wasn't hanging out at Gold's—a man of religion poring over scripture in preparation for his next sermon or consoling widows or inspiring teenagers, or whatever he was supposed to be doing for the people who were paying his salary at M'kor Shalom.

But some guys at the gym took Fred seriously. Some even envied him. He seemed to have everything: power, prestige, respect, and women falling all over him. When the cops asked Peppy if Neulander "seemed to take pleasure in telling you about these affairs," Levin chuckled admiringly. "I would assume so," he said. "I would take pleasure."

Peppy was the only one of Neulander's gym buddies who actually got to meet Neulander's girlfriends instead of just hearing about them. In early 1994, Neulander took Elaine Soncini and Rachel Stone, separately, to watch him play racquetball. The women's presence, said Peppy, encouraged Neulander to play extra hard. "If one of his women was there," Peppy said, "he'd beat the hell out of me. If they weren't, I'd beat the hell out of him."

Neulander didn't seem to care who was listening when he spoke about his mistresses. The message he gave was that his mar-

riage was already so bad that he had nothing to lose. He even told
Levin that he and Carol had discussed divorce, and that she seemed
willing to give him one. But then he'd have to figure out who to
marry next. Rachel, Fred calculated, would get about seven million
dollars by divorcing her husband; and Elaine had already inherited
over a million or so from her husband. Monetarily, it was a simple
decision, but his real passions were with Elaine.

Peppy Levin couldn't believe Fred's attitude. Forget about love,
he told the rabbi. It made no sense to marry either woman, even if
they were loaded, because they weren't Jewish—their conversions
hadn't occurred yet. Any rabbi who married a gentile, Levin said,
especially a rabbi who'd recently been divorced, would be thrown
from the pulpit onto the street.

"Fred," Peppy said, "you've got to be the dumbest fuckin' rabbi.
Are you stupid? Are you an ass? You're crazy if you think the people
at the synagogue are going to let you marry a *shiksa*. This doesn't
make any sense. Look what happened to that other rabbi. He
divorced his wife and married another woman and I helped him
get a job with a bank for thirty thousand or forty thousand dollars
a year, helping them bring in business from people he knew in
town. But I'm not involved with banks anymore and I can't help
you get a job. So what you're talkin' about isn't even a good business decision."

Peppy concluded the impromptu therapy session with a last
piece of advice. "What I want you to do is stick with your wife,"
he instructed Fred. "If you want to go out and get laid, go do it.
And come back home at night. If you divorce Carol, and there's a
popularity contest between you and her, you'd lose by a landslide."

But Neulander kept the divorce talk going with Carol—or so
he told Peppy—and Carol kept vacillating until finally declaring to
her husband that there would be no divorce. Neulander, Levin
later said, "was pissed off. Really pissed off."

One day in April 1994, Neulander slammed down his racquet after losing another game to Levin. "What the hell's wrong, Fred?" Peppy asked, thinking the rabbi was a bad sport.

"I wish the fuck I could go home and see my wife lying dead on the floor."

"What?" yelled Peppy.

"I'd like to go home and see my wife lying dead on the fucking floor. Maybe you could help me do it."

"Fred, get the fuck out of here."

Peppy was trying to stay straight, as he'd promised his kids he'd do and now a rabbi was asking him to get rid of his wife. He couldn't believe it. "Stop talking to me like this, Fred. Cut the bullshit. You're a rabbi. Stay a rabbi. Cut this shit out. You're fuckin' crazy."

Peppy walked out of the gym and got into the backseat of his car. He occasionally hired a man named Tony to drive him around town, or up to New York or northern New Jersey on billboard business. Today, Tony was behind the wheel. "Tony," he said, "that rabbi wants to come home and see his wife dead. What a fucking crazy son of a bitch." And Tony, who'd never been in trouble with the cops, just shook his head. "What the fuck is going on around here?" he thought.

14

"Advice for One DJ Under Fire: Cool It!"

As the summer of 1995 approached, things were going pretty well for Elaine Soncini. By then, the newspapers seemed to be losing interest in Neulander stories, the murder case didn't appear to be progressing, and Elaine's name had yet to be linked to Fred's. The papers did mention the rabbi's affair with a recently widowed woman, but the reference was too vague to lead even the most enterprising journalist to her door.

In early June, she married her former police protector, Larry Leaf, after she converted back to the Catholic faith she'd been born into. "Judaism is a wonderful religion," she said, "but I have to go home and Christianity is my home." Her speedy return to Christianity offended Gary Mazo, whose classes at M'kor Shalom had taught her about what it meant to be a Jew. He was certain that Soncini converted just so that people wouldn't complain that their new *rebbetzin,* should Neulander ever marry her, was a gentile.

Even if Elaine had been a "victim" of Neulander's, as Mazo later said, she was also a "participant in . . . deception" and had "defiled . . . the most sacred of ceremonies, the most potent of promises." Her conversion, he concluded, had been a "farce."

By midsummer, more than half a year had passed since Elaine had broken up with Fred. With her new husband and her return to Catholicism, she felt that she'd succeeded in distancing herself completely from the rabbi and all that he represented. Life was good again.

Then she got a call from a reporter at the *Philadelphia Daily News.* The paper had learned that Elaine was the previously unidentified recent widow who'd had an affair with Neulander. The secret she had been keeping for nearly three years was about to be exposed, whether or not she agreed to be interviewed. Hoping to put the best spin on the paper's story, she met with the reporter. The result of the interview appeared on August 18 in a splashy front-page story under the provocative headline:" 'I WAS IN LOVE. HE WANTED TO CONSOLE.' RADIO PERSONALITY SAYS SHE HAD TWO-YEAR AFFAIR WITH RABBI WHOSE WIFE WAS SLAIN." In the piece, Elaine came off as confused, maybe even deluded at the outset of an affair that began in the immediate wake of her husband's death. "I felt I was in love," she told the reporter. "Now I don't know if I was in love or in grief . . ." But she was undeniably furious at being unmasked. She had the names of all the other women involved with Neulander. "Why is my name the only one being discussed?" she wanted to know. "What hurts me to the very core is that I'm the sacrificial lamb."

The day after the story broke, Elaine launched a press campaign of her own—at Neulander's expense. On local TV, she accused her former lover of being "controlling," "manipulative," and "destructive"; she said he'd told her to lie to the police and he'd tried to handpick her lawyer to serve himself. To the *Philadelphia Inquirer,* she attributed her entry into the liaison to the vulnerability caused by extreme grief. "God was taking Ken from me and God was sending ... [the rabbi]," she explained. "He took on a larger presence to me at that time ... When you lose somebody who's a very pivotal part of your life, a great part of you shatters, and you're very vulnerable." She pleaded for understanding and empathy from the media, the profession to which she herself belonged. "I have found a new life, and I want that life to be private because everything else has become so public. First, my past with Ken is over and done and then, suddenly, my present is exploding. Don't take my future."

That, of course, was an exaggeration. Elaine still had her flashy job, a new marriage, and the fortune she'd inherited from Ken. The present was in turmoil, but in the long term the future was promising. It was her past that had been destroyed by her own actions, vulnerable though she may have been.

As for Neulander, the turmoil was unending and the destruction infinite. People who'd paid little attention to the case since it first broke were now riveted on the rabbi, thanks to the round-the-clock coverage in the press once Elaine's identity was revealed. There was, for instance, a Camden librarian who'd gone from indifferent in January to obsessed in August, reading everything he could find with the word "Neulander" in it. One day, he called a friend who belonged to M'kor Shalom.

"Well, well, well," the librarian said after his friend picked up, "looks like your rabbi had a bird on the side."

"A bird!" his friend snorted dismissively. "He had a whole aviary!"

On her first day back at WPEN since the *Daily News* story broke about her and Neulander, Soncini apologized on the air: she was "truly sorry" if her "errors in judgment" caused "discomfort or pain" to anyone. Yet—sticking to her self-imposed victimhood—Elaine also reminded her audience that she was "hurt more than anyone because I have to live with my mistakes every day—not just in my heart, but on television and in the newspaper." The moment she signed off at nine o'clock, the station's switchboard jammed. The calls, according to the station's general manager, were all "very, very positive. The view is that she's a victim. She was very vulnerable and she got had."

Soncini thought that by taking the initiative and meeting with reporters the day after the *News* ran its story, the press would back off, satisfied, and give her some privacy. No such luck. TV vans laid siege to her house, reporters followed her everywhere, and the only way she could leave the radio station the day of her mea culpa speech was by running out of the station's loading dock accompanied by ten bodyguards. So, still hoping to satiate the newshounds, she called a press conference. She looked fetching facing the cameras and microphones, wearing a skirt that came just above her knees, her hair as tidy as if she'd just come from a beauty salon. An occasional tremble in her voice was the only sign that she was less than composed.

From the outset of the press conference, Soncini went on the attack. She vented her fury at Camden County's acting prosecutor, who'd announced the day before that she had "a possible motive" for killing Carol. Elaine told reporters that this contradicted his assurances to her that he believed she "had nothing to do" with the crime. To suggest otherwise, she said, was "reprehensible and repugnant." She didn't spare the media, either, telling her audience, "You are relentless. This is a story I never wanted printed. People are pulling the levers, and I'm being bounced up and down and from side to side. All you have in this world, in this life, is your name. It's who you are and it's what you stand for. My name has been sullied. I sullied it myself. I don't want to talk anymore. I didn't want to talk in the first place. I'm talking again today. I want it to be the last time."

Elaine got what she wanted, in that sense; aside from occasional conversations with the police and a long, tearful appearance before a grand jury two years later, she enveloped herself in silence about Neulander. But her effort to spin the story to her advantage was none too successful. Friends were still calling her "sweet" and "vulnerable," but the general public referred to her in terms that would have been bleeped on prime-time TV. It didn't help to talk with reporters right after the *Daily News* story broke in an attempt at damage control, and then issue a broadside against the media a few days later for not respecting her privacy. She wanted it both ways, it seemed—spill her guts one day, shut her mouth the next. The *Philadelphia Inquirer,* fed up with her contortions, ran an annoyed editorial entitled "Too Much Talk? Best Advice for One DJ Under Fire: Cool It!"

"Let's see if we have this straight," the *Inquirer* asked,

> *A radio talk-show host calls in the media to complain that she is being harassed into talking about her adulterous affair with a rabbi whose wife was murdered last year . . . Then on Wednesday, she called in the media to beg them to stop trying to talk to her.*
>
> *Got all that? In a nutshell, that's where things stand with Elaine Soncini . . . Her recent comment/no comment gymnastics confirm that media manipulation is not restricted to politicians, sports figures and Bill Gates.*
>
> *No doubt, Ms. Soncini got a lot of sympathy from average folks when she talked about how wrenching it is when one's private affairs get swept up in a media maelstrom. It is, indeed. But it's a little disingenuous for a savvy media professional to paint herself as an unsuspecting victim of media excess.*
>
> *Perhaps for the moment, she's right: The best policy for her would be silence.*

Elaine apparently agreed; other than hosting her show five mornings a week, she kept quiet. Not that there was much for her to say at this point. Everyone within a hundred miles of south Jersey already knew who she was and what she'd done with her ex-boyfriend—a very bad rabbi.

15

Probe the Heart

With Soncini out of the closet and the Cherry Hill police chief
telling reporters about his theory that Neulander had hired a hit
man, it was Fred's turn to call a press conference. There, he denied
adamantly having played any role in his wife's death. The whole
idea, he thundered, was "inconceivable and repulsive." He
demanded an end to prosecutors indulging in "speculation" and
blasted journalists for relying on "unnamed and irresponsible"
sources. Neither the rabbi nor his lawyers directly acknowledged
the affair with Elaine, although one of his attorneys, Jeffrey Zucker,
said that her assertions "certainly address the ethics and morals of
Rabbi Neulander"—whatever that was supposed to mean. Zucker
added that the alleged "relationship would, in any case, have had
nothing to do with Carol's murder . . . unless someone is saying it
was a motive, which is absurd."

The day following Fred's press conference happened to be a Friday. If he attended Shabbat services that night, it wasn't at M'kor Shalom. Sitting in the midst of everyone you knew within twenty-four hours of denying to the world that you killed your wife would have been uncomfortable enough, even if you had been just another congregant. As M'kor Shalom's disgraced rabbi, it would have been intolerable, especially considering the Torah portion scheduled to be read that particular Shabbat—several chapters from Leviticus in which Moses warns the Israelites that to ignore God's commandments was to court disaster.

Congregants at M'kor Shalom had collectively endured nearly a year of traumatic events—and the subsequent emotional repercussions—stemming from their rabbi's private sins, the gravity of which was still emerging.

When Neulander resigned, most congregants stayed in the temple, although a good many of these grappled with their identity as Jews. They felt that something had corroded them from within and made them question the faith, even the very fact of being Jews. But some left the temple. They felt that M'kor Shalom's directors had betrayed their rabbi, and by extension themselves. Now they felt doubly betrayed by this man they revered when news of *l'affaire Soncini* came out. M'kor Shalom wanted them to know it was safe to return, that the temple *wanted* them to return. Few did. Some were too embarrassed, some were too devastated. A few didn't know where to direct their anger, so the temple remained an easy target for them.

For guidance in weathering this spiritual crisis, those who still belonged to M'kor Shalom turned to Gary Mazo, who was now, effectively, the leader of the congregation. One congregant who'd converted to Judaism under Neulander's supervision asked Mazo to "reconvert" her because she was convinced, after learning the truth about her former spiritual mentor, that her conversion had been tainted. Mazo shepherded her through the ritual bath where she'd had her original conversion. When a young congregant, a college freshman, came to Mazo and said she had decided to leave Judaism entirely because of her disillusionment over Neulander, Mazo listened. She told him that Neulander had presided over the burial of her grandparents and her own bat mitzvah; he had taught her, counseled her, consoled her: *he* had been Judaism. Now nothing seemed holy, just hollow, from the Torah to the Passover seder. Neulander had poisoned all that he had blessed. After she poured her heart out to him, Mazo praised her honesty and courage, then helped her to find meaning in the bitterness of her experience. "Judaism," he told her, "is a way of life. Judaism is the Torah, the holidays . . . the lessons and values your family, your heritage, and your rabbis have tried to teach you. We follow ideals, philosophies, and values, not individuals. No one *person* is Judaism."

The young woman stayed in the faith.

With the High Holidays of Rosh Hashanah and Yom Kippur—the holiest time of the Jewish year—approaching, Mazo wanted to deliver a sermon that spoke directly to the ongoing crisis rippling through the congregation. The ten-day period of reflection and atonement culminating in the Yom Kippur fast began with the blowing of the shofar calling everyone to God. They would pray, according to the liturgy, for "the power to transform the future."

"Everyone would be coming into that sanctuary with a lot of difficulty and a lot that was unsaid," Mazo later said. "I needed to address people's pain . . . I couldn't make believe nothing had happened." He decided that his sermon would center on the power and resilience of Judaism and its ability not only to survive but to transcend the failings of any individual Jew, no matter how severe the transgression—including adultery, and possible murder, by a prominent rabbi.

First, however, Mazo felt he should give fair warning to the implicit subject of the sermon, a man he expected would be there to hear it. Two weeks before Rosh Hashanah, Mazo called Neulander. "Fred," he explained, "I *have* to speak about these things. There's no way I can go into these holidays and *not* acknowledge what people are feeling."

"I don't agree with you," Neulander said, "and I am disappointed. But I do understand."

On September 25, the first day of Rosh Hashanah, Neulander attended services at M'kor Shalom with his children Matthew and Rebecca. (Benjamin, his youngest, was at school in Michigan.) They sat fairly close to the pulpit. Midway through the service, after the Torah reading and the return of the scrolls to the ark, Mazo began the sermon. Facing about two thousand people—an unusually large crowd at any other time in the Jewish year but routine for the High Holidays—he reminded his audience that the essence of Judaism was its belief in God and in Torah. "Sadly," he said, "I have heard time and again this year that Torah has lost its value . . . People look around their world and see that the words of Torah, the values of Torah, are not being lived out . . . They see their heroes fall . . . They draw the conclusion that if the messengers of Torah are no longer valid, then the message must no longer be valid . . . We need to remind ourselves that Torah is timeless. Just because the messengers of Torah are imperfect and perhaps disappointing does not mean that the message is bad . . ."

He didn't have to mention Neulander by name, of course everyone knew what the subtext was. People were almost holding their breath, wondering if Mazo, who was only thirty-one and had been at M'kor Shalom for just five years, could pull this off. In style, he was quite unlike the departed senior rabbi. While Neulander was impatient, imperious, and easily angered, Mazo was soft-spoken and almost unassuming. Many congregants thought that the younger man's gentle compassion and earnestness more than compensated for his relative lack of seasoning at the pulpit.

Mazo knew he risked infuriating half the congregation or causing Neulander to walk out midsermon, or provoking Matthew and Rebecca to tears. But he was convinced that the risk was worth it. He had to break into the anxiety and anger and sorrow that the congregation had been experiencing en masse since the previous autumn. The High Holidays were about renewal as well as atonement, and there could be no renewal for the members of M'kor Shalom without confronting reality and moving beyond it in a communal process of cleansing and healing.

Continuing on, Mazo assured his audience that they had already begun to mend their souls. "There is a will in us to go back to our roots and draw strength from God," he declared. "There is a will to reconnect with what has given our people stability over the years: . . . the wisdom of Torah. And there is a will to continue . . . ensuring our Jewish future by allowing . . . our children to connect with our Jewish past . . . We will continue to thrive . . . May we draw strength from one another."

Throughout the sermon, Mazo was deeply aware of the Neulanders, seated silently about twelve rows to his right. He didn't dare glance their way, in case their expressions or their body language distracted him from his mission or made him doubt its wisdom.

Mazo needn't have worried, at least not about anyone whose last name was other than Neulander. In the opinion of people who were there, Mazo would have earned a standing ovation—if such a thing could occur in a synagogue. "Gary gave us the outlet we needed," said one congregant. Like theirs, Mazo's faith—in Neulander, if not in God—had been sorely tested during the past year.

He, too, had suffered from the actions of M'kor Shalom's former leader, the rabbi sitting in the midst of people who were looking at him during the Rosh Hashanah service and thinking, "*This* is the man who taught our children the Ten Commandments?" But it fell to Gary Mazo, young as he was, to get up there and lead the others into the New Year—and a new year.

Fred Neulander may have come to temple thinking he was ready to repent, but first he had to examine why he had ignored Mazo's advice to tell his children that their father would be rebuked from the pulpit that day. In light of Neulander's latest misdeed, he could only consider these words from Jeremiah that were often read on Rosh Hashanah as a warning, if not a threat, from God:

> *I the Lord probe the heart,*
> *Search the mind—*
> *To repay every man according to his ways,*
> *With the proper fruit of his deeds.*
> *. . . All who forsake You shall be put to shame,*
> *. . . For they have forsaken the Lord . . .*

PART FIVE

CONSPIRING AGAINST GOD

16

"I'm Going to Nail That Bastard"

Not only was Neulander chastised by Mazo from the *bima,* he had also been officially suspended by the Central Conference of American Rabbis—one of the first rabbis to be affected by CCAR's new code about sexual misconduct. The code was a landmark: the first in any Jewish denomination that regulated rabbis' sexual behavior. For years, Arthur Gross Schaefer, a Los Angeles rabbi, had lobbied for such guidelines, arguing that sexual exploitation by a rabbi was more damaging than similar conduct by a doctor or therapist. "Not only is a congregant being abused by a powerful figure," Schaefer said, "but the tradition is abusing them and God is abusing them. Sadly, our community's reactions up to this point have often been based on keeping things quiet in an attempt to do 'damage control.' " He attributed the silence to a fear of lawsuits, bad publicity, and possible "outrage" against congregants "who dare to break ranks by speaking out . . . No one wants to hear that a beloved clergy person has acted inappropriately. The victim's character is put on trial."

The guidelines developed by the CCAR stated that rabbis who took sexual advantage of congregants were committing a sin against other people, as well as against God, even if the relationship appeared to be consensual. When responding to allegations of such behavior, the CCAR could determine that the charges were unfounded and dismiss them, or suspend a rabbi for two years from officiating in any Reform temple in the country, during which time he had to receive counseling from another rabbi and a psychologist. Their joint recommendation would determine if he could again lead a congregation, or it could expel him from the Reform movement.

The new guidelines were intended for rabbis with a pulpit. By the time Neulander was suspended, he had already resigned from M'kor Shalom. Suspension would just delay his efforts to find a position with another synagogue. Of course, if he encountered serious legal problems related to Carol's murder, suspension would be far too mild, and he would be among the few rabbis ever expelled by the CCAR.

In the late spring of 1996, there was widespread speculation in Camden County that Fred Neulander had just gotten the biggest break of his life. Lee Solomon, a Republican—and a Jew—had just succeeded Ed Borden, a Catholic, as county prosecutor. The scuttlebutt was that a Jew would not prosecute a rabbi. But Solomon had more *chutzpah* than many people gave him credit for: as far as Fred Neulander was concerned, he told his staff, it would be business as usual. When Neulander learned about this, he was particularly irked since he'd endorsed Solomon eight years before when he'd campaigned for freeholder, a position akin to county commissioner.

Assured of the backing of the new prosecutor, Marty Devlin, the lead detective on the Neulander case, started working a new angle when he learned that Peppy Levin—Neulander's racquetball buddy—had donated a Torah to M'kor Shalom in the memory of his late wife, Reta. The detective assumed that Levin had purchased the Torah himself; and since there'd been a rash of stolen Torahs around the country just a few years before, maybe Levin had donated a hot scroll. That might be in character, given his past criminal history. If Devlin could prove that, he could use his new leverage to convince Levin to reveal whatever he knew about Carol's murder.

In the fall of 1996, Devlin asked Gary Mazo to arrange for a Torah expert to examine the scrolls Peppy donated. On a quiet evening when the temple was almost empty, Mazo and his wife, M'kor Shalom's president and cantor, two detectives, and the consultant unrolled the scrolls on the altar in M'kor Shalom's sanctuary. The scribe was dismayed—the Torah was a patchwork, sewn together from pieces of other Torahs. It didn't satisfy the exacting standards for a Torah, and at the most it was worth maybe three thousand dollars. Mazo was almost in tears: the scroll, used just a few days before for a bar mitzvah, was tainted. Its words were holy, as they were with every Torah; but whoever had cobbled together this particular scroll had corrupted and defiled them.

Marty Devlin, on the other hand, who was Catholic, had never seen a Torah. As he looked at the scroll, he felt its holiness. It dated back to Sinai and Moses and even beyond that to a place where there was no time, if the mystics could be believed. Devlin went outside and breathed in the cool fall air. "I *know* we're going to solve this," he said to himself. "I can't explain it. But I *know* I'm gonna nail that bastard who killed Carol."

It was the pivotal moment for Devlin. He'd been working on the Neulander case for almost a year. He'd be on it another six years. But that moment on the autumn night after spending a few hours with the holiest writings of a religion he knew little about spurred him on, convincing him that, in this case, he had God on his side.

After confronting Levin, Devlin would learn that it was actually Neulander who purchased the scrolls. In 1992, Levin had told the rabbi that he wanted to make some kind of donation to the temple in honor of his wife.

"How much do you want to spend?" Neulander asked.

"Fifteen thousand, twenty thousand, twenty-five thousand. It doesn't make any difference."

"Well, how about donating a Torah?"

Levin gave Neulander sixteen thousand dollars. A few weeks later, the rabbi returned from New York with two scrolls—a Torah and the entire Book of Jeremiah, which is mostly about wickedness and hypocrisy. Levin had asked for one scroll; he was getting two. He was impressed.

But now, as it turned out, the Torah that Neulander purchased for Levin was virtually worthless, both financially and spiritually, and Devlin had to figure out what Neulander did with the balance of the money he'd received from Levin, and how that figured into Carol's death.

17

"Detective Perfect"

Before he joined Camden County's prosecutor's office in 1994, Marty Devlin had been a cop in Philadelphia for twenty-eight years. Working his way up through the ranks until he made detective, Devlin loved protecting the city in which he'd been born and raised. His favorite time of the day in the city was around three in the morning, right after it rained and the streets gleamed with the reflections of the neon and fluorescent lights. "Everything looks so clear and peaceful," he liked to muse, "yet there's a danger lurking out there that's exciting."

Before joining the Philadelphia Police Force, Devlin attended parochial schools, studied criminal justice at Temple University and, at age twenty-two, married a nice Catholic girl. He'd known her since he was sixteen. Together they had three kids, and when he wasn't teaching one of them how to ride a bike or out catching crooks, he was earning a black belt in karate. Even in Philadelphia's police department, with almost seventy-two hundred people on its payroll, Devlin stood out. He was a natty dresser. When he walked a beat, he wore his blues with panache: a bit of a tilt to his hat, an extra hitch to his belt so that his pants fit snugly, a new shine on his shoes. When he was promoted to detective and didn't need to wear a uniform any longer, his boss, Sergeant Larry Nodiff, had to get after him to wear a gun when going out on a case.

"Marty, do you have your goddamn gun?" Nodiff asked.

"OK, OK, Larry, I'll go back and get it," Devlin would say. Then he'd tug on his suit jacket to smooth out the wrinkles and turn toward Nodiff. "Damn it, Larry, there's a bulge when I put on a shoulder holster. It ruins the suit. And anyway," he'd add, holding up his hands, which had won him more karate matches in Pennsylvania and New Jersey than he could count, "what do I need a gun for? I have *these.*"

After all this teasing and grooming, Devlin always put his gun on. He had to: he was a cop.

Unlike some of the other detectives who were just killing time until they could retire with a good pension, Devlin refused to be chained to his desk. He hadn't become a cop to fill out forms. Like other dedicated detectives, Devlin rarely put in an eight-hour day. As one veteran detective said, "The idea of a 'shift' is crap. No one works a forty-hour week. A good detective works sixty, seventy, eighty hours a week. If you're not doin' that, you're not doin' your job." So Devlin worked as long as necessary when cracking a case, sometimes thirty hours straight, then went home to change his clothes to testify in court against someone he'd arrested the previous night.

Devlin moved fast. He took risks. He rarely screwed up. He relished knowing he had a really bad guy on his hands who'd made a really stupid mistake, which is why he often said, "There is *no* perfect murder. A lot of guys think they've committed the perfect murder. But there's always the little old lady next door who's looking out her window, right through the curtains and the carnations on her windowsill. She sees what you never wanted her to see, and there goes the 'perfect murder.' "

Devlin was teamed up with Paul Worrell. It was a good match: two Irish guys, both born in Philly, both about the same age. They'd first met years before when they were just beginning their careers in law enforcement. There'd been a break-in at a parochial school, Saint Carthage's, right across from Fairmount Park, six acres of greenery that sliced through the middle of the city. Worrell arrived on the scene first and started looking around to see if the culprit was still in the building. The school was silent as a morgue. Worrell cased the first floor and was halfway done investigating the second floor when a voice shouted from below, "I'm lettin' a dog loose. I'm lettin' a dog loose." Worrell heard a growling racing across the entire first floor of the school, then the sound was leaping up the stairs, and Worrell ran like hell, trying to find a place to hide. The only door that wasn't locked was a janitor's closet. As he jammed himself in, mops and brooms and Ajax tumbled down on him. He slammed the door shut. In a few seconds, a dog was scratching and yelping and pushing his weight against the door, and Worrell, twenty-four years old and almost as scared as when he'd been in an ambush in Vietnam, started yelling, "Let me out! Let me out! I'm a cop! I'm a cop!"

The guy on the other side was yelling, too, and the dog was howling, and Worrell continued shouting from inside the closet, and no one was making any sense anymore—just two guys screaming at each other in the middle of the night on the second floor of a Catholic school in northwestern Philly, and a goddamn mutt. The man in the hall finally dragged the dog away, fixed his gun on the door, and told whoever was in there to come out. When the fellow cornered in the closet staggered out, Canine Patrolman Martin Devlin, pride of the 93rd Precinct, came face-to-face with Worrell.

Little did he know that this guy, who'd almost peed in his pants inside the janitor's closet at Saint Carthage's, would become his partner in another eighteen years.

By 1990, Philadelphia's homicide rate, 525 a year, was one of the worst in the country; and Marty Devlin's conviction rate, the percentage of his arrests that resulted in a conviction, was one of the best on the force—95 percent. His excellent record could be explained in part by the fact that he rarely dropped a case until he was forced to by his superiors, and that he was such a clever interrogator that the thugs he questioned sometimes thought he was their best friend. One or two even thanked him for giving them an opportunity to unburden their souls, momentarily forgetting that the honesty that cleared their conscience was also the reason they were now going to prison.

Devlin almost brushed off Camden County when it tried to recruit him in 1994. He couldn't imagine working anyplace other than Philadelphia. But after he discussed the offer with friends, he realized that working in the county might be a stimulating new challenge. And, anyway, as Devlin later said, "cops are one big family. I'd be joining brothers I didn't know I had." Camden's plague of coke and crack and crooked politicians was about the worst in the country, and he assumed he'd rarely get beyond the city limits. But he started his new job about a month after Carol Neulander was killed, and a few days later he was working the case, out there in the affluent suburbs where he'd rarely expected to go.

By then, the rabbi was the chief suspect. Some of Devlin's best friends in Philadelphia, detectives who knew how good he was, were betting on Neulander—the guy was smart, clever, and his allies included Cherry Hill's power elite. Worse, he had God on his side: he was a rabbi. When Devlin told Larry Nodiff, his old boss from homicide in Philadelphia, that he was working on the Neulander case, Nodiff said, "Marty, you know I've *always* put my money on you. But you're up against a rabbi this time, and I'm putting my money on him."

"*What?*" shouted Devlin. "Let me get this straight. You're my friend? How long have we known each other? You're going with the rabbi? What kind of a friend are you?"

Nodiff smiled. "The bet is dinner at your favorite restaurant in South Philly—Varallo's. Marty, you're not gonna get an indictment. Neulander is good. He's very good."

Devlin got to work—fast. First on his agenda was chipping away at Neulander's confidence. To get the rabbi—and to win the bet—he had to throw Neulander off balance. He interviewed Larry Leaf, the cop assigned to bodyguard Elaine Soncini, and Soncini's sister and the woman who said Neulander was the creepy guy who answered her personal ad in the *Courier Post* and met her at Olga's Diner out on Route 70—a rendezvous she couldn't wait to get away from. He interviewed two of Neulander's kids: Rebecca told him about the "bathroom man" and Matthew told him about his parents arguing two nights before Carol was killed, this time adding that they'd started quarreling two months before the murder.

Devlin spread out the investigation, looking name by name down airline manifestos. He had a hunch that Neulander hired someone from Russia or Israel who'd flown in one Tuesday, the day the "bathroom man" first came to the house, and flown out the next Tuesday, the night of the murder. Devlin didn't find anyone who met his criteria. But there was one person—Leonard Jenoff—whose relationship with Neulander didn't make any sense. Jenoff was exactly the kind of person Neulander didn't ordinarily associate with. Jenoff didn't have a crummy reputation because he did bad stuff. He had a crummy reputation because he'd never gotten his act together: two wives had left him, the second because he drank too much. His weight was out of control. He'd drifted through all kinds of fringe jobs in South Jersey: selling cars, working at a fast-food joint, doing security in some casinos in Atlantic City, handling investigations—usually divorce-type stuff—for private detectives, and eventually starting his own private investigator business. He was friends with more state troopers and cops than most people talked with in their entire lives. Beyond that, he didn't have Neulander's charm or his education, and he didn't move—he *couldn't* move—in the affluent circles of most Cherry Hill Jews: he didn't have the right car, the right clothes, the right bank account. In fact, he barely had a bank account. About all Jenoff and Neulander had in common was that they were both Jewish.

After three decades as a cop, Devlin knew as much about character and personality as any good shrink, and he quickly sized up Jenoff as a goof. But he was perplexed that a smart guy like Neulander was bothering with a sad sack like Jenoff. Why, of all the private detectives in South Jersey, did Neulander hire this hack to help solve the case?

18

The Boy Wonder

Leonard Jenoff was born in Philadelphia in 1945, shortly before his family moved to Atlantic City. The city was a boomtown in those years, and the Jenoffs did reasonably well, first running a rooming house, then leasing a coffee shop. They served tourists who came from all over to see novelty acts like the amazing Diving Horse, which jumped off a platform into the ocean or to take a plunge in the blue-and-white Diving Bell, which fell twenty-five feet into the ocean (and from which they couldn't wait to escape because it was so hot and clammy), or to catch headliners—Benny Goodman, Mae West, Bob Hope, Frank Sinatra, the Supremes—at the Steel Pier.

Len's friends usually had a good laugh going up the steps to his apartment: it was rare that they didn't find him scuffling with his older brother, Gene, each boy calling the other "Fatty"—a name that applied almost equally to both of them.

To make up for his poor academic performance and lack of athleticism, Len devised all kinds of strategies to convince his peers that he was neat and cool. Like the time he told them he was a lifeguard—no mean trick for a twelve-year-old. The other kids almost believed him until they saw him at the beach "on duty," not running into the waves to rescue someone, but running from one lifeguard stand to another, taking orders for soda and candy.

In 1958, the Jenoffs moved to Phoenix, hoping the climate would help Betty's asthma. They stayed two years and Lenny hated every minute, missing his friends back in Atlantic City. When the Jenoffs returned to the city with the famous boardwalk, it was obvious that the town's heyday was fading—tourism was winding down, people were taking cheap flights to Europe and the Caribbean, and TV was saving them the trouble of traveling to places like the Jersey Shore for entertainment. Len's friends noticed that he, too, had changed over the past two years. He'd always had a knack for telling stories, but now he had a new one almost every day. One day, he had a black belt in karate and had to register his hands with the police; the next, he'd been hired by Cal Tjader, a jazz musician whose records Len played his bongos with; the day after that, he was having sex in hotel rooms with the pretty college girl who worked in the drugstore next to his family's coffee shop. One of his constant themes was that he was a spy or secret agent, which is why the kids called him "Junior G-man." And why, when *Dr. No*, the first James Bond film, came out in 1962, some of his friends left the theater begging, "Please, please, please. Don't let Lenny see this. He'll start calling himself 'Agent 008.' "

Jenoff would go to great lengths to make himself believable. In high school, he showed friends a scrapbook with headlines in large type that "proved" what a great football player he was: "JENOFF WINS BIG GAME," "JENOFF THROWS 30 YARDS TO WIN." Also pasted into the scrapbook were photos of football players that Jenoff said were him. It took his friends a while to realize that the scrapbook was a fake: the pictures were of professional football players, but they were taken so far away that their features were indistinguishable. And Len had had the headlines printed at a shop on the boardwalk that specialized in amusing headlines for tourists.

Then there was the time he wanted to bask in the adulation being heaped on swimmers in the annual twenty-two-mile marathon swim off of Atlantic City—the toughest in the world, a constant battle against tides, waves, and jelly fish. He had a sweatshirt printed up with the logo JENOFF/USA, laid it on a chair at a pool where some marathon swimmers were working out, and jumped in. After a brief workout, a small crowd gathered around the dripping-wet Len, asking his name and where he was from and how long he'd been training. Everything went well until someone asked why he'd developed such an unorthodox stroke: marathon swimmers didn't slap the water like he did. Oh, that's easy, shrugged Lenny. It keeps the sharks away. Everyone was satisfied with the answer, and a friend who just happened to wander onto the scene marveled at the brilliance of Len's quick thinking, although no one who was clustered around Jenoff knew that, since the seventeenth century, only a handful of people had been attacked by sharks along the entire New Jersey coast, and the last fatality had been back in 1926. The incident set a pattern for Jenoff: he learned how to blend pieces of reality into his own fantasies, fusing them to make people think he was a combination of the Hardy Boys, John Wayne, and J. Edgar Hoover. Friends told him to stop lying, but he couldn't—without his lies, he was like everyone else. If he had to be Leonard Jenoff, he'd be "Len Jenoff, the Wonder Kid."

Over the years, a lot of people tried to explain why Jenoff was like this. His favorite film stars were Humphrey Bogart, John Wayne, Steve McQueen, Clint Eastwood. All these were tough guys, champions of the good, loners trying to set the world straight. Although they set the tone of what Jenoff aspired to in his fantasy world, that information was insufficient to explain his peculiar psyche. For that, many people pointed to the relationship between Len and his brother. Even Len himself, many years later, would admit that he was "envious of Gene because his life was stable and on course." Gene was brighter and more of a go-getter; he had one very successful marriage, while Len would have three divorces. Amateur psychiatrists in South Jersey liked to theorize that Len tried to catch up with Gene with fantasies and daydreams, not with hard work. "Len was our Walter Mitty," said a cousin. "All the time, he was coming up with new schemes to get rich. Whenever he got some money, he went right through it. He was the opposite of Gene, who knew how to earn and how to save. Too much smoking was about all they had in common." Maybe the ultimate mystery of Leonard Jenoff wasn't *why* he had such a rich fantasy life, but that someone so ordinary could possess such an incredibly fertile imagination. It was as if his lies were his best protection from the dread that he knew lay inside himself. Better, he figured, to blot out this truth than meet it head-on.

At Atlantic City High, a massive building that took up half a block, segregation was determined less by race and ethnicity than by merit and potential. Students from the academic and vocational tracks didn't see much of each other. Their paths crossed in the cafeteria, where every week a new group gathered around Jenoff, mesmerized by his stories. When his old friends saw someone taking Len half seriously, they'd groan, "Oh, God! He's doing it again." Len was lucky his school had three thousand students: when one group got tired of hearing him, he moved along to the next.

In 1964, Jenoff entered Monmouth College in central Jersey. He flunked out after three and a half semesters, a dismal performance that affirmed the conventional wisdom that vocational-track students at Atlantic City High should not proceed to college.

Monmouth had changed nothing about Len, including his lying. In the late 1960s, a high school friend flagged him down at a traffic light in Atlantic City. Len pulled over, and as they were catching each other up about their lives, he bragged about his latest caper: doing undercover work for the police in Baltimore, where his parents had moved. "Look," he said, waving around a handset from a telephone, "the cops gave this to me." His friend took a good look at it.

"Len," Jenoff's friend said, "that's a Princess phone. You can't use that in a car."

"Oh, yeah," shrugged Jenoff, not missing a beat. "I know. But it *really* impresses the girls."

Despite all his lying, many who knew Len continued to feel kindly toward him. "Len was sort of a gentle, overweight giant," a neighbor remembered. "He'd do just about anything to help you. He was also very needy and even then saw himself as a failure, maybe as someone who always would be a failure." And a relative mused years later, "Len's a big fat teddy bear stuck in his own fantasy world." But there was also something disturbing about the way Len constructed his life. "Who can figure out how a mind like Len's works?" a friend asked in 2001, when Len was in deep trouble. "The possibilities are endless."

Clinically, Jenoff's lies weren't delusions. Unlike people suffering from delusions who might claim a dead relative had just visited them or that they were Napoleon, Jenoff always knew when he was lying. He was part of a long parade of people who seemed to thrive on constructing elaborate deceits, like Princess Caraboo in England in 1817, an exotic woman who appeared out of nowhere speaking an unintelligible language. Linguists believed she was from the East Indies, royalty had tea with her, and artists painted her portrait until a woman recognized her from a picture in the paper as a cobbler's daughter. These kinds of liars, who might seem dense when dealing with anything irrelevant to their deceits, are quick and clever when operating *within* the deception. In this one corner of their lives, they shape the world the way they want it to be, mostly because they are not prepared for the world in which everyone else lives. That's how it worked with Jenoff: his lies were so prodigious that when people caught on to them, often they shook their heads, not in admiration but at his extraordinary and tireless audacity.

PART SIX

LIES AND EXPIATION

19

"A Lousy Day"

When a reporter called him on September 10, 1998, Matthew Neulander gave him five words for his paper. They were a masterpiece of understatement: "It's been a lousy day."

A few hours earlier, Matthew's father had been charged with arranging Carol's murder and arrested. Neulander's accomplice was a mystery. The police had no murder weapon, no fingerprints, no witnesses, no money trail going from Neulander to a hit man. Just the idea that he'd hired someone to pose as a courier—the famous "bathroom man"—and kill Carol.

In the four years since the murder, the cops had been sifting through theories and tips and leads and always came back to the rabbi: the only person with a *plausible* motive to kill his wife. With Carol dead, he could marry Elaine Soncini—his "soul mate"—and enjoy the considerable inheritance she'd received from her husband. Moreover, his congregants' sympathy after Carol's horrible death would insulate him from criticism about his religious leadership, and his position at the temple would be more secure than ever.

But "plausible" wasn't airtight, and much of the case against Neulander rested on circumstantial evidence—arguing with Carol about divorce just two days before her murder; Elaine Soncini telling the rabbi she was leaving him if he didn't ditch Carol by the end of 1994; Peppy Levin saying Neulander asked him to have Carol killed; and Neulander making a point of being at M'kor Shalom the nights the "bathroom man" visited his house. All this was "plausible," but juries rarely convicted on the basis of plausibility.

Nevertheless, Marty Devlin pulled Neulander over around nine-fifteen in the morning. They were only three blocks from the rabbi's house. Neulander's short arms and thick body prevented Devlin from cuffing him behind his back, which he normally did when making an arrest. So he cuffed the rabbi in front and threw him in the back of his car. "What's this all about?" Neulander asked, without his usual bravado. "What's this all about?" Devlin retorted. "This is about Carol Neulander. And you're under arrest." The drama chafed Neulander's lawyers. "Letting us surrender wouldn't be good press," they complained.

Hours later, Neulander was standing before a judge. Gone were the blue slacks and striped shirt in which he'd left his house. He was now wearing an orange jumpsuit and high-top sneakers—standard issue for prisoners in Camden County Jail. His hands were cuffed in front of him, attached to a heavy chain around his waist. On Neulander's right were his two lawyers; a bit farther to his left was Lee Solomon, the thin-as-a-rail prosecutor. Solomon argued that the evidence against Neulander was "overwhelming," to which one of Neulander's lawyers countered that the evidence was merely "a thin tissue of supposition, opinions, and theories out of *True Detectives.*" The judge ruled that despite the case being circumstantial and lacking eyewitnesses, it was "not weak."

So the charges stayed, and Neulander, out on four hundred thousand dollars' bail, returned to 204 Highgate Lane. Since Carol's death, the house had lost its tidiness. Overgrown rhododendrons, some as tall as fifteen feet, hid the first-floor windows from the street. On the second floor, curtains and blinds were drawn so that reporters couldn't see in. The house was Fred's refuge from a world that was more and more convinced he'd broken a bedrock rule from the Talmud: "He who saves a single life saves the whole world. And he who takes a single life takes the life of the whole world."

Some people were already talking about "closure," but Neulander's arrest, said one of Carol's brothers, wasn't "bringing relief. I can't say that I'm surprised Fred was arrested. His name has been connected with the crime for four years . . . If he's guilty, we certainly hope that justice is swift."

However quickly justice came, the pain suffered by Carol's family could not be contained by courtrooms and magistrates. Life wasn't that orderly. Convicting Neulander would not satisfy the emptiness felt by his children or his in-laws or his former congregants. Suffering does not follow a neat timetable: there is no term limit on grief. It cannot be placed on a shelf or packed away in a drawer or sent out into the vestibule, where people can visit it at their convenience. Over time, it might lessen, but it will not be forgotten. People might shift from living within their sadness to living with it, but that would not necessarily brighten the shadow that descended on Cherry Hill in November 1994.

William Butler Yeats was right. Actors in a tragedy "do not break up their lines to weep." But this was no play, and by now, four years after Carol's murder, the pain had seeped into so many corners of so many lives that it was hard to escape. An eventual "resolution" in court might assure cops and prosecutors that they'd done their job, and done it well, but it would not end the sorrow in the deep recesses of the soul where the true pain from Carol's death resided.

———————

Matthew Neulander was torn about his father's innocence or guilt. What he was hearing from the rabbi and prosecutors was equally strong, he said a week after the arrest, and left him "questioning and doubting" his father, yet "not condemning him. The man has lost everything," Matthew said. "He's a shell of what he used to be. It sounds funny now, but he was my model of how to act. Nothing in the world would make me happier than to find out someone else did this. But if one word describes me, I'm a realist. I have to look at all the possibilities."

Neulander was meeting with lawyers, fending off reporters, trying to be a father to his kids, who'd already lost their mother and now, in a very different way, faced the possibility of losing their father. A few rabbis, mostly old friends, were counseling him. He tried to be cordial with his neighbors, never once mentioning his arrest. But his effort to avoid awkwardness upset them. They expected him to proclaim his innocence to everyone. He struck up a friendship (of sorts) with Barbara Boyer, a *Philadelphia Inquirer* reporter, who had several meals at his house. Since the murder, he told her, he'd had to "reinvent" himself. He was officiating at a few weddings and funerals, scouting out sites for a billboard company, and reworking a manuscript he'd written about the life of a rabbi (but not a *disgraced* rabbi). "It's either that or suicide or staying under the covers all day," he said. What would happen, Boyer asked, if he were convicted? "I can't answer that," he muttered. After an awkward silence, he added, "I won't answer that."

Run-ins with old friends were among Neulander's more awkward moments. As a close friend was walking his dog past Neulander's house a few weeks after his wife succumbed to a lengthy illness, Neulander came out, wrapped an arm around his pal, and

commiserated, "This is awful. I know what it's like to lose a wife."
His friend winced. With as much calm as he could muster, he said,
"This is different, Fred. I took care of a sick wife for many years.
You murdered yours."

Ignoring the comment, Neulander immediately asked how his
friend's son was doing. "The funny thing," the friend said a few
years later, "was that you could just never insult Fred Neulander."

20

"No Hit Man Goes to the House Twice"

Neulander was in exile in his own land. A handful of people still believed he was innocent, but they were getting fewer every day. Most people, especially former congregants, were furious. "This man was God's voice," said a member of M'kor Shalom. "How could he deceive us for all those years when he was disobeying God's law? How could he let down so many people who looked to him for guidance? How can we believe *anything* he said?"

Even while Neulander's ex-followers were struggling to come to terms with his deceit, some of them were among the last people in South Jersey to conclude that he was guilty. A year before, for example, Joel Rowe, a congregant who was close to Neulander, balked a few days before going to the rabbi's house for their annual breaking of the fast at the end of Yom Kippur. "I can't do this," he told his wife. "I can't sit there with that elephant in the room and pretend everything is normal." Rowe called Neulander and explained why he would not attend the meal. "You've been brainwashed by all those newspaper articles," the rabbi said. "Let me come over so we can talk about this." In about half an hour, Neulander was knocking on his friend's house. The two men sat down in the living room, and Rowe, who'd considered Neulander one of his best friends for two decades, laid out his reasons for concluding that he'd had Carol killed: the rabbi had inappropriately asked Rowe to give him funds that Rowe intended be used as a reward for information about Carol's killer; he never behaved like a grieving widower during *shiva;* he'd asked Rowe, a physician, to provide him with a letter explaining that medication he was taking for a heart problem would have caused him to fail the lie detector test he took in December 1994; and he had a motive. "You had everything to gain from Carol's death," he told Neulander. "Everyone would pity you; you'd be almost heroic. You'd be free of Carol. You could retain your elevated status in the community, and you would also retain your children's loyalty, which might not have happened if you'd divorced Carol."

Neulander's retort was brief. If he'd seemed unmoved during *shiva,* it was only because he was "a professional." He'd been trained to control his emotions. He wasn't immune to emotions; he just wasn't accustomed to showing them. As for a "motive," that was laughable: he'd loved Carol and had never intended to part from her in any way.

This exchange was completely surreal: two best friends discussing in a neat, comfortable, middle-class living room whether one of them committed murder. Their tone was friendly, calm; each man was in full possession of himself. It was as if they were talking about a book they'd recently read.

After listening to Neulander, Rowe said, "Fred, no matter what you say, I can't help but like you. You're charming and beguiling. But I think you're a psychopath and a murderer." Neulander stood up to leave, walked a few steps away, then turned toward Rowe. "Well," he said, with a half-smile, "nobody's perfect."

Like Rowe, half of South Jersey was putting together its own case about Neulander's guilt. The cops, for their part, thought the rabbi's relationship with Leonard Jenoff was particularly suspicious. Perhaps unlocking the mystery of why the rabbi placed such confidence in a second-rate private eye would yield the answers they were seeking. Neighbors often spotted Jenoff in the rabbi's backyard, the two of them smoking too many cigarettes and talking, it seemed, fairly secretively. But Jenoff was none too private about his relationship to Neulander, proudly announcing to anyone who would listen that he was "the rabbi's detective." He upheld Neulander's innocence and ridiculed the cops' idea that a hit man had killed Carol: "No hit man goes to the house twice. This is not a professional hit." The murder, he insisted, was a bungled robbery, done by "somebody who knew Carol went home at night with large sums of money. If the rabbi were going to have her killed, he would not have done it in his house, where he and his children were going to live and eat. You don't have it done in the sanctuary of your own home. A wife is a wife, but children are your blood. He loves his children."

Jenoff was also criticizing the police for having done a very sloppy investigation of the murder. Soon after Carol was killed, one of Neulander's children found a kitchen knife that had been missing for weeks. It was under a couch cushion in the living room, the same room where Carol was killed. If the cops had missed that, Jenoff asked, what else did they miss?

Devlin didn't like anyone saying the police were screwing up, especially someone like Jenoff, who was as entitled to call himself a private eye as a five-year-old with a Dick Tracy fingerprint kit. But that was one of the reasons Jenoff was pleased to be working the case. It let him appear to be the extraordinary detective he'd always wanted to be, the equal, perhaps, of professionals like Mr. Marty Devlin.

In reality, Jenoff was more of a drifter than a private eye. After dropping out of college, he worked as a salesman for a couple of companies and married a woman who lived in his apartment building. ("Irene was beautiful," said a cousin. "She was his prize. Len was proud as a peacock.") Len was devastated when she left him five months later. His parents asked him to move in with them in Baltimore. He was twenty-five years old.

Len's father, worried that his son needed a regular paycheck, made him "vice president" of his data processing company. Jenoff heartily embraced his new title; bolstered by the confidence it inspired in him, he was soon dating a new girl, who shortly became his wife. Phyllis Schwartz was a nice Jewish girl who "liked people who were adventurous," according to a relative. "*That's* how Len was presenting himself. It took us a while to figure out that he wasn't who he said he was."

Len was polite toward Phyllis's parents. And respectful. And kind. He wanted to make them happy. But they were Orthodox and kept kosher and observed every Jewish holiday, while Jenoff observed virtually nothing and could barely speak a word of Hebrew and never even had a bar mitzvah. What kind of a Jew had their daughter married, Phyllis's parents wondered? And besides that, what kind of ambition did he have? Phyllis's father, Hyman, had steadily worked at a massive Social Security complex near Baltimore for decades, yet his new son-in-law could barely hold a job. As a relative put it, "He cared about Phyllis. That was obvious. But he didn't care about anything else. That was obvious, too."

Yet, Jenoff believed he had finally landed his dream job when, unbeknownst to Phyllis (and just about everyone else), he started doing some undercover work for the Baltimore police department's intelligence unit—the Inspectional Services Division. The ISD reported only to the police commissioner, who forwarded dossiers to the mayor, the FBI, Army Intelligence, and the state attorney general's office. Some of its operatives worked directly with the CIA and the FBI and had learned at Fort Holabird, an Army base near Baltimore, how to tap phones and break into residences. Its twenty cops were supplemented with snitches that made easy money squealing on their friends or guys like Jenoff who always wanted to be spies. By the time the division shut down in 1975 because of adverse publicity in the press, it had spied on 60 organizations and 122 people—reporters, politicians, antiwar protesters, feminists, the NAACP, even striking cops.

Jenoff had convinced the police that the FBI had trained him to do intelligence work, and they gave him his first assignment. Jenoff was to befriend a defense lawyer, William Carrier, who was representing a local drug czar, so that the cops would know the case he planned to present in court. Jenoff also spied on the reelection campaign of black congressman Parren Mitchell, even while promising to work "morning, noon, night, and weekends" to send him back to Washington.

Some cops in the ISD couldn't figure out why their boss hired Jenoff. "He was always trying to make you think he was hot stuff," one cop said. "The funny thing about Len was that it wasn't in his nature to be quiet about anything. He was bragging so much that he was in the ISD that someone told the head of the division to keep an eye on him because he was mouthing off."

It wasn't surprising that when the *Baltimore News American* ran front-page stories exposing the ISD in late 1974, Leonard Jenoff's name quickly became part of the controversy. The stories jogged the memory of one of Mitchell's aides, who now recalled that he'd been in the Army Reserves with Jenoff, where the guy "almost advertised that he was into detective-type work and that he had assignments to follow people, that sort of thing . . . Jenoff was often absent—maybe for half a day, sometimes a whole day. Once he was absent from summer camp for half a week. He was never pressured about showing up. He didn't even wear a uniform all the time, but he did wear a little jacket. It was rumored he had a shoulder piece under it."

The spying didn't surprise Parren Mitchell, who fumed that "the government had been snooping on blacks for years. This is part of what many of us in the black community have suspected for a long time: information is being kept on certain people. There's no other way for me to think."

The governor and mayor maintained that the ISD was perfectly legal, and it took several years for dust from the scandal to settle. The city's mayor even shrugged that police *should* keep an eye on him. "The public," he said with a straight face, "should know if I've done anything illegal."

The last two months of 1974 were agonizing for Jenoff. His father succumbed in November to a heart attack—his fourth. He was only fifty-five years old. Then a barrage of headlines ended his spying for the city police. And finally, Jenoff was fired from the data processing company by his father's partner, who was disturbed by all the negative publicity. The sooner he broke his connections with Jenoff, the better.

Jenoff was infuriated. Within a few weeks, he'd lost his father, his job, and his undercover work with the police; the articles in the *New American* were so disturbing to Jenoff's wife that she had two miscarriages. He sued the paper, claiming he hadn't broken into Carrier's law offices as the paper claimed. Jenoff became obsessed with the lawsuit; he saw it as a way to salvage his name and reputation, although neither had been pristine before all this started. In 1981, he won the suit and got the biggest windfall of his life—fifty thousand dollars. Jenoff blew through the money fast, buying a gold Cadillac, some spy toys, and, most significant, a house in Marlton, New Jersey—a town right next to Cherry Hill.

Jenoff never told friends the real reason he was leaving Baltimore. He claimed that the FBI was shipping him out of state because he knew too much about what it was doing in Maryland. This sounded strange until people remembered all the headlines about Len and the ISD. But one cousin couldn't even *pretend* to believe Jenoff's story. "His tales were so bizarre," he said. "I had more important things to do than listen to a lunatic cousin." He wrote off Jenoff and never saw him again.

Jenoff moved into the same development in South Jersey where his successful brother, Gene, lived—Marlton Village, twenty-five acres of pale yellow town houses, pedestrian paths, swimming pools, and playgrounds. Jenoff hoped that being near Gene could repair the distance that three decades of Len's lies and fantasies had created in their relationship. If nothing else, family would be just a few blocks away to help Phyllis out: she and Len now had a baby on their hands, one-year-old Marty.

After a string of odd sales jobs, Len came down with "casino fever": the state had just OK'd gambling in Atlantic City and Jenoff wanted to get in on the ground floor. He had visions of scenes straight out of Hollywood—girls in skimpy costumes surrounding him while guys in sharkskin suits whispered tips in his ear about blackjack or craps, and, at the end of the night, coming home with more cash from his winnings than Phyllis could imagine. The Playboy Club gave him a nifty title—"executive casino host," which really meant he was a security guard—but he had better luck bedding bunnies than convincing management he was meant for better things. He split when they wouldn't promote him, and floated around for a while, working security at other casinos—the Showboat and the Taj Mahal and Resorts International—always just short of broke and praying, like any other gambler in this tourist trap come back from the dead, for the day the tables would turn for him.

There was no fortune for Jenoff in Atlantic City, but he figured there had to be some kind of payoff for watching other people clean up at roulette or slots while he was going home at the end of the week with a measly paycheck. Maybe his casino connections could impress the ladies? Not long after a young woman moved next door to him, Jenoff went up to her as she was leaving for work. "Y'know," he said, "I work in one of the casinos over in Atlantic City. One of the really big ones. I think you'd like it. But I can't tell you which one. They have this policy . . ."

"Big fucking deal, Len," she thought. "Who the fuck *really* cares?"

There was something silly about this slightly tubby guy in his late thirties trying to convince a neighbor he had a secret life. She had no idea that lies were Len's oxygen. Nor would Marty Devlin a couple of years later when he first ran into Len. By then—the mid-1990s—Jenoff was a licensed private investigator, mostly looking into divorces or car accidents. Nothing big. No break-ins, no muggings, no murders. Which is why it made little sense that Neulander trusted Jenoff to solve the mystery of Carol's murder. But the more Devlin learned about Fred Neulander and Leonard Jenoff, the more he realized they both had secret lives: Fred had his women and Jenoff had his lies. Maybe what was keeping them together was knowing more about the other than they should have.

21

A Savior Out of Nowhere

Marty Devlin wasn't the only one keeping an eye on Jenoff. Since Carol's murder, a *Philadelphia Inquirer* reporter named Nancy Phillips had been tracking down every lead she had about the case. Some people called it obsession, but others just called it good investigative reporting. At times, she had to convince some editors that following the case was the best use of her time, but her instincts told her there was more to the story—and more to Jenoff—than what even the police knew, or what they were saying they knew.

Phillips was smart. She'd graduated from New College, a small, tough school in Sarasota, Florida, in three years. One professor was so impressed with her writing that he critiqued her work privately two afternoons a week. "You know," he told her when she was a senior, "you should think about writing for the paper. You'd be great at it." He rang up the editor of the *Sarasota Herald Tribune,* who asked him to have his protégé in his office in ten minutes.

Phillips was wearing what college kids in Florida wear—a gauzy skirt and a top with little ties on the shoulders: not the best attire for a job interview. But her writing mattered more than her fashion, and the paper offered her an internship—an ideal way to spend the summer after graduating. Three months later, the editor asked her what every intern wants to hear: "Well, kid, would you like to stay?"

After two years at the *Tribune,* Phillips believed she'd outgrown the level of the editing being done at the paper: "I thought, arrogantly, 'Well, enough of this little pond.'" Returning home to Bucks County, just north of Philadelphia, she met with a metropolitan editor at the *Inquirer,* who signed her up for the paper's two-year program to train newcomers. Phillips eventually moved into the *Inquirer's* New Jersey bureau, where her brass-knuckle stories, like the one linking a mayor to a drug-related murder, copped some regional prizes for journalism. Phillips was on her way to being a star, and her looks and style didn't hurt: a perky nose, porcelain skin, a tall, slim figure, and miniskirts that revealed almost the full length of her legs. People wanted to sit down with her because she was a good reporter; certain men wanted to sit down with her because she was good-looking.

Phillips began writing about the Neulander case not long after Carol's murder. She didn't fully comprehend what the rabbi meant to congregants until his resignation was announced in late February 1995. "People were still reeling from a very violent death," she said, "and suddenly the rabbi was resigning ... People were crying. He was part of the fabric of their lives, as was Carol."

Around the same time, Phillips met Jenoff. She couldn't figure him out. Though he called himself a detective, he wasn't in the Yellow Pages under "investigators" and he worked out of his bedroom, a strange place from which to be running a business. When she checked him out with cops, lawyers, and other private eyes, their comments about his reliability, she said, were "not complimentary."

The reporter quickly realized that Jenoff's statements were not to be taken at face value. He said he fought in Vietnam; she learned he was a cook in the Army Reserves and never left the United States. The autographed photo in his wallet of Ronald Reagan on horseback was inscribed, "To Len Jenoff, a loyal friend & comrade in arms. Ron Reagan, 7/86." But the handwriting matched Jenoff's, not samples of Reagan's that Phillips obtained. And once, he introduced her to a friend who was allegedly a psychic. With his help, Jenoff bragged, he would solve Carol's murder. The psychic pulled out a sketch he'd drawn when visiting M'kor Shalom to pick up the "vibes." *This* is the guy who killed Carol, Jenoff's friend told Phillips. His drawing showed a man in his late twenties with prominent ears and an aquiline nose, wearing a wide-brimmed cap. If nothing else, the psychic sketched someone to whom most Jews could relate: the "killer" looked like an extra in *Fiddler on the Roof.*

However, some details Jenoff told Phillips did hold up, like the number of times he met with Marty Devlin at the prosecutor's office to discuss the case, or his visit to a friend who was a detective at the Evesham Township Police Department the night of November 1, 1994. Meanwhile, Phillips's suspicions regarding Neulander were growing, thanks to a source who slipped her details about Neulander failing a lie detector test in December 1994, and the cops briefly suspecting that Soncini was involved with the murder. Recognizing that Jenoff could be useful, Phillips began treating him like any other valuable source and taking him out to lunches on her expense account. She wanted to understand him; he wanted to get close to her. She said she was just a reporter, nothing more; he said she was like a sister to him. But ordinary reporters—especially reporters who are pretty and single—usually don't visit sources in the "office" part of their bedrooms. That's where Phillips went on November 1, 1996, the second anniversary of Carol's death and the day Jenoff said he would never reveal the "many secrets" he had about Neulander. Despite his vow, Len couldn't resist mouthing off. Neulander had once asked him if a pharmacist friend could recommend a fatal drug that could not be traced in the human body. If Phillips wanted to hear more about this, Jenoff said, prosecutors had to give him immunity.

Phillips was conflicted: she wanted to write a story that would solve the Neulander murder, but she'd assured Jenoff that all their conversations were confidential. Later, critics would charge that she was more concerned about being a reporter than a good citizen, although these were not necessarily mutually exclusive. Constitutional provisions guarding the press also safeguard the public's right to be well informed. If reporters began cooperating with the police, if they were perceived to be adjuncts of law enforcement officials, their sources would dry up. Journalists develop relationships because people trust them; if that trust erodes, fewer sources would mean that less information flows to the public. But Camden County's prosecutor had little patience with these principles when he finally learned about Phillips's secret conversations with Jenoff. "Why is there any question about what a reporter should do if you have evidence that somebody committed a murder?" Lee Solomon asked. "Journalists have an ethical and moral obligation to come forward. Cloaking themselves in privilege and allowing someone to get away with murder is unconscionable to me. Maybe it is legally permissible, but it's morally unconscionable."

Phillips developed a close relationship with investigators assigned to the Neulander case, and they all realized they were struggling with the same riddle: *Why Jenoff?* For the fight of his life, you'd think Neulander would hire the very best private investigator, not a guy whose clients rarely used him again. But the rabbi had met Jenoff a year before Carol was killed, and maybe there was more to their relationship than met the eye.

Jenoff had sought out Neulander for the same reason many people seek clergy: he needed help. By the early 1990s, Jenoff was living in a halfway house, sobering up after a five-year drinking binge triggered by fatally hitting a young man who was pushing his disabled car the wrong way on a busy highway. The courts exonerated Jenoff of manslaughter, but the accident shattered him. He often visited a neighbor a few days a week, crying, "The poor kid. The poor parents. I didn't mean to do it. I didn't mean to do it." He felt worse when the parents of the man he hit refused to meet with him.

In the months following the accident, Jenoff's wife began coming home for lunch to make sure he was sober; his friends began driving him home from bars because he drank until he was too smashed to get behind the wheel. Phyllis put him on an allowance, which he inevitably blew on booze. For a year or two after the accident, he was still a good father to Marty, often roughhousing with him on a mattress they dragged into the living room. But the drinking got worse, and Marty frequently saw his father puke in the sink, or at dinner he'd know that his father's glass was full of vodka even though Jenoff was claiming he was drinking seltzer.

Jenoff attended a few Alcoholics Anonymous meetings, but he hated them. He told Phyllis it was bullshit and he told Marty that his AA sponsor was gay and was hitting on him. By 1991, the Jenoffs were behind on their mortgage payments. Taking out a second mortgage so that he could pay for Marty's ten-thousand-dollar bar mitzvah hadn't helped. In the spring, Jenoff took his son aside. "Marty," he said quietly, "we lost the house." A few weeks later, Phyllis asked, "How would you like to move to Baltimore and live with Grandma?"

Phyllis's brother drove up from Baltimore with a U-Haul truck, filled it up with furniture and books and records and clothes and everything else from a marriage gone bad. They went to McDonald's for lunch. That's where it hit Marty: he was leaving his father, his home, his friends. Everything. He dropped his tray and started crying right in the middle of McDonald's. He was fourteen years old. It was August 4—the fifth anniversary of his father's car accident.

Jenoff telephoned his wife in Baltimore a few times, saying he was finally determined to stay sober. And he kept telling a neighbor he'd "do anything" to get Phyllis back, yet even as he spoke these words, his breath reeked of alcohol. And every time he drove down to Baltimore to visit "the love of my life"—Marty, his son—the boy went through the house, marking bottles that were stocked in his grandmother's liquor cabinet. There was always less in them after Jenoff left. He did start attending AA meetings again, that much can be said for him. But he was constantly breaking at least two of its twelve steps: "Make a searching and fearless moral inventory of ourselves" and "Admit to God, to ourselves, and to another human being the exact nature of our wrongs." So when Jenoff recited his usual stories about being a CIA veteran and helping Ronald Reagan and Oliver North devise the Iran-Contra scheme, his new friends at AA nicknamed him "Contra Lenny"—and worried about his commitment to the program. Alcoholics who don't recover, warns the Big Book, AA's catechism, are usually "constitutionally incapable of being honest with themselves. There are such unfortunates. They are not at fault; they seem to have been born that way. They are naturally incapable of grasping and developing a manner of living which demands rigorous honesty." Jenoff appeared to be one of those "unfortunates"—he was about as skilled a bullshitter as anyone at the AA chapter in Cherry Hill had ever encountered. It was clear that if he was ever going to break his addiction, he'd need the help of someone else, someone stronger than he was.

Some good did come from attending AA. Richard Hyland, a lawyer whom Jenoff met there, was disturbed by Len talking about becoming a Christian. Jenoff was telling him there was no place in the Jewish world for a drunk; even when he'd asked Jewish Family Services for five hundred dollars to enter a halfway house, they suggested he try Catholic Charities. "Fuck Judaism," Jenoff told Hyland. "I don't need this shit." Hyland thought Jenoff's grounds for leaving his faith were pretty thin. "This was more a resentment than an epiphany," Hyland said later.

Hyland asked a friend to help Len. "I hear you have a lot of issues about being Jewish," the friend said when he telephoned Jenoff. "I want you in my office at nine o'clock on Wednesday."

Two days later, Jenoff was sitting in Fred Neulander's study. His first impression of Neulander was that he was short; his second impression was that he was "cool." "He didn't say he was a rabbi," Jenoff said later. "He introduced himself as Fred Neulander. And he gave me this warm handshake. I started getting chills." The man was everything Jenoff needed: "He was my rabbi, my father, my confidant. Everything wrapped up in one. He came over from behind his desk and sat down next to me on the couch, and this might sound stupid—I'm certainly not gay—but it was like instant love. I was captivated by his charisma. He knew how to push every button."

At a particular low moment in Jenoff's life, this big-deal rabbi—a total stranger—was spending *three hours* making him feel special. If this important man saw possibilities in him, maybe anyone could? Neulander couldn't reunite Jenoff with his wife and son, but he could make him feel wanted and assuage his bitterness about being Jewish. You now belong to this congregation, the rabbi told him. Start coming to Friday night services. See me for counseling. It won't cost you anything. If having a bar mitzvah is important to you, you'll have one. But understand that you're not a "bad" Jew if you don't have one—bar mitzvahs weren't even common until a few centuries ago.

Jenoff left Neulander's office rejuvenated, almost jaunty. This wonderful rabbi had come out of nowhere and Jenoff felt confident he could help him turn his life around. People like Jenoff, down and

out and with no self-respect to draw from, often search for someone who will "give" it to them. At the age of forty-six, Len Jenoff
finally stumbled upon the man who would give him what he
couldn't give himself: a sense of self-worth. That first meeting with
Fred Neulander, he later remembered, "blew my mind. When he
gave me a hug, I felt like I'd known him for twenty years." Two
weeks after his initial session with the rabbi, they met for another
hour and a half, again in Neulander's study. Then he got a note from
Neulander: "I hope to see you often at services. Should you ever
want to see me again, all you have to do is call." Jenoff had tears in
his eyes when he read these words. This man *really* wanted to help
him. Len was counting on that for his salvation. He knew he
couldn't rescue himself.

22

In the Confessional Booth

In the months following that first meeting, Jenoff often saw Neulander at the temple, where they usually walked outside the rear of the synagogue to hide their smoking from kids attending the temple's nursery school. During their meetings, Jenoff lied to the rabbi all the time, telling him the usual stories about being in the CIA. "Blowin' smoke up his ass," Jenoff called it. "Bullshittin' about being a fucking secret agent."

Maybe Jenoff was still telling lies, but he had stopped drinking and started working again: waiting on tables at Denny's, driving a cab, collecting bills for $6.50 an hour—"big time for me," he later noted. Len hoped he and Phyllis could work things out. If she would only spend time with him in South Jersey, maybe come to services with him, she'd see how he'd come up in the world. When Neulander shook Jenoff's hand or hugged him as he was making his rounds of the sanctuary on Friday nights, Jenoff imagined that "all the rich Jews" were looking at him, thinking, "Wow! This guy must be important." How could Phyllis *not* see that he was a new man, a better man?

Reuniting his family was Len's dream. But Marty Jenoff didn't want his parents to get back together. Marty was growing into a tall, thin boy, with none of his father's bulk and much of his mother's sweetness. He was afraid that if his parents got back together, his father would start drinking again.

Now that his father was sober, he was fun to hang out with and Marty enjoyed visiting him in Jersey. They went to movies, ate at restaurants, and threw a football around, and once, his father introduced him to this rabbi who meant so much to him. They ran into Neulander at a shopping center near his temple. Fred was in a good mood: he'd just saved a box turtle that was about to waddle onto a busy highway. It wasn't every day that a rabbi saved a turtle from being crushed by traffic. Neulander thought that was pretty funny. So did Marty and his father.

Life can crumble all around you if you're not careful; for years, Jenoff's life had been almost nothing *but* crumbling. To all appearances, he was now piecing himself together, giving himself a fresh start, rearranging his mental furniture so that there was some semblance of order. There was even a new woman in his life—June McDonald. Slightly shorter than Jenoff, she was blonde and trim— an almost Barbara Eden/*I Dream of Jeannie* look-alike. Mutual friends recommended he get together with her to improve his credit: after recently retiring as a vice president of a local bank, she was advising people with poor credit. She also managed a health food store. With her combination of knowledge about money and vitamins and organic food, she was exactly the sort of person Jenoff needed to restore him to health—physically and financially.

After a few consultations with June at her condo, she asked him to stay for dinner. The two quickly fell in love. He called her

"Honey" and "Sweetie" and "Darling" and it was obvious that he adored her. For her part, June thought Len was an easy guy to get along with, and maybe, she figured, he was a better match than her first husband. Which is why she accepted an engagement ring from him on Christmas Day, 1996.

Eight months later they were married, and Len was happier than he'd been in years. He had a prize of a new wife. His private-eye business was still struggling, but he was getting enough new clients to help June out with payments on her condo that he'd moved into. And as much as he could, he doted on Marty, who was the one really good thing he'd done with his life.

But just four years later, in early 2000, these happy early days of his third marriage seemed light-years away. Jenoff started spending a lot of afternoons alone in the condo—weeping. Nancy Phillips knew why he was crying, but she couldn't tell anyone. Jenoff had confided in her that nearly six years before, when he'd thanked Neulander for all his help, the rabbi had responded, "Maybe one day there will be something you can do for your rabbi." A few weeks later, Neulander asked him to murder a woman who was a threat to Israel.

Jenoff couldn't say no to this guy. He'd fallen in love with Neu-lander, not erotically, of course, but because the rabbi was kind and thoughtful and treated him like he was a mensch. "If I was a woman," Jenoff said, "I would have been sleeping with him. If he asked me to jump off a bridge, I would have said, 'Which one?'" What's more, Neulander promised that if he killed the woman, he'd pay him thirty thousand dollars—cash. That would erase all of Jenoff's debts and maybe, since this was before he'd met June, it would also help him get Phyllis back.

When Jenoff told this to Phillips, he was relieved. "I've held this in for so long," he told her. "You don't know how many times I've come close to telling this to you." Then he begged for mercy.

"Please don't hurt me with this, Nancy. I can't ruin my life. I may have to take this to the grave."

Phillips found herself in a very difficult position. She'd heard a lot of crap from Jenoff, but she was convinced this was the truth. However, the conversation was protected by their deal that everything he told her was confidential. "In this profession," she observed later, "we live and die on our ability to keep every promise we make . . . When we laid down the rules, I obviously didn't know what was going to come out of his mouth. These were gut-wrenching moments."

A few weeks later, Jenoff called Phillips with new details: the killer's initials were PMD. In a later conversation, Jenoff told her they stood for Paul Michael Daniels, one of his roommates at his halfway house in 1994.

Then one morning in February 2000, Jenoff telephoned Phillips. Would she like to have lunch with him and Daniels? Scared, she said she was busy. Around noon, Jenoff showed up at the *Inquirer's* office in Cherry Hill with someone Phillips had never seen before—a guy in his midtwenties who didn't say much and whose eyes were slightly glazed, maybe from medication. Jenoff introduced this man as Paul Michael Daniels and again asked Nancy to join them for lunch. She said she was on deadline. He handed her an envelope and asked her to give it to her rabbi. When he left, she realized the envelope was empty.

Shortly after leaving her office, Jenoff called Nancy. "Don't be mad at me," he said. "I just felt that after all these years of wanting to know who did it, you'd want to meet him. But you were afraid. So I thought you needed a push."

Jenoff gave her more of a scare than a push. She remembered that the "bathroom man" gave Carol Neulander an empty envelope the first Tuesday he came to her house, saying it was for her husband. Phillips was scared that Jenoff was telling her that the killer knew exactly where she was and that if she squealed on him, she was next on Daniels's hit list.

Phillips started losing sleep. So did Jenoff. "This is like a nightmare," he told her. "It's been a nightmare for years. I've been trying to put it out of my mind."

The pressure was building on Jenoff to come clean. A date was finally set for Neulander's trial—June 19. As the middle of June got closer, more articles about the rabbi were in the local papers. To Jenoff, each article was a reproach to help the state present the best case possible. "I absolutely didn't believe the prosecution had a strong case," Jenoff later said. "I was one hundred percent convinced that Neulander would be found not guilty."

The little time remaining for Jenoff to confess was also putting a strain on Phillips. Though she couldn't divulge what she knew because of her off-the-record deal with Jenoff, in April 2000 she visited Lee Solomon, the county prosecutor, nervously asking what he had on Jenoff. Solomon was trying to leave his office early for a Passover seder, but he figured from Phillips's questions that she had something juicy. When she left, he turned to his chief homicide detective, Marty Devlin. "You know, Marty, you might be right. Maybe Jenoff's got more to say than what he's given us."

On the last Friday in April, seven weeks before Neulander's trial would start, Phillips and Jenoff had lunch at the Top Dog Restaurant in Cherry Hill, a cross between a singles bar and a sports club, with live bands at night, dollar drinks on Tuesdays and Thursdays, and bikini contests every few weeks during the summer. Over pizza, Jenoff told Nancy he couldn't keep quiet about the murder anymore. "I think about this every day," he said. "I ask God every night to forgive me. There've been times when I thought of killing myself, times when I prayed for cancer, prayed for a heart attack so

I wouldn't have to go on keeping this inside of me." He'd confess on Monday, he assured her. He just needed the weekend to muster up his courage.

After lunch, Phillips and Jenoff headed toward Philadelphia in his silver Dodge Caravan. He wanted to show her two sites that he said figured in the murder. While passing through Camden, the county seat, Phillips asked if he would rather confess right then. Surprisingly, he asked her to call Lee Solomon on her cell phone and propose they meet for coffee. Solomon's secretary patched the call through to her boss, who was getting a haircut. The prosecutor agreed to meet in half an hour at Weber's Colonial Diner in the town of Audubon, not far from his barber's. He had no idea what Jenoff wanted, but he trusted Phillips. If any reporter in South Jersey "owned" the Neulander story, it was Phillips. She'd been on it since Carol was killed, following up lead after lead, talking with dozens of people, getting close to Carol's siblings. She'd been as diligent and unwavering as any good detective.

Weber's has a long salmon-colored counter in the front with twenty swivel stools and a bank of booths facing the street. More tables are in the rear. Above each booth is a stained-glass lamp, and ivy dangles from hanging planters. There's nothing "colonial" about Weber's. In New Jersey, what's most important about a diner is the simple fact of its existence, not its name, which rarely described its décor and never described its cuisine—fatty and fried and cheap and quick.

Out of the way, it was a good place to meet Jenoff. Weber's had fewer Jewish customers than Ponzio's, the most popular diner in Cherry Hill. It was also less hectic than Ponzio's: even the waitresses moved about with a lethargy ill-designed to elicit extra tips. Here, Solomon and Jenoff could talk quietly and unobtrusively.

Jenoff and Phillips were the first to arrive at the diner. "I haven't been this scared," he told her, "since November 1"—the night

Carol was killed. At around three o'clock, Solomon walked in with Marty Devlin. They'd agreed that Devlin would do most of the talking, since he knew more about the case than Solomon.

For privacy, Solomon asked for a table in the back. The hostess showed them to a booth in the rear left-hand corner. Solomon and Devlin sat on one side; Jenoff and Phillips sat on the other. No one needed the seven-page menu. Solomon and Jenoff both ordered coffee and the $1.35 fruit cup. Fruit in the mid-afternoon was part of Solomon's routine: he needed the sugar for extra energy.

Jenoff was squirming on the red vinyl upholstery, spooning away at his fruit cup, trying to figure out where to begin, trying to stop his leg from shaking, trying to light a Newport Light—the first of many. Realizing they had a nervous wreck on their hands, Solomon tried to focus Jenoff on why they were there: "I'm here to listen to you . . ." Jenoff took a deep breath, paused, and blurted out, "I'm really not a bad person . . ." To prove that, he said he was concerned about how what he would say would affect his wife and son. Solomon and Devlin couldn't answer that. They didn't even know what he was going to tell them. But it was obvious that whatever it was, it was fiercely serious.

Jenoff repeated the story he had told Phillips several months before—the rabbi, the money, the woman who was a threat to Israel, the horror, and then the guilt. There were also some new details, like Neulander telling Jenoff that if he pulled this off, there might be a job for him with the Mossad, Israel's legendary spy agency. In his fertile imagination, Jenoff had imagined running a bookstore as a front for the Israelis or collecting raw intelligence for them. "I'm very good at that," he'd thought. Jenoff also told Solomon and Devlin that Neulander had driven him past the house where he claimed the victim lived, then past a house around the corner that the rabbi said was his. As Jenoff told it, he balked and stalled as the date for the hit got closer. But Neulander goaded him on, once saying, "Sometimes, people have to die for a cause."

Jenoff took a long sip of coffee. He lit another cigarette. He didn't want to continue, but the three people he was with, people he both respected and feared, were waiting for what came next.

Lee Solomon had never heard a confession with a reporter present, but he let Phillips stay. "When you're trying to get at what someone has to say," Solomon reflected later, "and it's remarkably difficult, as it was with Jenoff, you give them whatever support is available. In this case, the support came from a reporter."

The entire situation was so unorthodox—a guy coming forward on his own, six years after the fact, gulping down coffee and puffing his way through half a pack of cigarettes in a family restaurant on a Friday afternoon—that Solomon just kept thinking, "Holy shit! Holy shit!" There was no interrogation, no pressure. In some way, it was too easy: Solomon and Devlin didn't have to sweat this stuff out of Jenoff. Carol Neulander would finally have justice. And Jenoff? What would he have? This guy sitting across from Lee Solomon in Weber's was begging for forgiveness, for relief from the secret he'd been sitting on for six years.

Few cops have read *The Compulsion to Confess* by the psychoanalyst Theodore Reik. And even fewer of them have heard of Reik. But their instincts tell them Reik was right when he said "Confession is the criminal's first step back to society." A confession is usually not an end in itself, but a way to appeal to certain authority figures for absolution, maybe even for affection. A member of Freud's inner circle, Reik framed confession in traditionally Freudian terms: just like a child's confession "unconsciously represents a new wooing for love," a criminal confesses because he wants "to re-enter society by declaring himself worthy of punishment. [He is] the outsider on his painful detour back to the family of man." Confessing was maybe Jenoff's last chance to enter that family, to stop being an outsider.

Jenoff's reputation as a liar didn't bother Solomon. In some ways, Jenoff was like a lot of criminals who minimize their involvement with a crime when they first confess, not willing to admit it to themselves or hoping prosecutors will never find out the real truth. But in time, the whole story (more or less) comes out, almost like there's a compulsion to purge themselves. Experienced prosecutors know the pattern, and as long as key parts of Jenoff's story could be confirmed from other sources, Lee Solomon would stand by it.

If Jenoff's story held up, it meant that Jenoff and Neulander had conned each other, Jenoff with his stories about spying and killing and knowing Ronald Reagan and Oliver North, and Neulander with his stories about a terrorist living on Highgate Lane in Cherry Hill who had to be killed for the sake of Israel and the Jewish people. They kept feeding off of each other's lies, and the symbiosis that developed was as improbable as it was fatal.

Weber's was still fairly empty: it was that in-between time after lunch and before dinner. A family came in for an early supper and sat down a few tables from where Jenoff was confessing. The brother was throwing French fries at his little sister and their parents were trying to keep them under control.

Their waitress was getting antsy. These four customers at the back table were hardly ordering anything. She'd gone over a few times to refill their coffee cups, especially for the fat guy who was doing most of the talking and was drinking coffee like it was going out of style. After a while, the thin guy with suspenders and the crisp white shirt and the rep-striped tie just told her to leave her coffeepot on the table. It didn't seem like they were ever going to leave. About the only one who went anywhere was the fat guy, and he just got up—often—to go to the bathroom. The other three just sat there, glancing at each other once in a while. What the waitress didn't know was that as they drained the coffeepot, three of those people at the back table were witnessing a bizarre confession that connected all the missing pieces of the Neulander case.

Jenoff plunged ahead with his story. On the last Tuesday in October, he went to the house Neulander had pointed out. The rabbi said the woman would be there alone. He waited in the bushes until she pulled up in the driveway, then approached her, not realizing until he tapped on her car window that she was talking on her cell phone. He said he was delivering a letter for her husband and asked to use her bathroom. Once inside the house, he lost his nerve. Exiting the bathroom, he gave the woman an empty envelope and drove away.

The other people at the table stirred: Jenoff was claiming *he* was the "bathroom man" whom Rebecca Neulander had overheard her mother speaking to as the two of them were on the phone on two consecutive Tuesdays in the fall of 1994.

Jenoff lit another cigarette and continued. The day after the bungled murder attempt, he met Neulander in a parking lot behind a Sheraton on Route 70. Neulander was furious. The veins in his neck were bulging and he shoved his face into Jenoff's. He'd already given him about seventy-five hundred dollars for the hit, he bellowed. Jenoff was a coward. If he didn't kill the woman, Neulander would kill *him*.

Jenoff panicked. He couldn't kill anybody. Back at his apartment, he asked Paul Michael Daniels to help him with the hit. Daniels was sitting in an easy chair in the living room when Jenoff came up behind him and showered money down on him that he'd gotten from Neulander: some fives and dozens and dozens of tens and twenties. A confetti of cash like the two of them had never seen. As the money fluttered down, Daniels screamed, "Motherfucker, motherfucker, this fucker is *serious*. That bitch is dead." Jenoff knew he was going to make his friend, the rabbi, very happy.

After their AA meeting the next week at M'kor Shalom, Jenoff and Daniels drove in separate cars to the woman's house. Jenoff knocked on her door, assuming she would recognize him from his previous visit and let him in. She did. Daniels followed Jenoff into the house. When the woman turned her back to them, Daniels slammed her on the head with a lead pipe. Jenoff left the house just before Daniels hit her. He drove to a parking lot at a nearby shopping center, where Daniels caught up with him in his car when he had finished his job. The woman back at the house was dead, he told Jenoff, handing him a duffel bag with the lead pipe, the woman's purse, and a blood-splattered windbreaker.

As Daniels drove home, Jenoff threw the bag in his trunk and filled up his car at a gas station (making sure to get a timed receipt for the purchase). Then he went about his usual Tuesday night routine: picking up a few cups of coffee at a convenience store and taking it to a good friend, a detective in the Evesham Police Department. The first half hour Jenoff was at the police station, he was a nervous wreck; somehow, he calmed down and spent over two hours there. The detective was "the best friend I ever had," Jenoff would recall a few years later. A devout Christian, the officer was "always preaching love, forgiveness, and goodness, and trying to get me to accept Jesus." If the detective had known that night what Jenoff had done, his forgiveness might have been sorely tested.

As Jenoff was telling all this to Lee Solomon and Marty Devlin, he had to sometimes fight to get the words out; at other times, he was almost unable to stop talking. Confession was a relief, but the combination of shame and guilt and fear about what would happen to him next made him stop so many times that the sum of his pauses almost equaled the sum of his actual confession. And yet, he continued:

Around midnight, Jenoff left Ed Brown at the police station and drove to the rear of a Pep Boys auto supply store in Cherry Hill, where he threw Daniels's lead pipe into a metal recycling container. Next he removed several thousand dollars from the murdered woman's purse and dumped that and Daniels's windbreaker into a trash bin near the Philadelphia side of the Benjamin Franklin

Bridge. The next morning, Jenoff said, he turned on the radio. Every station was talking about the murder of Carol Neulander. Jenoff vomited. Until then, he thought he was killing a terrorist, carrying out, in his words, his personal "raid on Entebbe," comparing the murder to Israel's 1976 raid on the airport in Uganda where the PLO was holding 105 airline passengers prisoner. Israeli commandoes saved every passenger and killed the terrorists. Looking around the table at Weber's, Jenoff insisted he "never would have murdered her if I'd known it was Fred's wife. You have to believe me. I loved the man. I was a poor Jew with no one to love me. No rabbi ever spent more than five minutes with me, and Fred would sit with me for hours."

At a condolence call to Neulander's house a few days after the murder, Jenoff said, the rabbi slipped Jenoff more money for the hit. He promised to pay the rest in two years. To launder the money, he hired Jenoff as his private investigator.

Some customers in Weber's recognized Lee Solomon and asked the manager why he was there so long. But no one could identify the heavyset guy sitting across from Solomon who was constantly twisting, turning, fidgeting, squirming, shoving another half-smoked cigarette into the ashtray, drinking pots of coffee, going to the bathroom, coming back from the bathroom. It was as if the only way Jenoff could get his story out was by squeezing it out—scene by scene—with calisthenics worthy of the tenacity of his secret.

Solomon was in no rush to charge Jenoff, not that night. In his career, he'd had more than one person confess to a crime he didn't commit. He needed some kind of proof, especially since Jenoff implicated someone else—Paul Michael Daniels.

Exhausted from his tormented confession, Jenoff drove Phillips back to her office in his van. Along the way, he released her from their agreement that prevented her from writing about anything he'd told her.

Two hours later, the sun was going down. It was the start of the Jewish Sabbath and Jews around the world were reciting an ancient blessing while lighting the candles that marked the beginning of the day of rest: *Barukh atah Adonai Eloheinu, melekh ha'olam, asher kid'shanu b'mitzvotav v'tzivanu l'hadlik ner shel Shabbat* ("Blessed are You, Lord our God, King of the Universe, who has sanctified us with His commandments, and commanded us to kindle the light of the holy Shabbat"). Jenoff telephoned Phillips. "Say a prayer for me, Nancy," he asked. "Say a prayer that God will help us. Say a prayer that I won't be that badly punished."

23

"He's Gotta Have Ice Water in His Veins"

The day after Jenoff confessed, the phone rang at the home of Frank Hartman. It was the middle of the afternoon. Picking it up, Hartman heard a woman crying, pleading for help. The voice was slurred. Hartman didn't recognize it. Whoever was calling sounded like she'd been drinking too much. Hartman told her she had the wrong number.

Hartman was a fixture in South Jersey, where he'd been a lawyer for forty-seven years. He was now in his early seventies, a burly man, with silver hair and a beard that matched it, and as devoted to his law practice as he was to his family. Some local cops deemed him a "character." He loved charming jurors—spinning down-home stories for them, or launching into a digression about the derivations of, say, a phrase like "Hobson's choice," then sliding into a tightly woven argument about why the twelve good men and women to whom he was talking had only one choice, of course, and that was to acquit his client. At one time, Hartman had seventeen lawyers in his firm, but he eventually decided that was too many to manage. By the mid-1990s, he'd winnowed the firm down to three other lawyers and set a national precedent while doing so: all three were his daughters.

A few hours after Hartman hung up with the mysterious crying woman, he got another unexpected call. This time it was Leonard Jenoff pleading to see Hartman that night. Hartman was on his way out the door to an Italian restaurant with his wife and a daughter. Although he'd concluded over the years that most people who said something was "urgent" were alarmists or tended to exaggerate, he asked his family to go to the restaurant without him. He'd catch up with them later.

Hartman had met Jenoff in the late 1980s when he defended him on charges stemming from his fatal car accident. He lost track of him over the years, then hired him as an investigator in the early 1990s when another lawyer—a member of Jenoff's AA group—told him that Jenoff needed work. Hartman found him competent and dogged, but was annoyed that Jenoff sometimes "got showy" and told too many people he was working on a case.

Jenoff arrived at Hartman's around seven-fifteen, and gave him an abridged version of what he'd told Lee Solomon and Marty Devlin at Weber's. Midway through their conversation, Hartman figured that the woman with the blurry voice who'd called that afternoon was Jenoff's wife. Hearing that her husband had confessed to killing Carol Neulander was sufficient to make her pick up a drink, despite her years of abstinence from alcohol.

Oddly, there were many similarities between Jenoff's story and a previous, very public case that Hartman had worked on earlier in his career. In 1984, Robert Marshall, a prominent insurance agent in Toms River, a small town along the New Jersey coast, was charged with hiring hit men to kill his wife, Maria. Marshall was having an affair with a school principal, was saddled with $300,000 in gambling debts, and had recently taken out a $1.5 million life insurance policy on his wife. While driving home from a casino in Atlantic City, he pulled into a densely wooded picnic site just off the Garden State Parkway. He later told cops he'd had a flat tire, and that while putting the spare on the car, someone had violently robbed them, shooting his wife and striking him on the back of the head. But the police didn't buy it. Even though Maria's purse was missing, she was still wearing all her jewelry. Any good thief would have taken all he could grab. Investigators gradually focused their search on a former Louisiana deputy sheriff, Billy Wayne McKinnon, who said Marshall originally hired him as a private investigator to keep an eye on his allegedly unfaithful wife, but then asked the ex-sheriff to kill her. McKinnon said he'd hired another Louisiana man, Larry Thompson, to do the actual murder.

The court issued Marshall a death sentence, McKinnon got five years in jail, and Larry Thompson walked after six witnesses said he was in Louisiana at the time of the murder. Thompson's lawyer was Frank Hartman.

The case was front-page news all over New Jersey. Joe McGinniss wrote a best-seller about the case—*Blind Faith*—which was adapted into a TV miniseries. In the book, McGinniss called Frank Hartman an "old warhorse, whose many battles before the bar had left him seasoned, mellowed, perhaps scarred just a trifle, but possessed of both tolerance and wisdom in full measure." An apt rendering, and nearly sixteen years after Maria Marshall's murder, Jenoff hoped this "seasoned warhorse" could deliver the same results he had for Thompson. Hartman's job was to teach Jenoff how to convince a jury that confessing was the single redemptive moment in his life: this *one* time, Jenoff was telling the truth, a truth that would seal Fred Neulander's fate as much as Jenoff's.

On Monday morning, three days after Jenoff's confession at Weber's Diner, investigators brought Paul Michael Daniels into the station for questioning. Hartman and Jenoff were already there, meeting with prosecutors, trying to work out a deal.

"What are we getting for cooperating?" Hartman asked.

"Nothing," prosecutors said. "He's already confessed."

The police had a confession, but not necessarily one that was credible, given Jenoff's penchant for lying and the lack of corroboration from his alleged accomplice. All day, Daniels had been stonewalling them. So detectives put a wire on Jenoff and sent him into the room one floor down where Daniels had been telling cops all morning that he didn't know anything about the murder. Daniels was a twenty-six-year-old paranoid schizophrenic who'd been struggling with cocaine and heroin abuse since he was sixteen. He heard voices, saw visions, and had never been able to keep a job. Despite the twenty-eight years separating them, Jenoff was his buddy. They spent a lot of time together—going to movies and watching TV and just goofing around. It wasn't quite a brother-brother or father-son relationship. It wasn't even an uncle-nephew relationship, despite Michaels calling Jenoff "Uncle Lenny." It was really more of a counselor-camper relationship, with Jenoff advising Daniels about how to get through the day and relishing the rarity of someone, even a paranoid schizophrenic, looking up to him.

When Jenoff walked into the interrogation room, Daniels looked at the first familiar face he'd seen in hours. Fleetingly, he thought everything would be all right. Before Marty Devlin left the two men alone, he warned, "Both of you guys are telling different stories. I would suggest that both of you get your shit together. Talk. Do whatever you want. But get your shit together." Then he turned and slammed the door shut.

Daniels was upset, and he wasn't shy about telling Jenoff why. For hours, the cops had been telling him that Jenoff was saying Daniels was the only one who'd hit Carol.

"They said that I said that?" Jenoff asked.

"Yeah."

"They're both lying to us. You and I know what happened. I drove and I hired you . . . The fucking rabbi is going to put all the blame on us. Now is the time we fuck him . . ."

Daniels kept begging Jenoff not to crack. "Don't break down, Lenny. Don't break down."

But Neulander was setting them up, Jenoff said with feigned outrage. No doubt the rabbi was another thirty feet down the hall, working out a deal for himself: "Think about this, Paul. Who gave them your name and my name? The fucking rabbi. Don't you see what's happening? That motherfucking rabbi set us up. You and I are in jail and he'll be back in his four-hundred-thousand-dollar house . . . You always looked up to me like uncle and nephew . . . Trust me here, trust me here . . ."

Daniels was adamant. "I'm not saying I did it."

"We both did it, Paul."

"I'm not saying that. I'm not saying that."

Jenoff kept pressing him. "You're going to let him get acquitted next month at his trial and they're gonna charge us. I think if we come clean—if we say I drove you there—that's the best way to go . . ."

Daniels stubbornly continued to hold out. "We got the rabbi by the balls," he insisted.

"How are you going to have him by the balls?" Jenoff asked. "You have a history of mental shit and drugs and I'm a drunk."

"So that don't mean nothing," Daniels said.

"He's a respected rabbi," Jenoff countered.

"So that don't mean nothing."

"People paid his bail. We better say we were there and he hired us to do it. That's the only salvation we have."

"I ain't gonna do it . . . I ain't ready for that. I ain't ready for that, Uncle Len."

"You're not ready to admit the truth, huh, Paul?" Jenoff prodded.

"Don't fuck me, Lenny, because I ain't going to jail today."

For another five minutes, Jenoff leaned on Daniels and Daniels pushed right back. Exasperated, Jenoff pretended he was about to call his lawyer, only to return a few minutes later with an angry Sergeant Devlin. "Let me explain something to both of you," Devlin growled. "I'm not playing around anymore. We know what happened and we know who was involved. So get together right now and hash it out. I'm not coming back in here twenty times. Understand?" Then he left the room.

This time, Jenoff put more pressure on Daniels, insisting that Neulander was telling the cops that Daniels hit Carol " 'cause I chickened out. We'll cut a deal, Paul. Give him up . . ."

"I guess," said Daniels, not too convincingly.

"You gonna tell them you were there with me?'

"Yeah. Fuck him."

"I'll tell them he approached me, paid me, and I hired you. That's the true story. You went in and did it . . ."

That's when things went bad for Jenoff. Daniels wasn't going to let him get away with this. "You did it, too, Len. You hit her. You hit her one time."

With the cops listening on the wire, Jenoff now desperately tried to get Daniels to retract his statement. So he prompted Daniels, "I'll tell them . . . you went in and did it and I pushed her down or tripped her and Carol struck her head on a coffee table and you finished her off."

"No," said Daniels, holding his ground, " 'cause you said, 'This is the knockout punch,' and you smacked her one time."

They went back and forth like this for a while: Jenoff reiterating that Neulander hired him and he hired Daniels; Daniels reiterating that *both* of them hit Carol and he wouldn't be the fall guy. Jenoff was in deeper than ever now, but at least he'd accomplished his mission. When Marty Devlin returned, Daniels admitted that he'd been with Jenoff the night of November 1, 1994.

At 5:22 that afternoon, Marty Devlin again interrogated Paul Michael Daniels. Much of what Daniels said corroborated Jenoff's account of the murder, but new details added nuance—or contradicted what Jenoff was telling Devlin. Daniels claimed that Jenoff originally told him a vending machine salesman was hiring them, but two days before the hit revealed it was actually Neulander. He also maintained that Jenoff was the first to whack Carol with a pipe; Daniels took one look at her and knew she was dead, but he hit her twice "just to make sure." After the murder, according to Daniels, Jenoff told him the rabbi was "putting on a big crying spree and stuff like that, trying to fool everybody." In the months ahead, the rabbi paid them "in little small bunches. Like seven hundred here. Eight hundred there . . . Three, four, five times." But he never paid them the full thirty thousand dollars he promised.

In the coming years, that debt would gnaw at Jenoff. At first, Neulander asked for two months in which to pay it. After he resigned from M'kor Shalom, he asked for two years. Jenoff agreed, thinking, "He won't stiff me." But Neulander kept telling him he was broke after paying his lawyers and, anyway, he argued, Jenoff was reaping new business from all the publicity about Carol's murder. "Lawyers believed that if I was Fred's private investigator," Jenoff later said, "then I had to be good. Many lawyers hired me because I was Neulander's PI." While there was a certain truth to the rabbi's argument, there was a countertruth: the man still owed Jenoff roughly half of what he'd promised him.

By 1997, Jenoff realized the rabbi was never going to pay him. About eighteen months later, Jenoff investigated Neulander's finances and learned the rabbi had almost $290,000 in stocks and cash. He invited Neulander to a diner for coffee and showed him these accounts. The rabbi's eyes bulged and he insisted the money was being reserved for his lawyers and children. That was the last time they discussed money. "He conned me good," Jenoff realized. "I loved that man for four years, and now he's ruined my life."

The night Jenoff and Daniels were arrested, a reporter knocked on Neulander's door. He was surprised to see Barbara Boyer, the *Inquirer* reporter he'd allowed to visit a few times over the past year for some off-the-record conversations.

"What brings you here?" he asked.

Boyer told him about Jenoff and Daniels. Neulander was stunned. "Len Jenoff was arrested?" he asked. "This is ridiculous."

Neulander's lawyers arrived an hour later and had to run a gauntlet of TV crews that were already camped outside the house for what would be an all-night vigil.

The following day, Boyer returned for a ninety-minute interview with Neulander. Jenoff's story, said the rabbi, was unbelievably "fabricated." Neulander knew he was innocent, and he was certain that Jenoff was, too. But why, Boyer asked, would Jenoff invent such a story? "You'll have to ask him," Neulander said. Maybe Jenoff had been "scheming" all along, just waiting for the right moment to turn against the rabbi. Neulander also said he'd never counseled Jenoff: "I listened, made some referrals, made some suggestions. But I don't counsel. If you don't have a [counseling] degree, you don't counsel someone." And while he never hired Jenoff as his private investigator, he did pay him twelve hundred dollars for "stuff I never asked for."

Neulander dismissed Jenoff's claims that they were friends. He explained that he was just a rabbi doing his job, and that Jenoff was just a recovering alcoholic supposedly rehabilitating himself. Neulander emphasized that he was really perplexed about Jenoff's "confession" because he'd gone to such lengths to help the man, like offering him his house for his wedding in the summer of 1997. "He told me he had no money," the rabbi said, "and I had an empty house. End of story."

Not quite. The wedding was, indeed, held at Neulander's house. Upstairs, the rabbi's daughter, Rebecca, helped the bride get dressed; downstairs, about thirty guests, including an FBI agent, an IRS agent, a few local cops, and the manager of a strip club, were kibitzing and admiring the three-tier wedding cake that Neulander had bought from Classic Cakes, the bakery Carol started. When the ceremony started, Jenoff and his two best men came forward. One was Len's son; the other was June's son from her previous marriage. June came down the stairs and turned left. Everyone was waiting for her in the room where Carol had been killed.

Jenoff and Neulander had initially agreed to have the ceremony in the family room. But when Jenoff arrived at Neulander's that day, the rabbi had already arranged chairs for guests in the living room. He said he was too embarrassed to officiate in the family room because a leaky pipe had damaged the ceiling. Jenoff walked back to the den where, indeed, a two-by-three piece of the ceiling had collapsed. He reconciled himself to the situation but was not happy about where the rabbi said he and June were to take their vows.

Neulander delivered a wonderful sermon about love and relationships and caring and commitment. Though the guests were visibly moved by the rabbi, what was more notable was what they were preoccupied about—being in the living room. "It was spooky," acknowledged a member of the wedding party. "But we were there to celebrate a new marriage, not to dwell on the past. There comes a time when you move on. This room couldn't be cordoned off forever."

One person couldn't avoid the obvious. A friend of Jenoff's pulled him into the living room a few minutes before the ceremony started. They were the only people there. "Not to be morbid," he said, "but morbid's my personality. Where was Carol's body?" While other guests were filling up on hors d'oeuvres and June was getting dressed upstairs, the groom stretched out one leg, pointed to the carpet with his foot, and said, "Well, you see, her head was here and one arm was here and her legs were down this way . . ." A few minutes later, the ceremony started and June stood exactly where Carol's battered head had come to rest.

The friend who'd asked Jenoff about where Carol's body had lain was in law enforcement. Driving home after the ceremony with his wife, she asked if he'd seen any signs of police surveillance around the house. "Nothing," he said, "but if that rabbi did have his wife killed, he's gotta have ice water in his veins to have a religious service in the same room where it happened."

24

"Dismiss Whatever Insults Your Soul"

The cops figured they had a pretty good case even before Jenoff's confession, but now their indictment suddenly got stronger. However, it wasn't a closed book—Jenoff was a notorious liar. And Daniels—a paranoid schizophrenic who'd been using heroin and coke for a decade—could hardly be called reliable. It was difficult to predict how these loose cannons, who were now a centerpiece of the state's case, would perform in the witness box when faced with Neulander's lawyers.

But most people in Cherry Hill had already drawn their conclusions about Neulander's guilt. Jenoff's confession had merely confirmed their darkest suspicions. Even a statement issued by M'kor Shalom suggested that it had more faith in the U.S. legal system than in its former rabbi: "Our tradition venerates the pursuit of justice for all, as exemplified by the biblical command, 'Justice, justice shall you pursue.' These recent arrests and turn of events have surprised and disturbed our entire community. However, we must still remember that our system of justice requires that all persons are presumed innocent unless and until proven guilty. It is our prayer and hope that, when the proceeding is concluded, justice will be served." In Philadelphia's *City Paper,* a young man who'd been raised in Neulander's temple voiced what was on everyone's mind. Over the years, he wrote, only a "handful" of M'kor Shalom congregants hadn't been "playing Agatha Christie," trying to figure out whether Neulander killed Carol. Now there was "a real, live human being in the parlor"—Len Jenoff—"detailing how it all went down . . . My easy first impression of Len Jenoff is that he's not playing with a full deck. But it doesn't matter: the cards he's brought to the table effortlessly complete the hand I've been playing semi-privately for years . . . The game seems almost over, but the endgame that was supposed to bring relief has, for me, just made things worse: looking at this kind of blunt truth is a game that's no fun and without winners."

The confession was certainly no parlor game for Jenoff's son, Marty, who was tormented by his father's confession. Marty's mother had paged him while he was working at his college's TV station: "Call your stepmother." When Marty reached June, she was hysterical. He pieced together the few words and phrases he could understand until he realized his father was in jail for murder. A friend at the station glimpsed Marty on the phone. He looked like he'd been hit by a train.

Unlike Len's brother, Gene, who disowned him, or June, who would divorce Jenoff in another two years, Marty's loyalty for his father after the confession was steadfast. But it wasn't easy. Like a good son, Marty had grown up accepting his father's words as the truth. He had never questioned Jenoff's stories about being in the CIA and the FBI, but now Marty didn't know what to believe.

_____

By early June, Jenoff's lawyer had successfully reduced charges against his client. Now charged with aggravated manslaughter, Jenoff would be eligible for parole in about two years if he got the minimum sentence. Daniels, who was charged with aggravated manslaughter and robbery, could be in prison as long as fifty years. Daniels's bail was set at four hundred thousand dollars; Jenoff's at two hundred thousand dollars. "I can get out of this," Jenoff told Hartman. "Friends'll help." However, even with friends chipping in and his wife maxxing out their home equity loan, Jenoff couldn't raise the bail. Instead, both he and Daniels waited in jail for the end of Neulander's trial, when the judge would sentence them. If the rabbi was acquitted, their lawyers planned to tell the judge that the sentences should reward their effort. Jenoff and Daniels's job was to confess, and they had done that well. It wouldn't be their fault if Neulander's jury didn't believe them. Jenoff's lawyer would also argue that by persuading Paul Michael Daniels to confess, Jenoff had saved the state the expense of a long trial.

In jail, Jenoff had much time for reflection. One of his regrets was the timing of his confession. Had he held out and "gone to the prosecutor with my attorney the first day of the trial," he would have had an extra six weeks of freedom. With that, he would have attended his son's college graduation in Maryland, then joined him for the graduation present Jenoff had arranged: a family trip to Mexico. Instead, he was locked up in Camden County's jail, and the probability of being in Mexico soon were as slim as getting a film deal that he kept praying would financially offset the worst disaster of his life.

Highgate Lane was now Cherry Hill's biggest tourist attraction. Neulander still lived there, and drivers slowed down as they passed the house, TV news vans frequently parked outside, and journalists pigeonholed neighbors. Everyone wanted the scoop on "the man you love to hate," which is what Neulander once called himself when talking with a reporter. One day, boys on dirt bikes gathered at the end of Neulander's driveway, daring each other to ring his doorbell. Egging each other on, they moved closer to the front door, never quite getting there. One boy, riding around in tight circles, hit Neulander's trash cans with every pass.

Seven weeks after Jenoff confessed, the rabbi was charged with capital murder. Until Jenoff and Daniels had confessed, the worst sentence he could have received was thirty years in jail. Now he faced life—or lethal injection. On June 21, two of his kids— Rebecca and Benjamin—slept over at his house, knowing those might be the last few hours of their father's freedom: the next day, a judge would rule on a motion by prosecutors to revoke his bail. Shortly after noon, the three of them walked over to Rebecca's Honda SUV, which was parked in her father's driveway. She handed the keys to Neulander, and the rabbi drove to his lawyer's offices in Camden. This was the last time Neulander would ever drive a car.

In the courthouse, prosecutors argued that Neulander killed Carol to avoid a divorce; the defense contended that it was absurd to revoke bail just because a "bizarre, psychotic" guy like Jenoff had "confessed." He'd already told three different stories about the murder.

Judge Linda Baxter wasn't moved. The threat of capital punishment gave Neulander "an enormous incentive to flee," she ruled, and Jenoff's confession improved the chances of conviction. "For a person to come forward and implicate himself in a murder without any promise made to him," she said, "persuades me that the statement is reliable." She ordered Neulander to prison.

Carol Neulander's siblings gasped. After six years of rumors and innuendos and revelations, they were still stunned that this man who'd been part of their family for forty years was going to jail. Within days after their Thanksgiving dinner with Fred in 1994, a mere three weeks after Carol's murder, they'd started to hear about his affairs; by the end of that year, some siblings were certain that he'd killed their sister. And yet, there was still a tremendous dissonance between what their hearts were telling them—and Judge Baxter sending the man who married their sister to prison to await trial for her murder.

Guards slipped handcuffs on Neulander's wrists. Rebecca and Benjamin watched silently from the third row in the courtroom; their older brother, Matthew, was in the last row with his fiancée. As he left the courtroom, Matthew paused in the doorway. For about ten seconds, he stared at his father's back, whispering contemptuously to his fiancée, "Watch him. Just watch him."

Outside the courtroom in Camden, Carol's oldest brother, Ed, made the family's first public statement since their sister was killed. "It's an obvious understatement . . . that Carol's murder was the most devastating event in our lives . . . Now that the evidence has become so overwhelming . . . it is the right time to make a statement in support of those who have worked so diligently to solve this crime . . . From the very beginning, we as a family sought only two things: justice and closure. Maybe, just maybe, we are finally getting to that point."

Matthew Neulander was less sanguine. For six years, Cherry Hill had been watching the almost Oedipal dance between Matthew and his father. Since Carol's murder, Matthew had been the most visible of the Neulander children. His sister had gotten married and moved to Connecticut; his brother had graduated from college and moved to Brooklyn. Matthew never left South Jersey. He had friends here, he fell in love here, he got engaged here, he went to medical school here—and now that his father was in jail, he moved back into the house where he'd grown up. He tried to bring 204 Highgate back to life: friends often visited; a baby gate kept his two large dogs from the living room where Carol was killed; the bushes

that Fred allowed to grow helter-skelter for privacy from neighbors
and journalists were trimmed. Though sunlight streamed in once
again, Matthew couldn't expunge the aura that enveloped the
house, and that probably always would.

While Matthew spent his nights in the house he'd once shared
with his parents, his father slept on a mattress on a stainless steel
bunk. His nine-by-eight-foot cell on the northeast block of the
Camden County Correctional Facility also had a stainless steel toilet, a portal window overlooking the cell block, and a window
with narrow slits overlooking the street.

If Neulander's cell had been on the opposite side of the jail, he
could have seen the row house that Walt Whitman bought in 1884.
Whitman wrote in an upstairs bedroom here, scratching away with
a quill pen on a pad braced against a knee and listening to children
and peddlers below: his American song. This most gentle of poets
beheld God "in every object" and "every face," but what would he
say of a certain rabbi who had served in Cherry Hill for too many
years? Perhaps, borrowing a line from his finest poem, *Leaves of
Grass*—"dismiss whatever insults your own soul"—he would conclude that Neulander had finally reached his proper destination.

Neulander was luckier than most prisoners. He had a cell to
himself. Frozen kosher food was sent in from the outside and
warmed up for him in the kitchen. Friends, including two rabbis,
visited him regularly. Taking full advantage of a law entitling every
prisoner to an hour of recreation every day, he jogged and played
basketball in the prison's seventh-floor gym. Which is not to say
that there weren't certain deprivations: his harmonica, which he'd
recently started learning, was confiscated. "No instruments," said a
guard. He rarely watched his favorite TV show, *The West Wing*—
another inmate enjoyed Black Entertainment TV and Neulander
quickly learned it was wise to defer to those bigger and stronger
than him. Generally, though, his notoriety was acknowledged by

other inmates who gave him a wide berth and would enthusiastically tell their lawyers, "Wow, I saw the rabbi today."

While Neulander was somewhat of a "celebrity" within the confines of Camden County Correctional, his notoriety outside the jail was growing as well. But any sympathy or goodwill toward the rabbi had evaporated. In a diner on Route 70, a college kid told his girlfriend, "Hey, on the way to my parents' house, I can show you the house of that rabbi who killed his wife." "Wow," she said, her face lighting up, "I've been reading about him. What an asshole." Newspapers published letters calling Neulander a "brutal creep . . . Unload this guy as soon as possible." Some people blamed Elaine Soncini for Carol's murder and wanted her radio show canceled. The *New York Post* dubbed the Neulander case "The Ten Commandments Trial," while the *Philadelphia Daily News* ran a cover story about Neulander's life in jail entitled "Among Sinners." And Carol Saline, a senior writer for *Philadelphia Magazine* and probably the last journalist in America who believed Neulander was innocent, confessed that she'd been duped.

Saline had known Neulander for twenty-five years. A member of his temple, she'd relished his "charisma," his "thoughtfulness," his "wonderful" sermons. He'd come to her family seders, officiated at her children's baby-naming ceremonies, delivered a "tender eulogy" at her father's funeral. In her first article about Neulander, published a year after Carol's murder, Saline concluded that the investigation was botched. She noted that newcomers without contacts in South Jersey had been assigned to the case, and that seasoned forensic experts scoffed at the theory that a hit man killed Carol—professional killers use guns, not the kind of blunt instrument that smashed in Carol's head. Lastly, she cited one psychiatrist who believed there was rarely a correlation between adultery and murder. "Sexual impulse," he said, "is driven by power, not aggression. I can't imagine someone who isn't a psychopath plotting the death of his wife. An act of rage, an irresistible impulse, maybe. But nothing in this rabbi's life shows that kind of criminal mind."

With Neulander in jail, Saline wrote a second article about him. As before, she turned to a psychiatrist, hoping he'd say that Neulander didn't know what he was doing when hiring Jenoff, that he was in a dissociative state. No such luck. The psychiatrist concluded that Neulander was a sociopath—aggressive, arrogant, bull-headed. This diagnosis, coupled with new evidence about Neulander, convinced Saline that he was consumed by "overweening hubris."

In an interview for Saline's first article, Neulander affirmed that his beliefs were intact. "I have not lost my faith in God," he stated, "but my faith in people has been shaken." Now, five years later, it was Saline's faith that was shaken. "It is painful," she wrote, "for anyone . . . to admit that even in our most intimate connections, we can never see deeply into another human being . . . Promises get broken. Friends betray us. We learn that good people lie and cheat, and thus, eventually, we come to appreciate the fragility of trust. To protect ourselves, we increasingly place our faith in the few people we think we know and love. That is our safety net. And mine now has a gigantic hole."

In the court of public opinion, Neulander was a dead man. In addition to public censure, the rabbi also received a scathing anonymous letter a few days after Jenoff and Daniels confessed. The writer identified himself as a Jew, although as he admitted, "not a very smart one." (He'd barely graduated from high school and he never finished college.) And he'd only seen Neulander once, at a bat mitzvah where the rabbi "walked up and down the aisle with glasses hanging from his neck." It was obvious Neulander thought "he was hot shit . . . But I could see right through you . . . I know you were probably a really good person once because the people in this town respected and loved you . . . But you became evil. You wanted something so bad that you came up with a scheme . . . You did what Hitler did—found a person you knew was weak and talked that person into doing something evil. Just like Hitler. Well, I hope the sex was worth it because, you see, you risked everything for sex. You have killed your wife, and your poor children will now know that you followed a man who had six million Jews killed."

Being an accessory to the Final Solution is perhaps the most horrific accusation anyone could level at a Jew. But in the fashion characteristic of a religion that emphasizes the possibility for forgiveness and redemption, the letter writer offered Neulander an out: "You need to talk with God and tell him what you have done and ask for forgiveness. He will know if you mean it or not . . . You need to admit to your children what you have done and accept the punishment that will be given to you. Your children will understand this better if they know the truth . . . You see, you were starting to believe you were better than God. You were not."

Five weeks after Neulander went to jail to await his trial, Jenoff met with Sergeant Devlin. He'd remembered details about Neulander that might help investigators. "A lot of it," Jenoff told Devlin, "I had, like, put out of my mind and it's coming back to me." He'd also deliberately lied about parts of the murder when confessing at Weber's. "I was still too scared to be totally honest," he later conceded.

Len told them of the time Fred asked his "dear, close friends" David and Patsy Brandt to include him in Rosh Hashanah dinner at their house. This was two months before Carol was killed. Jenoff felt out of place. All the guests were "very wealthy"; he was a recovering alcoholic who was so ashamed of his broken-down 1980 Oldsmobile that he parked it halfway down the block. Ten days later, the Brandts, again at Neulander's request, invited Jenoff to their house to break his Yom Kippur fast. At both events, the rabbi introduced Len "like I was his fair-haired child." Neulander's unsaid intent was to show Jenoff all the wonderful things to which he would have access, if he just listened to his good friend, the rabbi.

Neulander, said Jenoff, had cleverly given himself a foolproof alibi: plan the murder for a night when his son Matthew was almost guaranteed to race home in his ambulance and find his mother dead on the living room floor. The rabbi was certain that no one would believe he was so heinous as to do that to his son.

This rabbi was always scheming, always plotting, Jenoff told Devlin. In the midst of the murder investigation, the rabbi sought revenge on his newly acquired enemies: Nancy Phillips, whose *Inquirer* stories he believed were biased against him; Peppy Levin, whose grand jury testimony damaged Neulander; and Devlin, who was a tenacious son of a bitch. The rabbi had formulated ways to revenge them all. If Jenoff seduced Phillips, Neulander would get her fired from the paper for having inappropriate relationships with her sources. "As your rabbi," he counseled, "I'm telling you to be loyal and faithful to your wife. But as my friend and investigator, if you can get Nancy to bed, go ahead and do it." As for Devlin: What kind of cop would quit Philadelphia's elite homicide unit? Devlin must have been fired. Jenoff's job was to find out why. And then there was Levin. Walking around Neulander's backyard one day, the rabbi ordered Jenoff to kill Levin with a stun gun. With Peppy's heart condition, Neulander figured, the gun might be powerful enough to kill him if placed over his heart. Neulander nagged Jenoff about these plots for weeks until Jenoff finally shut him up. "Fred," he reasoned, "forget about it. You're in enough trouble already."

So Phillips was never compromised, Devlin was never scandalized, and Levin was never killed. But Neulander was still planning to denounce all of them at a press conference he would hold on the courthouse steps immediately after the acquittal he was sure he'd get. That was before his bail was revoked and he was sent to jail. From there, Fred Neulander couldn't get revenge on anyone. The most he could hope for now was freedom.

===== PART SEVEN =====

THE TRIALS

25

"A Piece of Dung"

Fred Neulander's trial started in mid-October 2001—seven years after Carol was killed, six years after Neulander resigned from M'kor Shalom, four years after an investigative grand jury had been convened to look into the case, three years after the rabbi was indicted, and fifteen months after Leonard Jenoff confessed that Neulander hired him to murder Carol. While Neulander's lawyers were claiming that their client had been "slandered and smeared for years" and was eager to have his day in court, they had been doing everything possible to delay the trial: filing for a change of venue; trying to subpoena Nancy Phillips's notes from her interviews with Jenoff; demanding that a psychiatrist examine Jenoff; attempting to bar Rebecca Neulander from testifying about conversations with her mother about the "bathroom man." Every motion failed. Judge Linda Baxter ruled that Neulander could still find an unbiased jury in Camden County, despite massive pretrial publicity; that the First Amendment protected Phillips's notes; that the prosecution's argument prevailed and shielded Jenoff from psychiatric tests—"Normal people stretch or disregard the truth . . . to advance their own interests and to make themselves look good. There are not enough psychiatrists in the world to examine such prevaricators, nor do they need to be examined." And an appeals court and the state supreme court both refused to hear arguments that Rebecca's "bathroom man" testimony was hearsay.

Neulander had a strong defense team—Leonard Goldschmidt, a psychologist and jury consultant, and Jeffrey Zucker and Dennis Wixted, two of the best defense lawyers in South Jersey. The two attorneys made an odd couple. Zucker was short, slightly pudgy, almost avuncular; Wixted was over six feet tall, with shoulders as straight as his haircut—a flattop left over from the 1950s—and a more severe, less playful demeanor than Zucker.

Opposite them was a lone veteran prosecutor—tall and rangy Jim Lynch. He'd begun his career in private practice, then served in Camden's public defender's office for eighteen months. In 1982, he became a prosecutor. After twenty years, he still liked that side of the law. "We try to do what's right," he said. "We don't fill out time sheets and we don't worry about personal financial interest. And largely, the victims' survivors we deal with are good, empathetic people."

Lynch was living only a mile and a half from the Neulanders' house when Carol was killed. In 1996, he was asked to review the Neulander case. Even a "cursory" review, he later said, "raised serious questions about the rabbi." Since Jenoff's confession, Lynch had been designing a strategy contingent on persuading jurors that the state's case rested on more than the credibility of this man with a very dubious character. Jenoff was both a liability to the prosecution and a boon to the defense, which saw his decades of lying as the rabbi's best opportunity for acquittal. For someone who'd been a virtual nonentity a year before, Leonard Jenoff was now in the center of the most notorious rabbi trial in the history of the United States.

On the day of the trial, Neulander wore a dark suit; he looked anxious and flushed. The rabbi's three children sat about ten feet behind him; to their right were Carol's brothers and sister. While Neulander didn't turn around to look at anyone, he occasionally surveyed the jury—nine women and seven men, including the four alternates. The men were all white; three women were black. Almost everyone was middle-aged.

In their opening arguments, the defense and prosecution agreed on one thing: Neulander was consumed by passion. But they differed on the consequences of that passion. Neulander, Lynch said, was "brilliant," a "wonderful speaker," "extraordinarily successful," but he could not be sated. "Overwhelmed by lust, greed, arrogance, and betrayal," this man who "had it all . . . wanted more. And he plotted to kill." Lynch previewed some witnesses, like Elaine Soncini, who was one of the people to have fully experienced Neulander's amorous desires and had been told by the rabbi that she was "far superior" to his wife. Lynch proposed that a twisted obsession had motivated Neulander to discuss the murder many times with Len Jenoff—"how to do it, how to pull it off, how to do it neat, how to do it clean, and how to make sure under any circumstances suspicion was deflected from this defendant, the husband, the man who wanted Carol Neulander dead." He warned jurors of Neulander's insincerity on the tape of the 911 call he made the night of the murder ("You're going to hear clutches in his voice, hesitations, moaning, groaning . . . You're going to hear what sounds for all the world like genuine emotion . . . This was phony play-acting . . ."). In the end, Lynch concluded, the evidence would be "damning" of Neulander, who "was the architect of his own fate."

Next, Jeffrey Zucker conceded the obvious—the rabbi, by being unfaithful to his wife, "betrayed" his family, his synagogue, and his religion. "But it's one giant step from adultery to murder, ladies and gentlemen, and that's where the prosecutor and I part ways." Neulander might be "humiliated," "embarrassed," and "disgraced," but "the evidence is going to show you as clear as the nose on my face that he's not a murderer." Zucker urged jurors that the tape of the 911 call would depict a man struck by "horror and terror," that Elaine Soncini "enhanced her stories as time goes on," and that Len Jenoff, the state's key witness, was a "sick, demented person" who can't "sift between truth and fantasy." As Zucker concluded, the defense attorney retuned to his opening theme, "Fred Neulander is not on trial for being unfaithful. Fred Neulander is not on trial for betraying his wife, his religion, or his children. Fred Neulander's on trial for the most serious crime that we know—capital murder . . . Listen carefully," he asked of the jurors, "as I know you will, to both sides of the case and I have no doubt that you'll find this case full of reasonable doubt."

With that, the prosecution started calling the first witnesses: a consultant to Carol's bakery, one of the last people to see Carol alive at a meeting barely three hours before her murder, and some law enforcement officials who described the crime scene and the jewelry Carol was still wearing even after the beating. Lynch showed jurors photos of Carol's battered, bloody body. Glancing briefly at them, Neulander took his glasses off, his hands slightly trembling. And finally, at the end of the day, Lynch played Neulander's famous 911 call. The courtroom was absolutely still. About the only movement was in the third row of the spectators section where Neulander's children were tightly clasping each other's hands.

The next day, Elaine Soncini was on the stand—all day. A heart-shaped necklace dangled from her neck, a cocoa-colored pant suit accented her figure, shoulder-length hair neatly framed her face. Speaking with the verve of a veteran broadcaster, she called Neulander "brilliant," "maybe even a genius." She explained that she had converted to Judaism partly because of him, showered him with presents, imagined a life with him. He had called her his "soul mate" but was afraid he'd be fired from his job "instantly" if their affair became known. "It would jeopardize his standing," said Soncini. "He was preaching family values." And yet, Soncini said, after she gave Neulander her ultimatum—choose her or Carol—he said he'd seen a lawyer, who counseled that a divorce was "no problem." The rabbi had told her he and Carol were planning to work out a separation. However, after "some people in the community" warned that divorcing Carol would "jeopardize" his position at M'kor Shalom, Neulander took back his promise to split with Carol. "Where would I go at my age to get a job?" he asked Soncini.

From the witness box, Soncini also described her only face-to-face encounter with Carol. Neulander had asked Elaine to meet him and his son one Saturday afternoon at the F&M Deli in Cherry Hill; they'd pretend it was "a chance encounter." As planned, by the time she arrived at the deli, Neulander and Matthew were already there and they made room for her at their table. But then, to Soncini's surprise, Carol arrived with Rebecca. Then Benjamin, the Neulanders' other son, showed up, too. Elaine recalled thinking that she couldn't get any more uncomfortable—until the conversation turned to *The Age of Innocence,* Martin Scorsese's just-released film about the rigid social code among upper-crust New Yorkers in the 1870s. Just that morning, Neulander had telephoned Soncini to say that if he couldn't see the film with her, he'd go by himself; and now Carol was saying, "Freddy and I just saw the most wonderful film." Soncini, distraught, paid for everyone's lunch and dashed outside. Hours later, Neulander tracked her down at the nursing home where she was visiting her mother. He apologized for not telling her that he'd seen the film with his wife. "Just don't lie to me, Fred," Soncini said. He promised never to lie again.

After testifying for three hours, Soncini was wilted. Judge Baxter called a lunch break. Dennis Wixted, one of Neulander's two lawyers, used the time to telephone his office from a pay phone. "How's Elaine doing?" his secretary asked. "She's very dramatic," Wixted answered. "The jury's eating it up."

In the afternoon, the questioning turned to November 1, 1994—the day Carol was killed. Neulander came to Soncini's house for their daily tryst around noon; that evening, he made his usual good-night telephone call to her. She recalled that he had sounded calm. The next morning, Wednesday, he called her at the radio station less than an hour after she had learned about Carol's murder. "Are you frightened?" she asked. "I'm afraid I'm going to lose you and my children," he responded. "Fred," Soncini inquired, "why would you lose us?" He didn't answer.

Soncini testified that in the weeks following Carol's death, she'd had sex with the rabbi a few times but broke off with him after police gave her the names of Neulander's other mistresses. However, he had written to her frequently. At that, Lynch, the prosecutor, handed Soncini some letters she'd received from Neulander—an apology for "the pain I caused you," a lament that "losing all contact with you is unimaginable . . . I weep for you and with you . . . Never forget who you are." On the stand, Soncini cried while reading these last lines.

During cross-examination, Zucker's opening question implied exactly what he thought of Soncini's performance in the courtroom: "Have you ever taken acting lessons in New York?" It turned out she had—briefly when she was seventeen, only in Philadelphia, not Manhattan. That was the most gentle question he would ask her for the next two hours. Didn't she have "low moral standards"? After all, she'd had an affair with a married man, then continued after his wife was killed. "Looking back on it now, yes," Soncini answered, who was as harsh on herself as Zucker was.

"Do you agree with me that it takes two, ma'am, to commit

adultery?" Zucker continued. "I have always agreed with that," answered Soncini, "and I have always said that I am an adult and my immoral behavior is something for which I take full responsibility."

"As a grieving widow, Miss Soncini," Zucker said, "were you in some kind of a vulnerable position because of the fact that you had just become a widow and you let your guard down and you made an error in judgment? Is that what you're saying?"

"I think it was a conscious error in judgment on my part," admitted Soncini. "And I take full responsibility for that . . . [It] speaks more to my own moral lack of character than the fact that I was grieving or not grieving." Ultimately, she told the court, she wanted to know the truth about Carol Neulander's death as a way to atone for her affair with Carol's husband.

"I wanted to know," she testified, "if this man, for whom I had such great regard, could have been involved in something like this. I dishonored his wife in life and I was not going to dishonor her in death."

The day after Soncini's testimony, Thursday, Lynch played a tape of detectives' interview with Neulander just a few hours after he found Carol's body: several times, the rabbi denied having any infidelities. The balance of the day was filled with prosecution witnesses. Rebecca, Neulander's daughter, recounted the "bathroom man" story. ("I was on the telephone. Mommy said there's somebody here to drop a letter off for Daddy . . . Daddy told me to expect him . . . The very strange thing is that he needs to use the bathroom . . .") Anita Hochman, the cantor at M'kor Shalom, described Neulander's visit to her choir class at the temple the night of the murder. ("This was rare, very rare. He was in an 'up' mood.") And Myron "Pep" Levin, the ex-gangster who played racquetball with Neulander, testified for over an hour in a weak voice—he'd had a stroke and two heart bypass operations in recent years. His memory was faulty and he kept mixing up dates and forgetting the federal crimes for which he'd been convicted. But in typical gangster style, he sprinkled his testimony with expletives and even some humor. (Judge to prosecutor: "Remember, you're talking to a witness who's seventy-seven years old." Levin proudly correcting the judge: "Seventy-six.") Nonetheless, Levin was certain of one thing: three months before Carol was killed, Neulander said, "I wish I could get rid of my goddamn wife and have her killed, see her on the ground when I go home someday."

"What are you? Fucking crazy?" Levin recalled he'd responded.

"Do you know anybody . . ." Neulander began asking, when Levin suddenly interjected, "Get the fuck out of my head, you crazy bastard. You're nuts. Fred, forget you even told me about what you said. Stay away from me. You got a lovely wife. Stick with it."

On cross-examination, Neulander's lawyer concentrated on Levin's motivation for telling this story. Hadn't he and Neulander ended their friendship on a sour note after Peppy learned about the despoiled Torah the rabbi had sold him, threatening Neulander with "legal problems" if he didn't get his money back?

"I don't recall," Levin answered. "What's your point there?"

"My point," explained Zucker, "is that because you felt you had lost the money on your Torah, you made things worse and worse as time went on for Fred Neulander, didn't you?"

"I made it worse and worse?"

"Yes."

"No," Levin maintained, "not in my opinion."

At this point, Judge Baxter intervened, concerned because Levin was sweating so profusely. She then explained Zucker's line of questioning—Levin had changed his story to get revenge on Neulander for swindling him in the Torah sale.

Levin blanched for a moment, then said with some disgust, "That is so sick."

With no one vouching for Levin—just his word against the rabbi's—the defense had successfully raised some uncertainties about his motivation. Hoping to bolster Levin's credibility, prosecutors produced Cynthia Sharp-Myers, an ex-girlfriend of Levin's, who recalled that in 1994 Peppy told her Neulander wanted his wife dead. When first approached by investigators, she had denied knowing about the rabbi's comment. "I did not take the conversation seriously," she told the court. Prosecutors also flew Levin's former driver up from Florida. With his bulk, his deep New Jersey accent, and his fractured grammar, Anthony Federici resembled most of the characters on the HBO crime show, *The Sopranos*. He waddled to the stand, took his oath, and stated that Peppy had told him three times in 1994 that Neulander wanted to find Carol dead when he came home someday, and that the rabbi was searching for someone to kill her. In one of these conversations, according to Federici, Levin paused after mentioning the rabbi's search for a killer. "I believe Mr. Levin was asking if I would kill Mrs. Neulander," Federici told the court. "He was implying that. He wasn't saying it directly. He was trying to see if I would bite." And why had Federici withheld this information from investigators for several years? "I had concerns that Myron Levin had the reputation of someone you don't cross. I was afraid of my life and my family's life."

Matthew Neulander sat silently through these testimonies. Now a resident physician in North Carolina, he had arrived in Camden fairly certain about his father's guilt. For several years, he'd been trying to apply the same threshold of certainty to the rabbi's possible involvement that a jury would use—reasonable doubt. After all, Matthew called himself a realist. But realism was almost impossible to maintain when trying to determine if your father killed your mother.

When he took the stand, Matthew told Lynch that two nights before the murder, he'd witnessed his parents arguing about ending their marriage. In an instant, he saw their relationship go from "fine to not fine." The next morning, Matthew recalled, his father was "vague and noncommittal," "distant and aloof." When Matthew tried to get him to explain what was going on, Neulander just mumbled a few generalities about the future not being clear.

The next night, November 1, Matthew had come home to share a pizza dinner with his father, and again he tried to discuss the Sunday night argument. Again his father had clammed up. Matthew returned to work around six-forty; approximately two hours later, he overheard the dispatcher sending an ambulance to his house. Matthew raced there to 204 Highgate, where he finally found his father standing in the driveway. He remembered peppering him with questions. "What's the matter?" "Where's Mom?" "Is she OK?" "Do you know what happened?" "Did you see her?" To each, Neulander had given the same answer: "Everything's going to be OK."

Matthew's testimony suggested that his father was callous, insensitive; Zucker's job when cross-examining was to show that Neulander was caring, compassionate. Zucker himself took on a gentle demeanor when questioning Matthew, lest Matthew perceive him as hostile. Zucker asked Matthew to think back to the advice his father had given him when Matthew had been subpoenaed to testify in 1997 for the grand jury looking into his mother's murder.

"He told you to testify honestly, didn't he, Matthew?"

"Yes, sir."

"And isn't it true, Matthew," continued Zucker, "that throughout your upbringing and up to the time you received the subpoena that your dad has always instilled in all the children that honesty is important?"

"Yes, sir."

And wasn't Neulander so concerned about his son that the

rabbi had paid for Matthew's lawyer? The rabbi's son bristled at that suggestion. He wasn't sure who'd paid the lawyer, but definitely not his father.

By the time Matthew left the stand, he'd proven to be one of the more stubborn witnesses before Zucker that day. Even the point about Neulander instilling honesty in his children could work against the rabbi; if Matthew had, indeed, learned that lesson well, then every word from him was gospel, even his account of his parents fighting forty-eight hours before the murder, an incident his father never acknowledged.

The next witness wore a bright orange jumpsuit, courtesy of the Camden County jail. Leonard Jenoff—oval shaped, peering out of oversized glasses, bewildered at how his life had turned out—would testify for the next three and a half days. Dennis Wixted would hammer away at Jenoff, trying to shred whatever self-respect still resided in the ex-alcoholic, chronically prevaricating, publicity-seeking confessed killer-for-hire. He wanted jurors to find Jenoff unbelievable, erratic, risible, lying as he'd always lied. Lynch, on the other hand, was hoping jurors would distinguish between a lifetime of lies and Jenoff's insistence that he was now telling the truth. Given Jenoff's history, Wixted had the easier job.

Jenoff detailed the past twelve years or so of his life: the fatal accident that wasn't his fault, his subsequent drinking, his divorce, meeting Neulander in his study at M'kor Shalom, and being "overwhelmed" by the rabbi's "graciousness." Neulander was "taking my shame away," helping him "feel like a worthy Jew," Jenoff told the courtroom. Seeking to impress the rabbi, Jenoff explained he had lied to him about being in the CIA and committing assassinations. In 1994, Neulander began asking Jenoff about killing— "Would you kill for Israel?" "Would you fight against the enemies of the Jewish State?" Then he confided that an enemy of Israel lived in Cherry Hill who had to be killed. Jenoff told the court that he asked Neulander for more details before taking the job. "There's no need for details," Neulander reportedly said. "Either you're the man for the job or you are not the man for the job ... This woman is evil." In midsummer, Jenoff testified, Neulander identified the "enemy" as his wife—a deviation from Jenoff's confession back at Weber's Diner, where he'd said that he didn't know the real identity of his victim until he turned on the radio the day after the murder.

Jenoff stated that he kept stalling, not wanting to go ahead with the murder, at one point telling Neulander he needed an accomplice. Fine, the rabbi had said, but the payment would remain as they'd agreed—not a dime more. Jenoff explained that he'd then hired Paul Michael Daniels. They had gone to the Neulanders' house twice. The first time, Jenoff chickened out, but at least he established himself with Carol as a friendly presence by saying he was delivering a letter for the rabbi; the second time, Carol had invited him inside. Jenoff told all this matter-of-factly—no drama, no histrionics, no great emotion. But everyone in the courtroom knew what was coming up—they'd read his confession in the papers the year before—and they braced themselves for it.

Jenoff continued with his testimony. Carol, he said, had led him into the living room, where "she turned and put her back to me ... I put my left hand on her shoulder. I pulled out the lead pipe ... and whacked her on the back of the head."

For almost a minute, Jenoff was too choked up to speak. Carol's children and siblings were sitting about twenty feet in front of him—kneading their hands together in anguish, breathing quickly, almost painfully. Then Jenoff pulled himself together and continued. After he struck Carol, he said, "she started to stumble. I heard the words, 'Why? Why?'" Ignoring the plea, he had left the house and waited outside while Daniels finished the job. "I heard thumps," Jenoff said. "It seemed like forever." Then Daniels came to the front door and surprised Jenoff by saying he had to make sure Carol was dead. Jenoff walked into the living room. Afraid to touch Carol, he bent over her and heard "a noise. It was like a gurgling, a regurgitation, a hissing." It was the sound of blood pouring out of Carol's head.

Jenoff said that on one condolence call that he made to the Neulanders, the rabbi slipped him a manila envelope stuffed with about $7,000 in cash. Later, they had agreed to launder the balance that was due to Jenoff by having him bill the rabbi's lawyers for phony investigative work. But Neulander's attorneys eventually fired Jenoff when they chose their own investigator. After that, he received two personal checks from Neulander totaling $935, and in 1997, the rabbi paid him another $200. According to Jenoff, Neulander still owed more than $12,000 for the contract hit.

Jenoff was tailor-made for a cross-examination, and Wixted made the most of it. "When you lie, does your nose grow?" the defense attorney inquired. "How can anyone tell if you're lying or telling the truth? No jury can tell when you're telling the truth or lying because you do both the same way." For the two days that Wixted grilled Jenoff, he returned to those lies again and again. Didn't he lie to the grand jury? "I tried to answer the questions," Jenoff hedged, "so I would not be arrested." Didn't he use mob movies to "embellish" his life, like adopting "Deuce," a name he heard in a gangster film, as a nickname for himself and Daniels? "That could have happened," Jenoff admitted. What about those bills totaling almost $2,500 that Jenoff sent Wixted's firm for investigating the Neulander case? "The whole thing was a sham, Mr. Wixted," Jenoff responded, as if talking to the lawyer over a business lunch. "Your client was paying me cash for killing his wife . . . He gave me $18,000 total. If I submitted a bill to you . . . for the balance, you would have wondered what the hell it was for." And then there was his résumé—a pack of lies? "I got the whole world to believe it," answered Jenoff, almost proud that he'd pulled the wool over everyone's eyes.

Wixted had gotten Jenoff to retract just about every story he had ever told in his life—except his involvement with Carol's murder. Cynics might ascribe such narrow determination to Jenoff's singular talents as a liar: he intuitively knew that to make that one story credible, he had to stick with it, even if that meant divesting himself of all the other crazy tales he'd told over the years. One lawyer who'd watched Wixted square off against Jenoff was impressed—with Jenoff. "Dennis never rattled Jenoff," the lawyer commented shortly after Jenoff stepped down from the stand. "Let's face it. At this point, the defense doesn't have much to work with. As of now, there's a very credible case against the rabbi. Everyone in this room believes Jenoff killed Carol. What they have to do is make the leap from Jenoff to Neulander."

Paul Michael Daniels testified on the last day of the prosecution's case. Pale, thin, barely monosyllabic from his antipsychotic medications, Daniels said he'd only had to think "a minute or two" when Jenoff asked him to help with the murder. On November 1, 1994, he "smacked" Carol twice in the head, then "ran out of the house." During cross-examination, Wixted asked if he personally knew whether Neulander had anything to do with the murder. No, Daniels said, then he remembered that when he'd attended Carol's funeral at the temple, "the rabbi came up to me and asked if I was OK."

"You took that to mean he was involved?" Wixted asked.

"Yes," said Daniels. "I think that's what he was trying to tell me."

Wixted would regret asking that last question.

While the prosecution rested, the defense stepped up and presented a case that was swift and almost surgical in its precision—witness after witness in quick succession. Jenoff and Daniels' roommate from 1994, who never saw any signs that they had come into a windfall; *Inquirer* reporter Nancy Phillips, who read excerpts from articles she'd written based on conversations with Jenoff that contradicted some minor details in his testimony; two jailhouse snitches, one claiming that Jenoff told him Phillips had promised him a "lifetime of sex" and a Pulitzer Prize for implicating Neulander, the other alleging that Jenoff bragged that he'd framed the rabbi; and finally, of course, Fred Neulander himself. Dressed like a cleric—dark pinstripe suit, white shirt, red-and-green patterned tie—he sounded like one as well, confident, articulate, sincere, humble. At first.

Neulander was barely seated in the witness box when Wixted asked if he'd had his wife killed. "I'm innocent," Neulander emphatically declared. But he didn't deny his affairs: "I betrayed my community, my synagogue, my family. I betrayed my profession . . . I was selfish and arrogant." But it was a selfishness, he said, born from a need: he and Carol were no longer intimate. They'd agreed to an open marriage. Yet with all his amorous activities, he never considered divorcing Carol, he said. As he explained, there was no need to. "The situation with Carol was stable."

On the stand that day, Neulander played many roles: grieving widower, contrite philanderer, innocent victim, and even preacher, looking at jurors occasionally to explain Jewish holidays and traditions. At one point, asked why he'd opened his house to Jenoff in 1997 for a marriage ceremony, he recited a parable that illustrated why Jews avoid succumbing to the gloom of death. Great sages, Neulander said, tell about a funeral and a wedding procession approaching an intersection at the same time. Who goes first? Neulander asked, then proceeded to deliver a sermon, almost like he was on the *bima*. Common thinkers, Neulander said, humbly noting that he was among them, would let the funeral cortege go first out of respect to the dead and concern for the mourners. But the sages—the uncommon thinkers—taught that the wedding procession goes first: it represents life and hope and "the attempt to find meaning when it's very hard to find meaning, especially in a death that's tragic."

Judaism, continued Neulander, instructed him to choose life; that's why he offered his house for Jenoff's wedding. Judaism "knows we are all going to experience death and grief and sorrow and pain," but if we grieve too much "death wins . . . and there's another death—not physical, but psychological or spiritual."

It was a good sermon and it proved why he had been such an effective rabbi: he was precise, pedantic, poised. In the afternoon, within minutes after Lynch started cross-examining him, he was a different person—barely audible, rarely capable of completing a sentence, constantly faltering when trying to keep pace with Lynch, who was famous for shredding witnesses under intense questioning. Why had he lied to police about his affairs the night Carol was killed? "I was humiliated," Neulander answered. "Humiliated and embarrassed."

"Your personal interests were more important to you than solving the murder of your wife?" Lynch asked.

Neulander was silent for almost a minute. "Yes," he finally answered.

The rabbi kept stammering and contradicting himself. He called Peppy Levin a "semi-friend," then admitted he'd invited him to his daughter's wedding. He denied he'd told Soncini that she was "the most wonderful thing that ever came into my life," then was made to listen to a tape from Soncini's answering machine on which he'd used those very words. Still, he insisted that he never loved her, then squirmed while Lynch read a romantic poem Neulander wrote to Elaine two months after Carol's murder. "I guess I loved her at the time," Neulander admitted.

"Did you love her?" Lynch continued to press the point the next day.

"I can't say," said Neulander this time, hedging. Then he paused. "Yes, you can say I didn't love her."

The denial caught Lynch as he was pacing away from Neulander. Wheeling toward the rabbi, Lynch shouted, "You weren't lying to this jury yesterday, were you, sir?"

"I gave the wrong impression," Neulander admitted. "I used the wrong words."

"Well, you said something a hundred and eighty degrees different than what you're saying right now, didn't you? It's totally and completely different, isn't it, sir?"

"I had feelings for her," persisted Neulander.

"Sir, excuse me," Lynch said sarcastically. "Do you recall my question?"

"Yes. And I don't know what a hundred and eighty degrees means."

"Well, a hundred and eighty degrees—I'll explain it to you, sir. If I'm going in one direction and I turn around and go in the opposite direction, some people refer to that as a hundred-and-eighty-degree turn. Do you understand now?"

"I did not love her," he said.

Lynch, realizing the opportunity Neulander's admission gave him, asked several times if phrases Neulander had used in letters to Soncini—"I will pay any price, wait any time, to keep my promise," "I need you to know that I will not, because I cannot, love another"—were "lies and misrepresentations." Each time, Neulander said, "I simply wanted to continue the relationship." Lynch finally asked the judge to direct Neulander to answer his questions.

"I don't know how to answer other than how I did," Neulander argued with Judge Baxter. "I wasn't—"

"The answer that the question calls for," explained Baxter, "is 'Yes, Mr. Lynch, you're correct' or 'No, Mr. Lynch, you're not.'"

With that admonishment, Neulander quietly admitted, "Yes, they were lies."

The Fred Neulander who left the witness stand was chastened and tired, a shell of the man who'd walked into the stand the day before. Spectators and family who'd watched Neulander were astounded. Everyone had expected Jenoff to psychologically collapse on the stand; instead, it was Neulander, the brilliant man full of charm and charisma. One quality now united both the rabbi and the hit man: they were now admitted liars.

The closing arguments were emotional—and brutal. Dennis Wixted, the rabbi's own lawyer, called him "disgusting," "despicable," "a hollow man . . . who looks shiny and bright from the outside, but when you open him up and look inside, there's nothing of substance there—no honor, no decency. My only appeal to you is to challenge not that Fred Neulander . . . was a miserable little piece of dung as a human being, but that he did not set up the killing." Wixted underlined that there was no physical evidence, no paper trail, just the word of Leonard Jenoff, an accomplished liar.

The prosecution had the last word. Lynch reminded jurors of the synagogue staff who had observed Neulander at M'kor Shalom on a Tuesday night, an evening when he was rarely there. His presence at the temple that night was Neulander's alibi, and it worked for a while. But his true character was revealed by the company he kept, people like Leonard Jenoff and Peppy Levin, who were most unsavory. And by the selfishness that animated him. "In this man's mind," Lynch shouted, "the sun, the moon, and the stars have to revolve around him. Nobody else's life is important . . . except his own . . . He not only failed the fundamental test of human decency; he failed the human test. You don't take the life of another person."

Three hours after the jury left the courtroom to deliberate, the forewoman sent a note to Judge Baxter: What if they couldn't reach a unanimous decision? The question was "premature," Baxter said, noting the complexity of the case and the forty witnesses and sixty exhibits that jurors had to properly consider. "Keep deliberating," she ordered.

The jury did just that. While waiting for a decision, Matthew Neulander called his father from his home in North Carolina. He'd watched Neulander's testimony on Court TV and was furious at the lies he'd heard. Over the phone, Matthew went down his list: his father's claim about Carol agreeing to an open marriage, his denial that he'd given Matthew a list of lawyers to choose from, his portrayal of his relationships with Peppy Levin and Len Jenoff as something other than close friendships. To each question, Neulander quietly said, "I don't remember it that way" or "Who made you the ultimate arbiter of truth?" Fred Neulander did not retract a single statement he'd made on the stand. At that moment, Matthew was certain his father had killed his mother.

On the fifth day of deliberations, jurors asked to hear readbacks of testimony from several witnesses, including Jenoff and Matthew Neulander. That afternoon, they told Judge Baxter they'd reached a "complete standstill." Soon they sent another note: they were deliberating again. Finally, after a total of forty-four hours, the jury concluded that they would never get a unanimous vote. They'd had three ballots, and each put them closer to a hung jury: 11–1, 10–2, 9–3. Baxter declared a mistrial, and Neulander, who had been stoic for nearly the entire trial, broke into an elated grin.

Fighting back tears, Carol's brother Robert told reporters that Neulander would now "sit alone with his arrogance and wonder whether there are twelve other people somewhere who will fail to recognize the truth." Lee Solomon, the county prosecutor, immediately announced plans to retry the rabbi. Lynch, who had executed that searing cross-examination of Neulander, was too tired and dispirited to relish a retrial; he'd been working on the case for five and a half years. For him, the hardest part of the mistrial was "explaining to Carol's family that we're going to start from scratch. The emotional investment was immense." Then he saw a picture in the paper of Neulander "grinning from ear to ear, like he had won the state lottery. After I saw that, I was energized. I was ready to start picking another jury that afternoon."

26

"How Many Are the Days of the Years of Your Life?"

After the media circus at the previous trial one year earlier, the retrial was moved to where it might be easier to seat a jury—fifty-five miles to the north in the town of Freehold. This was the anti-Camden: small, bucolic, pastoral, affluent. Freehold had a population of just thirty-one thousand, fifty thousand fewer than Camden's, but a median income of seventy thousand dollars, three times that of the larger city's. This was clearly a different universe. Freehold's streets were lined with so many Victorian homes that *Meet Me in St. Louis* could have been filmed there. Patrons in the small cafés along Main Street kept their eyes out for Bruce Springsteen, who lived nearby. Bruce sightings weren't common, and when people did spot The Boss, they tried not to squeal like teenagers. Springsteen appreciated that and donated a fire engine to Freehold, not only because this was his hometown but also as a thank-you gift for treating him like a regular guy.

Beyond the change in venue, there had also been a change in legal representation: Neulander had a new lawyer. Zucker and Wixted bowed out after the first trial, claiming that they'd underestimated the flat fee they'd charged Neulander and that, after representing him for seven years, they'd actually lost money on the case—and he couldn't afford them now. Mike Riley, the rabbi's new attorney, was tall and slim, more revealing about himself in private than Zucker or Wixted and less dramatic in courtrooms. While Zucker and Wixted had been the right guys for a Camden jury— they got Neulander a hung jury, the next best thing to an acquittal—Riley's demeanor could be more effective with a Freehold jury, a more straitlaced, conservative town. But almost regardless of the verdict, Riley could benefit from representing Neulander. He'd been in private practice for only three years after serving as a tough prosecutor for almost two decades, and this was the case of a lifetime. Already, every TV network in the country was knocking on his door for interviews, some promising that he'd be sitting down with the best correspondents money could buy.

Riley's strategy was simple: at some point during this whole saga, "just about everyone's been lying, even Fred, who originally saw no connection between his affairs and the police thinking he was a suspect." Over the years, most key witnesses had changed their stories: Peppy Levin, when detectives threatened to indict him; Elaine Soncini, when she panicked after lying to the police about her affair with Neulander; and especially Leonard Jenoff, who, Riley asked, "never hurt anyone in his life and now this? People don't change this drastically so late in their life." Despite being able to bolster his defense by pointing to so many discrepancies in the testimonies, Riley still worried about the chances of winning Neulander an acquittal. "I wake up at three o'clock in the morning, wondering whether I'm adequate to save this man's life."

To prepare for the retrial, prosecutors had been trying to step back and reassess their strategy at the first trial, ready to revamp it if necessary. "The temptation," Lynch said, "is always to take a case back to the drawing board and change everything." But this time, they weren't ready to make a complete overhaul; they were convinced that the evidence was sufficiently damning to Neulander.

Despite the change in venue, Neulander still drew plenty of attention from the press. A week before the trial, the *Philadelphia Inquirer* ran an article about the rabbi's new girlfriend—Victoria Lombardi. "Ms. Vicki," as she was best known, had experienced much media scrutiny before she became associated with Fred. In 1969, 45 million people watched Lombardi marry the ukulele-playing falsetto Tiny Tim on *The Tonight Show*, wondering if this sweet looking seventeen-year-old knew what she was doing. Eight years later, she divorced, moved back home to South Jersey, worked intermittently as a go-go dancer, a model, and the proprietor of a New Age gift shop. Yet she continued to be known as Ms. Vicki, if only behind her back. As early as 1998, Neulander's neighbors had noticed a slender woman who appeared several years younger than the rabbi visiting him often at home; they eventually recognized her as the legendary Ms. Vicki. Now the *Philadelphia Inquirer* was exposing the romance between the divorcée and the rabbi. They'd met in 1998, either at a cocktail party or through a relative of hers. He courted her, sending flowers. They dated. She believed he was innocent. After his bail was revoked, his mail was forwarded to her house—and she drove around in the Toyota Camry that had been Carol's. ("It's a car," she exasperatedly explained after Neulander's trial. "It's not like I'm wearing her nightgown.") While there was nothing inherently wrong with two people of consenting age dating, his choice of Ms. Vicki said as much about her as it did about him.

Then, on the very eve of the trial, the UPN cable channel aired a three-year-old episode of *The Practice*. The timing couldn't have been coincidental. The episode, titled "Do Unto Others," was about a rabbi in New England tried for allegedly raping a black woman. The TV rabbi was an enormously popular figure in his fictional community, and after he had become obsessed with the black woman, his temple had offered her $1.2 million to drop charges against him. When first broadcast, the Anti-Defamation League protested that the show perpetuated the stereotype that Jews placed a higher premium on money than truth. But a New York rabbi had a different opinion. "A rabbi on trial for rape?" asked Jonathan Pearl. "How absurd or offensive is that when a rabbi in New Jersey is the prime suspect in the murder of his wife?"

Most of the thirty or so prosecution witnesses had testified at the first trial. Among them were cops who investigated the murder scene, all of whom Riley tried to portray as bumblers; Rebecca Neulander, whom Riley barely questioned, afraid a tough interrogation would produce a backlash of sympathy for her; and Peppy Levin, more dapper and less mentally confused than he was a year before.

But the trial was more than a repeat of the previous year's. Lynch had managed to find a handful of new witnesses to strengthen his case. Five members of M'kor Shalom testified for the first time, all of them doing their former rabbi no good. Beverly Weiss said she had been intrigued by a strange man who had been with Fred on both of her *shiva* calls to the Neulander house. The two of them had been absorbed in a very quiet, very private conversation. She later realized it was Leonard Jenoff. Therefore, she had been surprised at the first trial when Neulander stated that he barely knew the man. Weiss had more to tell the jury. A few months after the murder, she said, Neulander invited her to his house for tea. He knew that she was close to Soncini and that Elaine had already confided in her about their affair. Midway through their conversation, Neulander asked Weiss to assure Soncini that other than Carol, he hadn't been sleeping with anyone else while seeing her, an awkward request from anyone whose wife had just been killed, and—as Soncini already knew, thanks to the police—an outright lie, since Neulander's affair with Rachel Stone overlapped the one he'd been keeping up with Elaine.

Another congregant who testified was Sheila Goodman, the temple's president at the time Carol was killed. When Goodman raced to the Neulander's house around eleven that night, she cried out "Why?" as soon as she found the rabbi. Almost matter-of-factly, he blamed the murder on immigrants who worked at Carol's bakery. "Those Colombians," she remembered him muttering. "They'll rob you for a nickel." Then he added, "You know, Carol didn't suffer. She died with one blow." Goodman did not ask Neulander how he knew that.

The most devastating new testimony came from Elaine Soncini and Matthew Neulander. Once again, Soncini was the most elegant witness of the trial: every hair in place and an ensemble straight out of *Vogue*: a navy blue pantsuit with gold buttons on the sleeves and a scarlet handkerchief in the left breast pocket. Immaculately parsing every sentence, precisely enunciating every syllable, she could have been emceeing her old radio show, but for some tears and a growing impatience with Riley's tenacity during cross-examination. Mostly, she reiterated what she'd said at the first trial, except for one new detail. In the spring of 1994, she said, Israel's new counsel general in Philadelphia called, asking to discuss WPEN's coverage of Israel. As the station's news director, she was the person who oversaw reporting about the Middle East and she agreed to meet the envoy for lunch. She invited Neulander, thinking he might ask the Israeli to speak at the temple. The lunch went well, with the two men pleasantly chatting away in Hebrew. Neulander didn't mention the Israeli again until September, when Soncini told him about a strange man she'd met at a dinner party the previous night who'd claimed he was an antiterrorist agent. "Sure, that's Len Jenoff," said Neulander, who'd also attended the

party. "I've been talking with the counsel general about him, trying to get him a job with the Israelis." The story corroborated
Jenoff's account that, as a reward for killing Carol, Neulander was
trying to get him a job with the Israeli government, particularly
with the Mossad, the Israeli spy agency.

Factually, Matthew Neulander's testimony was identical to the
previous trial's. It was his emotion—raw and explosive—that gave
it new power. He'd come to Freehold determined that this time
justice be done, unlike last time. Ever since deciding that his father
was guilty, twelve months earlier, he'd been bottling up an enormous amount of anger. His forty-five minutes on the stand gave
him an opportunity to vent the rage he'd been feeling toward his
father, whom he called "a piece of shit of unimaginable propor-
tion" in an e-mail to a friend. An almost perfunctory question was
sufficient to send him on a tear. His mother was "wonderful,"
"funny," "great," "terrific," "loving," "caring." His father was shifty:
in 1995, Matthew remembered Neulander telling him he'd had
one "meaningless indiscretion," then reversing himself a few days
later, saying he'd cherished the affair and he'd had others. His father
was cold: as Matthew scrubbed Carol's blood off the couch in the
living room, he asked Neulander what thoughts raced through his
head when he'd found her battered body the night before. Neulander said he'd been "too repulsed," "too scared," "too sick" by the
sight to help Carol. "That's strange," Matthew muttered, incredu-
lous that his father—that *anyone*—wouldn't have tried to comfort
Carol, no matter how horrible she looked. After telling the court
about that exchange, Matthew stared directly at Neulander on the
far side of the well. Looking like he was ready to leap out of his
seat and thrash his father, Matthew cried out, "I would give my
right arm to hold my mother's hand and let her know I was there."

Everyone in the courtroom winced; some cried. Even Marty
Devlin, the detective who believed he was thoroughly "hardened"
after solving dozens of murders, teared up. Mike Riley, Neulander's

lawyer, shifted uncomfortably in his seat and thought, "Matthew's a loose cannon up there. He obviously has it in for his father." It was also obvious that Matthew didn't recognize Neulander as his father anymore, never calling him "Dad," always "Fred." If even a shred of the father-son relationship had been intact before Matthew's testimony, nothing remained when he was finished.

The coup de grâce came with Jim Lynch's last two questions to Neulander's son. "Over the course of your medical career, how many people have you dealt with who suffered a traumatic loss?"

"Hundreds."

"How many reacted as your father did?"

"None."

With that, Matthew was dismissed. It was one of the best testimonies Lynch had ever heard from a prosecution witness, and such a bad day for the rabbi that a TV technician cracked, "Fred'll soon be swimming with the gefilte fishes."

It had been such a dismal week and a half for Neulander that when Judge Baxter announced at the end of the proceedings on Tuesday, October 29, that the trial wouldn't resume for another day or two because of "legal matters," more than trial-goers speculated that Neulander might change his plea. But, in fact, without the jury present, the lawyers were arguing whether Riley could ask Jenoff about possible involvement with another unsolved murder in South Jersey. Janice Bell had been fatally stabbed in her home in Voorhees, a few miles from Cherry Hill, about thirteen months after the Neulander murder. The similarities between the Bell and Neulander killings were chilling: both women were found lying in a pool of blood in their own homes, the husbands of both women quickly emerged as suspects, and Jenoff was on the sidelines of the investigations for both killings—in 1994, Neulander hired him to "solve" his wife's murder; in 1996, at a hearing for the Bell case, Jenoff introduced himself to her family as an available private eye, an offer they accepted a few months later. Just as Jenoff had for Neulander, he arranged for the Bell family to meet with a psychic in hopes of catching the killer. Now Riley was telling the court that a prisoner claimed Jenoff had told him that he'd killed Bell. Riley wanted permission to grill Jenoff about the Bell case. Lynch, in turn, argued that discussing the Bell murder would turn Neulander's trial into a trial within a trial—one to determine if the rabbi killed his wife, another to determine if Leonard Jenoff killed Janice Bell. It would also put the prosecutor in the awkward position of defending Jenoff in one case and prosecuting Neulander in another case.

The next day, Judge Baxter ruled that Jenoff could only be asked if he'd ever talked with the prisoner, David Beardsley, about the Bell case. Questioning beyond that would only confuse the jury. This was no great victory for the defense, but at least Riley had slowed down Lynch's blitzkrieg. For ten days, the prosecutor had set the pace, casting Neulander as a liar, a creep, a murderer, and making jurors visibly upset or angry. As successful prosecutors do, Lynch had managed to get the jury emotionally invested in his case. But he might now have to work extra hard to get them as mad as they'd been before Riley's motions put everything on hold.

Four days later, Leonard Jenoff took the stand; he would be there for the next two days—sixteen hours in all. As before, it was embarrassing, humiliating, degrading: he had to renounce almost everything he'd said in his life, except for the events leading up to Carol's murder. Lawyers from both sides grilled him even more savagely than back in Camden. When Jenoff said, as he had at the first trial, that blood pouring out of Carol's head made a "hissing sound," Lynch was prepared, and whipped out a twenty-by-sixteen-inch color photo of Carol lying in an immense pool of blood. "Is that how she looked?" Lynch yelled. Jenoff turned away. Burying his face in his chest, he began crying. *"Is that how she looked?"* Lynch yelled again. "Yes, sir," Jenoff managed to say.

The photo, the most gruesome exhibit of the entire trial, disturbed one juror so much that he couldn't stop swiveling in his chair the rest of the day; another juror who was related by marriage to Holocaust survivors kept wiping her nose with the cuffs of her oversized sweater. Every trial has a moment, an epiphany when things begin to cohere, and this photograph and Matthew's anguished plea to have been able to help his mother were it. Nothing put jurors into the Neulanders' living room on the first two days in November 1994 as emphatically, and as horribly. Months later, some jurors still hadn't gotten that image or Matthew's words out of their heads, and they never expected that they would.

Mike Riley had to somehow defuse the tremendous impact that Matthew had made on the court; his strategy was to turn Jenoff into a joke—a man so unreliable that the jury would be more likely to laugh at his lies than believe a single word he spoke. The best opportunity to do that lay with Jenoff's résumé, which Riley picked apart—lie by lie and fantasy by fantasy. Jenoff didn't really testify before the Senate Select Committee on Intelligence, did he? Or the President's Commission on Organized Crime? Or train at the FBI's national academy in Quantico, Virginia? He hadn't even graduated from Monmouth University, as the résumé claimed, had he? Jenoff admitted that all of these were falsehoods, and Riley kept hammering away at him, falling into a rhythm, sliding back and forth between Jenoff's fabrications on his résumé and his stories about Neulander, hoping to rattle him and get him lost in the thicket of his lies.

Surprisingly, Jenoff sometimes gave as good as he got, just as he had at the first trial. Why, asked Riley, should anyone accept his word that he and Neulander had discussed killing Carol if no one else had heard these conversations? "When you're talking about a murder," answered Jenoff, "you don't invite a lot of people." Pressing on in his efforts to prove Jenoff was entirely unreliable, Riley questioned: Hadn't he told the grand jury he planned to show Mossad recruiters a photo of himself, dressed up like an Arab, posing with the Smothers Brothers at a casino in Atlantic City so that they would know he'd make a fine undercover agent? "I was joking," insisted Jenoff. Hadn't he betrayed his friends who'd signed his application to be a private investigator, friends who'd given him jobs, loaned him money, sobered him up when he was drunk? "No," shrugged Jenoff, "not at the time." And didn't Jenoff take real people and real places and invent stories about them? Didn't his lies become his reality? "No, no, no," Jenoff protested. "I always knew the truth." Riley wanted jurors to conclude that Jenoff would betray anyone—his good friends, even a rabbi who'd counseled and aided him—to get some kind of purchase on life, an endeavor at which he'd been notoriously unsuccessful.

Riley did his job, and he did it well; in the end, the jurors couldn't stomach Jenoff. "A lost soul who would cling to anyone who might elevate his feelings of self-respect," said one juror after the trial. "A jerk, a piece of shit," chided another. "His whole life was a big lie." Yet the one puzzle that gnawed at everyone was why Jenoff would possibly confess to killing Carol if he hadn't done it. His confession went against the pattern of his lies, a pattern that had been established since he was a kid: he used lying to make himself look better than he was, better than he could ever be. Lynch honed in on this discrepancy and raised a question that made an indelible impression on the jury: in April 2000 when Jenoff confessed, he was sober, happily married, and earning, at last, some decent money. It had taken him too long to get to that point; why would he risk losing it? To most jurors, the answer was simple: Jenoff came forward and confessed not so he would be a hero, the guy who brought Fred Neulander to justice, but to acquire some measure of peace, to somehow get the horror of what he'd done off his back. Confession was a cleansing, an expiation.

The prosecution was almost ready to rest. But first, portions of

Neulander's testimony from the first trial were entered into the record. Lynch and his team had agonized over the best way to do this, eventually vetoing playing video excerpts of the testimony because these might be too distracting: Lynch wanted jurors to focus on the content of Neulander's answers. So for ninety minutes Lynch read certain questions he'd asked Neulander, and a fellow prosecutor, sitting in the witness box, read the rabbi's answers. A clever tactic, this put the rabbi between a rock and a hard place. If Neulander took the stand, he would essentially testify against himself. If he chose not to testify, jurors still got to hear his most troubling testimony from the previous year: he never went to Carol's aid—"I knew not what to do." He had sex with Soncini several times after the murder. He told her to lie to investigators. He loved her; he didn't love her. State law precluded Riley from rebutting anything that was being read into the record from the first trial. With that, Jim Lynch rested.

On the thirteenth day of the trial, with his lawyer standing next to him, Neulander almost whispered, "I will not be taking the stand." He could barely be heard two rows away. Every lawyer wants his client to look jurors in the eye and swear that he's innocent; that's a basic principle of Criminal Law 101. But Neulander was scared that he'd do as poorly as he had at the first trial, maybe even worse, especially since Lynch had been prepping for a whole year to go up against him again.

Without Neulander testifying, Riley worked with what he had, which wasn't much. One witness said she had run into Jenoff at Weight Watchers a few weeks before he confessed; he said he was trimming down for some upcoming appearances on television—a sign, Riley suggested, that Jenoff was a publicity hound (and a vain one). Three inmates Riley called to the stand had encountered Jenoff in prison and claimed he'd told them that the murder started out as a robbery and Neulander had nothing to do with it. One of these inmates was David Beardsley, whose accusations against Jenoff had already assisted the defense by allowing them to stall the proceedings and argue that testimony about the Janice Bell murder be allowed into the trial. Baxter's ruling that Bell-related questions had to skirt the specifics of the case reduced Riley to this general exchange with Beardsley:

"Did Jenoff ever tell you he was involved in another murder?"

"Yes."

"Did he tell you it was a woman?"

"Yes."

That was about as inconclusive as any questioning of the entire trial. It certainly did nothing to plant suspicions that Jenoff had more homicidal tendencies than he admitted and that these may have led him to kill Carol Neulander without her husband inciting him.

As the day was ending, Lynch was getting furious that he wouldn't have another round with Neulander. He displaced his anger on the last of the defense witnesses—yelling at them or slamming down papers directly in front of them. His ire reached its peak when probing James "Mickey" Rooney, a friend of Jenoff's from AA, about his efforts to garner publicity from the Neulander tragedy. "How many times have you been on Court TV because of this case?" Lynch shouted.

"Three or four times," answered Rooney.

"You weren't involved with the murder of Mrs. Neulander," persisted Lynch, turning his attention to Rooney's offer to help Jenoff get a book or film deal. "You just wanted to make money from the murder of Mrs. Neulander. God forbid you wouldn't get your share."

"Yes," agreed Rooney. "I wanted that money as bad as you want the rabbi."

With that, Lynch lost it, bellowing right into Rooney's face, "You don't know me. You don't know anything about me." The jury was stunned. For four weeks, they'd admired Lynch and Riley, each lawyer quick and swift, clever and ethical. And now Lynch was having a temper tantrum just a few feet in front of them. Some jurors blamed it on the strain of the trial; others on Lynch's frustration with the rabbi. Yet one juror thought the shouting worked to Lynch's advantage. "Rooney was a sleazy character," the juror later explained. "He was in it just for the money. When Rooney questioned Lynch's motives and character, Lynch lashed out, just like I would have. It showed that Lynch was a real person, just like all the rest of us."

Seconds after Lynch's outburst, Rooney was dismissed. Closing arguments would be presented the next morning. Neulander returned to his cell, exhausted yet relieved. After what Lynch did to Rooney, he knew the prosecutor would have eviscerated him had he testified.

The next day, Riley reduced the prosecution's case to "emotion and passion." He argued that the state wanted jurors to dislike Neulander; the greater their contempt, the easier it would be to convict him. Neulander was "flawed," but his infidelities "did not translate into murder." Some witnesses, Riley pointed out, were almost as flawed as the rabbi, and testimony from them was illogical. Riley focused on Soncini's statement that Neulander wouldn't divorce Carol because his kids were fragile. If this was accurate, why, Riley asked the jurors, would the rabbi murder their mother: "Was it easier to have her murdered than divorce her?" And if Neulander was so concerned about his children's well-being, why expose his daughter to Jenoff—"this monster"—and let her hug him at the wedding held at the Neulander home? Lastly, Riley asked for *proof.*

Pacing directly in front of the jury, Lynch provided the proof that Riley had requested. He displayed four-by-three-foot charts delineating how witnesses corroborated Jenoff's testimony and contradicted Neulander's. Lynch was more sarcastic than Riley, ridiculing the idea that Carol's murder started out as a random robbery: "Eenny, meeny / miney, moe / I'll steal this house / Ho, ho, ho!"; mocking Neulander's theory about the murderer: "Does 'drug-crazed psychopath' describe anyone in this case? Was he thinking of Paul Michael Daniels? What a remarkable coincidence!"; pondering why Neulander told Carol's sister the case would never be solved: "Was that a prediction, ladies and gentlemen? Or was that a wish?"; reserving his greatest scorn for Neulander: "Let's be realistic about Fred Neulander! He *is* a cut above. He's *Rabbi Neulander!* He puts on a suit and tie after having pizza with his son, goes to temple to visit some classes, and he's above suspicion the night his wife is killed. He's *Rabbi Neulander.*"

Riley had *almost* persuaded a couple of jurors that Neulander was innocent; now Lynch undid the defense lawyer's handiwork. Lynch's two-hour closing left most jurors certain that this rabbi was lying about his role in the murder, ignoring a key passage from Isaiah, "I will go before thee and make the crooked places straight."

At 10:45 A.M. on November 15, the jury—seven men and five women—retired to a small antechamber just off the courtroom. Four hours later, they emerged to hear Rebecca Neulander's testimony read back to them. The prosecution was buoyed. Rebecca was essential to their case: her knowledge of what transpired between her mother and the "bathroom man" on two consecutive Tuesdays made her the only other person besides Paul Michael Daniels who, in any way, could corroborate Jenoff's story about "delivering" a letter to the Neulanders'. And highly medicated, ex-junkie, paranoid schizophrenics weren't the most reliable people.

The jury recessed for the weekend. On Monday, when it voted for the first time, some jurors were squeamish about using the words "guilty" or "innocent," so they all agreed to substitute "yes," "no," or "maybe" on their ballots. Nine voted "yes," three voted "maybe." No one voted "no." On Tuesday, they voted again: eleven "yes," one "maybe." Neulander's lifeline was getting thinner. By Wednesday, some jurors were beginning to fear there might be a mistrial. To help the one holdout reach a decision, they reviewed everything that might contribute to "reasonable doubt," then rebutted it, point by point. "It was obvious Fred was guilty," a juror later said. "Take your pick—Jenoff, Daniels, Soncini, the fight with Carol two nights before the murder. It was overwhelming!" When they asked the holdout what else was needed to reach a decision, they only got a mumbled "I'm still not sure," and a request to ease up on the pressure. "Too bad," one juror remembered saying. "From now on, there are no more fucking 'yeses' and no more fucking 'noes' and no more fucking 'maybes.' We vote 'guilty' or 'not guilty.' If we don't agree, we tell the judge."

The jury took its last vote and, at 3:30 P.M., filed into the courtroom. Two of the younger women on the jury were holding hands. No one looked at the rabbi. Neulander stood up to receive the verdict. The forewoman read:

"Guilty to capital murder."

"Guilty to felony murder."

"Guilty to conspiracy."

Neulander sat down, removed his glasses, and looked vacantly into space. A few rows back and on the opposite side of the courtroom, Carol's family sat, dazed, then rose in silent tribute to the jurors. It had taken a few minutes for the decision to sink in: eight years is a long time for justice to be reached.

Up in New York City, a woman in her mid-fifties nodded her head as she watched the verdict being read on Court TV. On November 2, 1994, she'd turned on her radio and heard that the wife of a prominent rabbi in South Jersey had been killed the night before. She'd rarely heard the name Neulander since dating Fred at Jamaica High back in Queens, but she immediately called her son, who lived in Baltimore.

"Fred did it," she told him.

"Look, Mom," he said, trying to calm her down, "you haven't seen this guy in years. His wife was just killed yesterday and there's *no* evidence that he did it. What are you talking about?"

"Listen to me," she insisted. "I *know* Fred. I *know* his character. He will do anything to get ahead. I *know* he killed her."

This woman had broken up with Neulander because she'd detected something rotten in him, something unprincipled and opportunistic. Apparently, she figured, Fred hadn't changed much over the years.

When the court reconvened the next day to determine Neulander's sentence, it was as if all the air had been sucked out of the room: a man might be sentenced to death here. Four witnesses spoke on behalf of Neulander—his son Benjamin recalled how his father had sent him "down a good and strong path," and how he'd created "something out of nothing" at M'kor Shalom; two congregants recalled Neulander helping thousands of people; Neulander's former assistant rabbi, Gary Mazo, begged that compassion and holiness, the holiness of life, prevail. Judaism, said Mazo, deems nothing more sacred than human life. Mazo also had a more personal reason for asking that Neulander be spared: he'd seen in him "that spark of God that is now buried somewhere very deep inside of him." Mazo pleaded that jurors help Neulander "reclaim that spark."

Then it was Neulander's turn. For a month, he'd sat implacably, rarely reacting to witnesses' testimony. Other than one whispered sentence telling the judge that he wouldn't testify, this would be the first time he would speak. No one knew what to expect.

Neulander sat down in the witness stand, adjusted the microphone, smiled at the jury, and greeted them with "Good morning, ladies and gentlemen." None of the jurors knew what to do. Should they smile, too? Should they wish him a good morning? They were silent. "Good morning," Neulander repeated, more firmly than before. He was treating them like bashful students at Hebrew school. A few jurors mumbled, "Good morning." Neulander looked pleased.

"I am here," he said, "to offer a plea for my life." Then he launched into a teaching about the first meeting in ancient Egypt between Pharaoh and Jacob. Instead of asking the patriarch his age, Pharaoh inquired, "How many are the days of the years of your life?" *This* was how Neulander wanted to be judged: how had he spent "the days of my life"? Had he made a difference in the world? Before November 1994, Neulander told the court, he'd had "great blessings"—good friends, a fine career, and "my wife, Carol." Neulander's *chutzpah* jolted everyone: saying Carol's name to the people who'd convicted him for killing her was almost blasphemy. Then it got stranger.

Carol, said Neulander, was "remarkable," "bright," "funny," and endowed with "class." "When you were in the company of Carol Neulander," he said, "you knew you were in the company of a lady, and you behaved like that." The two of them had even perfected a little routine—an affectionate song-and-dance—about spending the rest of their lives together. One would say, "I want to grow old with you," and the other would respond, "I want to grow old with you, too. But let's do it slowly." Then, after a pause from Neulander came a confession (of sorts) to the jurors who would decide his fate: "I miss her and I loved her and I love her."

For a man whose brilliance and sermons were renowned, whose speeches invariably possessed perfect pitch and could move people to tears or laughter, Neulander sounded phenomenally oblivious to the gravity of the situation. He expressed no remorse, no contrition, no humility. Several former congregants who watched him on Court TV were disappointed: they'd heard his "days of the years of your life" sermon at least twice before. Even in this life-or-death appeal to the jury, Neulander was recycling old material, speaking more from his rabbinic posturing than from his heart.

Neulander's nerviness continued. If jurors let him live, he would teach prisoners how to read, help them earn their GEDs, encourage them to develop their artistic or musical talents. If that happened, Neulander told the jury, they, in turn, would have enriched *their* own lives by helping him change "the days of the years of the lives of so many men I have yet to meet." Interestingly, he never spoke about changing *his* life or attitudes, only about changing others'.

With that, Neulander left the witness box and sat next to his lawyer. Riley was vexed. Neulander had told him that he would develop a theme around the "days of your years," but the lawyer never anticipated that the rabbi would invoke Carol. "Can you believe that?" Riley thought. "He *loved* Carol? They wanted to grow old together? Half an hour ago, I was pretty sure he wouldn't get the death penalty. Now I don't know." Riley would have been more worried if he'd known how angry jurors were with Neulander. "How dare this murdering son of a bitch lecture to me?" a juror said a few weeks later. "How dare he 'importune' me to do anything for him? The man is a worthless carbon life-form."

The jury deliberated for almost two hours. No one tried to change anyone's mind: you don't twist arms when deciding whether to execute someone. There was no voice vote. Opening the written ballots, the first was marked "death." The second was marked "life." A death sentence has to be unanimous. The ballots were flushed down the toilet so that the exact tally would never be known.

After the forewoman announced that Neulander would spend the rest of his life in prison, a few jurors glanced toward Carol's siblings, who silently mouthed, "Thank you." With that, members of the jury knew they'd reached the right decision. But Matthew Neulander was not so generous. After Matthew heard his father's "galling," "maddening" allocution, his father's life meant nothing to him. Execute him or let him rot in prison—either choice was "ultimately acceptable" to Matthew.

Congregants at M'kor Shalom had been living under the shadow of Neulander's crime for almost a decade, so when several members saw a rainbow near the rabbi's house soon after his conviction, they interpreted it as a sign that their burden had been lifted. God had showed Noah a rainbow as a promise that there'd be no more floods. The congregants who saw the rainbow embraced it as a promise that the hell delivered to them by their former rabbi had finally ended.

Two months later, Neulander was formally sentenced. As usual, he tried to control the situation, asking to be excused so that he wouldn't have to listen to the victim impact statements. The judge refused. Then, one by one, Carol's siblings came forward. Her brothers, Ed and Robert, called Neulander the "basest form of humanity"—a "liar," a "coward," a "cheat," a "sociopath," a "disgrace." "Were it in your provenance, Your Honor," said Robert, "I would ask you to sentence him to anonymity so he could suffer his narcissism in silence." Carol's sister, Margaret, called him "a monster beyond human comprehension." Perhaps the harshest words came from his children Rebecca and Matthew. Their father—a "worthless, soulless, pathetic shell of a man"—would "never comprehend his egomaniacal and selfish acts." Matthew asked the judge to relegate him to be "an outcast and afterthought forever."

Then Neulander offered not a mea culpa, but contempt. He was impervious, invulnerable. Distinguishing between his "external" self and his internal self, he admitted that the outer Fred had been hurt and embarrassed by the verbal assaults of his children and relatives. He could be "assaulted," he could withstand "tyranny"—the tyranny of losing his family, of enduring the "pathological lying" of Leonard Jenoff, of suffering the slander of an overzealous prosecution. But he alone knew what no one else knew: he was innocent.

"I know in my heart and mind that the verdict is wrong," he stated. "I cannot express remorse for something I did not do. That place that is so private knows the truth. I, and only I, know that I am innocent."

With that, Neulander sat down. Judge Baxter immediately reprimanded him. "You received a fair trial," she said firmly.

It was a classic Neulander performance, harking back to his childhood when his father modeled a stolid, impenetrable machismo; to his decades of swaggering through sermons; to a lifetime of aspiring and achieving—the kid from Queens who always beat the odds. Spectators in the courtroom were disgusted by his arrogance, and the judge, now revealing herself for the first time after two long and difficult trials, said she was appalled at the rabbi's conduct leading up to Carol's murder, conduct "so cold to throw a shiver down the spine of any civilized person"—planning the murder for a night when Matthew would be driving an ambulance; seething, not being relieved, when Jenoff didn't kill Carol that first Tuesday; getting into bed with Carol every night even as these plans were being laid. Then she condemned Neulander to prison for the rest of his life. He would be eligible for parole when he was eighty-eight years old.

Leonard Jenoff and Paul Michael Daniels were sentenced two weeks later. Daniels apologized, blaming his participation on drugs. "It wasn't me," he said. "I was on the stuff." Almost in tears, Jenoff expressed his "loathing and pity" for Neulander, whom he had "worshiped" for several years. He apologized to Carol's siblings and children by name, knowing that he had "deprived Carol Neulander of a full and fruitful life . . . Regardless of what you sentence me to, your honor, for the rest of my life, I will live with this guilt and shame."

Attorneys for both men tried to shift some of the responsibility for the murder away from their clients. Frank Hartman, Jenoff's lawyer, said Neulander "used Len Jenoff as he used so many other people, and he played Len very well." Moreover, without Jenoff, Hartman argued, the prosecution not only would have had a weaker case against Neulander, but it would not have known about Daniels. Craig Mitnick, Daniels's lawyer, recounted a life of sexual abuse by his client's father, substance abuse beginning at age ten, a life of halfway houses and therapies that culminated with the Oxford House when he was eighteen, where he met a fatherlike figure he called "Uncle Lenny," in whom Daniels's trust was "tragically misplaced." Mitnick argued that Jenoff was responsible for the destruction of both Carol Neulander and Paul Daniels.

Carol Neulander's children and siblings were adamant: no mercy should be given these men. Both had a choice, and they chose to kill. As the Neulander children said in a joint statement, "They chose to dress in a certain way, drive certain cars to certain locations, approach and enter the house a certain way, and flee a certain way . . . These men are not star witnesses . . . These men are cold-blooded murderers." Carol's brother, Ed Lidz, requested thirty-year sentences for each man. "No one forced them to enter Carol's home to kill her . . . They accepted the price for a human life that Fred had set when he hired Len Jenoff to set up this vicious, idiotic crime."

Judge Baxter was more lenient than Lidz desired, sentencing each "cold, calculating murderer," as she called Jenoff and Daniels, to twenty-three years in prison. Baxter appreciated Daniels's corroboration of Jenoff's testimony, but blaming his participation in the murder on his psychological and drug problems was gratuitous. "That pertains to you," said Baxter, "not to the crime." Jenoff was given less than the maximum of thirty years because his cooperation with prosecutors exceeded anything Baxter had ever encountered; he was the missing link in what otherwise would have been a circumstantial murder-for-hire case. However, the sentence severely disappointed Jenoff, who'd expected a fifteen-year sentence, with eligibility for parole in five years. Since he'd already been in prison for three years, his most optimistic scenario was that he would be released in just twenty-four months. Now he couldn't appear before a parole board for at least seven years.

Jenoff was now face-to-face with his mortality—inmates don't live to a ripe old age. "I will be sixty-five years old in May of 2010" [the earliest he could be paroled], he said a few weeks after sentencing. "My father died of his fourth attack at age fifty-five. My brother, who is sixty-one, has already had two attacks and double bypass surgery." If his health didn't fail, there were other ways he might meet his death. He'd already been beaten up three times in prison—inmates don't like snitches, and he'd snitched on Neulander. Money and other personal items had been stolen. He was an easy target for hardened prisoners—innocent in the ways of serial criminals and hardcore thugs, and so wracked with remorse and guilt that, in a letter to an acquaintance, he quoted Psalm 51, the most famous of the seven penitential psalms written by King David:

> *Have mercy on me, God . . . , in your abundant compas-*
> *sion blot out my offense.*
> *Wash away all my guilt; from my sin cleanse me.*
> *For I know my offense; my sin is always before me.*

But beyond concern for his own death, Jenoff mourned the time he was losing with his son, Martin. "It hurts me deeply to think about doing seven more years," he lamented, "and probably missing Marty's wedding and the birth of his first child. He deserves so much more than that. Some days, I wish that I wouldn't wake up in the morning, but I have to stay strong for my beloved son's sake."

After the sentencing, Ed Lidz said he was satisfied with the judge's ruling. "There was never any question that the person we wanted to be held most responsible, and to get the most punishment, was Fred," said Lidz. "He's the one who instigated the whole thing."

Epilogue

Fred Neulander was sentenced to life in prison on a Friday. That night during M'kor Shalom's Shabbat services, Neulander wasn't mentioned, not even obliquely. That would have been too harsh a reminder about what happened in Freehold a few hours earlier. The rabbi and cantor preferred to be more subtle, developing, through music and prayers, a theme of reconciliation, not with Neulander but with themselves, so that they could find peace at last. Luckily, the Torah portion that was read that evening was most appropriate—it was about the reunion between Jacob and Esau. After not seeing each other for years, Esau met Jacob as he was entering Canaan with his wives and flocks. Jacob prostrated himself before Esau, atoning for stealing his birthright from their father. Esau had once threatened to kill Jacob; now he hugged and kissed his brother and helped him feel whole.

For some eight years, congregants at M'kor Shalom had been

soiled and stained by Fred Neulander, and now, finally, it was time
to begin to be whole again, just like Jacob. Cantor Anita Hochman
picked up her guitar and sang, "Guide my steps and help me find
my way / I need your shelter now / Rock me in your arms, and
. . . help me make this day." The congregation sang along.

Shortly after resigning from his post as senior rabbi in 1995, Neulander had sent a handwritten note to some of the higher-echelon
staff, "humbly and sincerely" asking for forgiveness. The gesture
conformed perfectly to Judaism's rules of etiquette, in which the
sinner, rather than the victim of sin, must initiate forgiveness. But
the psychological wounds inflicted by this sinner cut too deeply for
forgiveness, or even sympathy, to be forthcoming. That was reserved
for the rabbi's three children, *not* for the man ultimately convicted
of killing their mother.

  Fred Neulander never admitted guilt and never showed
remorse. He never sought what is called in Hebrew *teshuvah,* the
turning away from sin. Authentic *teshuvah,* as the Talmudic scholar
Adin Steinsaltz defines it, must emanate from the "first crack of
awareness" of wrongdoing and from the "unease and disquiet" that
results. Leonard Jenoff managed to experience *teshuvah;* he came to
realize, during that eight-year interval between crime and conviction, that he would "forever live in shame and guilt." Oddly
enough, the awareness that became available to the congenital liar
and former drunk has eluded to this day the Jewish scholar, leader,
and teacher who hired him—Rabbi Fred Neulander.

"If," as F. Scott Fitzgerald wrote, "personality is an unbroken series
of successful gestures," then Fred Neulander excelled in gestures of
sham and deception. But from August 1995, when news of the
affair with Elaine became public, until Neulander's conviction in
November 2002, those who'd been taken in by the man's personality felt only shame and anger. Certainly, he managed to fool

many smart and educated people who knew and admired him. The man was a *rodef,* Hebrew for "pursuer," "follower," "stalker," and his followers were blind to his true character. Their anger was directed toward him; their shame toward themselves.

In the 1960s, Neulander had written to one of his mentors back in Hartford, where he'd attended college, that rabbis "can make a difference in the souls of their congregants. Rabbis can help make the darkness less frightening." Not for twenty years did the people of M'kor Shalom realize that their own rabbi, the man who'd written these words, had made the dark . . . darker.

In August 1994, Fred and Carol traveled to Portland, Oregon, with three other couples, all members of M'kor Shalom and good friends for more than two decades. Over the years, various combinations of these couples had vacationed together, shared dinners on major Jewish holidays, and celebrated each other's lifecycle events. Now they were heading to the wedding of the son of one of these couples, a young man who'd received his religious education under Neulander's stewardship and had naturally asked the rabbi to officiate at the ceremony. Coincidentally, the wedding was on Neulander's birthday, August 14. The rabbi's wife and friends sang "Happy Birthday" to him at the wedding rehearsal.

Afterward, the four couples rented a van and explored Oregon for a week, traveling almost the entire length of the state, from the Columbia Gorge in the north to Crater Lake National Park in the south. The weather was glorious, the scenery was extraordinary, and everyone enjoyed the respite from everyday stress in the company of friends. *This* was what vacations were for, and *this* was what friends were for, particularly these friends, who had been especially close since they'd met in the mid-1970s. Carol was wearing a walking splint because she had sprained her foot not long before the trip, and Fred was doting and affectionate, eager for her to be comfortable. As one member of the foursome later remembered,

"If you didn't know us, you would have picked out Fred and Carol as the couple most in love. There was a lot of hand holding, a lot of calling each other 'Honey.' Of the four husbands, he was the most solicitous, the most attentive. He just about put the rest of us to shame."

When they returned to Cherry Hill, two of the wives all expressed the same sentiment to their husbands. In fact, they used almost the exact same words: "Why can't you be more like Fred? He is *so* nice to Carol."

Three months later, Carol Neulander was dead.

Acknowledgments

Before I started this book, I'd never been to Cherry Hill. I'd whizzed by it many times—one of the host of towns along the New Jersey Turnpike that you did your best to ignore while en route to someplace else that had to be more interesting. If through some fluke you did stop, it was brief—for gas or to fix a flat or to grab a quick bite at a diner, New Jersey's gift to wandering and hard-pressed gourmets.

While working on this book, I made many stops in Cherry Hill. I spent many nights there, as well. I discovered that the places we discredit and ignore and write off as mundane or boring or insignificant possess as much color and texture and complexity as those places we deem thick with panache and allure, descriptions that, as it turns out, are usually ill-deserved.

This book demanded that I enter not just Cherry Hill but also the lives of literally hundreds of people. After the murder of Carol Neulander and what eventually emerged about her husband, many of these people had to rebuild their faith in themselves, in rabbis, and in Judaism; for some people, especially the children of the principals in this tragedy and Carol's siblings and their fine spouses, an entire lifetime of rebuilding will never replace what they have lost. The Lidz family—Robert and Barbara, Ed and Carol, Margaret and her husband, Louis Miele—endured eight years of incalculable heartache. Their parents would be proud to know how they fought for justice, and that Carol's memory is with them daily. The agony of the Neulander children—Rebecca, Matthew, and Benjamin—must be excruciating. So, too, the pain of Leonard Jenoff's son. Anyone presumptuous enough to pretend to understand what these four have endured is a fool.

I took no joy in writing about a rabbi who went bad, but I do take pleasure in recognizing, if only anonymously, my many friends who are rabbis who helped me with research and texts, sent me in the right direction with ideas and hunches, and scolded me—as only rabbis can!—when I veered off into completely stupid terrain that I erroneously believed was valid and valuable. Their preference to remain anonymous confirms that, unlike Fred Neulander, the vast majority of American rabbis seek not glory but truth.

Neulander is an aberration. He represents what can go wrong with the rabbinate and, indeed, with clergy from any faith. His misdeeds should be neither ignored nor forgotten. They should serve as cautions about what happens when hubris supplants candor and when we foolishly and persistently worship before the altar of the ego.

I've used pseudonyms for three of Fred Neulander's mistresses. Elaine Soncini, the only one whose actual name was used, was so publicly associated with the case that it made little sense to give her the blessing of anonymity. The others, who are relatively unknown, do not deserve to have their names permanently linked to Neulander. The less harm that can be inflicted by telling the Neulander story, the better. Joel Rowe is also a pseudonym for one of Neulander's best friends.

Also, Judge Linda Baxter's last name was Rosenzweig when she began officiating at the Neulander case. In the interest of consistency, she is referred to as Linda Baxter throughout the book.

Thoughtful guidance, wise suggestions, and/or illuminating stories came from Mark Panitch, Gene Rubin, Joel Glazer, Gary Mazo, Sally Amsel, Earl Kratsch, Bill Fleischer, David Geffen, Arthur Lesley, Larry Nodiff, Michael Tasch, Harold Kaplan, Helen K. Zeidler, Neil Kleinman, Alan Hart, Marlene and Sheldon Schwartz, Phyllis Jenoff, Tereze Gluck, Libby Crystal Rappoport, Marty Devlin, Joanne Barley, and the three Michaels—Michael Olesker, Michael Varbalow, and another member of that nomenclatural fraternity who just wants to be known as "Mike."

For two consecutive autumns, Judge Linda Baxter's fairness and firmness set the tone for Neulander's extraordinary trials. We never met; judicial code precluded interviews. But her courtroom was an example of clarity and, yes, judiciousness. Jim Lynch, the prosecutor at both trials, and Michael Riley, Neulander's attorney at his second trial, were gentlemen. Witnessing their mutually respectful courtroom jockeying was an honor.

Frank Hartman's generous help early on saved me from having a stroke later on. Mike Riley, although he's already been mentioned, and his wife, Tracy, deserve special thanks for their many kindnesses.

Multiple thanks to the almost two hundred people I interviewed who wish to stay off the record: friends of Fred, Carol, and
Jenoff dating as far back as their youth, present and former members of M'kor Shalom and Temple Emanuel, graduates of HUC-
JIR, cops and detectives and lawyers and prosecutors, community
leaders, politicians, and assorted relatives, some distant and some
quite close, of the central characters in this book.

George Anastasia, Rita Giordano, and Jim Nolan were good
company in the trenches. Loraine Agnew at the *Courier-Post* was
very helpful with photos. The folks at *Dateline* were terrific, especially Izhar Harpaz, Marianne Haggerty, and Jamie Bright. May
your Nielsens continue to soar.

David Hirshey, my editor at HarperCollins, steered me away
from my own worse inclinations. His patience was as extensive as
his talent. Pilots in World War Two had God as their copilot; I had
David. Also at HarperCollins, Emily McDonald rolled up her
sleeves at the last minute and pitched in. For her, a standing ovation, please. I'm also grateful to Susan Squire, who labored many
long nights to make this a better book. And finally, gratitude to
Mark Jackson, resident legal sage at HarperCollins. He is one man
whom I don't want to see in court.

A trio of Amys helped guide this book almost from its inception: savvy Amy Rennert, the Queen of Book Agents; canny Amy
Schiffman, the Queen of Film Agents; and indefatigable Amy
Rubin, the Queen of Researchers. (To be frank, "savvy," "canny,"
and "indefatigable" apply equally to all of them.) A supporting cast
of researchers include Ted Rand, Wendy Ward, Michele Siegel,
Ryana Smith, Lucy Bruno, David Blackwell, and three moles that
work in key institutions affected by the Neulander story and pre-
fer to remain unnamed. Stuart Horwitz: Thanks for your percep-
tive suggestions on the original proposal. Peter Handel: Thanks for
giving me Amy Rennert's phone number. I'll treat you to the best

bistro in Berkeley next time I'm in town. Harry Stein: If all else fails, you can always get a job with the Pony Express.

Perhaps the greatest guidance came from Helen, Sarah, Amy, Molly, Zeifus, Wild Thing, Desdemona, and Ichabod, all of whom heard more than their fill of Fred stories and quite sensibly kept me grounded and humble, and sometimes—God bless 'em—shut me up.